Francis Schaeffer wrote about worldviews, development specialists write about fighting hunger, and often the twain never meet. Discipling Nations *is the best book I have seen at uniting worldview analysis with sound perspectives on development.*

Marvin Olasky
Editor, World *magazine*

. —————— .

Joining Food for the Hungry about the same time 17 years ago, I have noticed and admired the author's focused study of Weber's thesis that "ideas have consequences" in all its ramifications. This book resulted from that study and would provide development practitioners the occasion to reflect on their experiences, to their immense benefit.

Ted Yamamori, President
Food for the Hungry International

. —————— .

The reality of what happened to Darrow's life in L'Abri these many years ago is a reality that has been repeated in the lives of a tremendous variety of men and women who have come from a great many countries, with differing backgrounds, ranging from strong atheism, liberal Judaism, and Mohammedanism, to liberal Christianity. One common denominator was their search for answers. This book would be your being able to pull back the curtain on the window of one man's search and his finding answers that fit.

Edith Schaeffer
L'abri Fellowship

D0391557

DISCIPLING
NATIONS

THE POWER OF TRUTH TO TRANSFORM CULTURES

DARROW L. MILLER

with Stan Guthrie

P.O. Box 55787, Seattle, WA 98155

YWAM Publishing is the publishing ministry of Youth With A Mission. Youth With A Mission (YWAM) is an international missionary organization of Christians from many denominations dedicated to presenting Jesus Christ to this generation. To this end, YWAM has focused its efforts in three main areas: (1) training and equipping believers for their part in fulfilling the Great Commission (Matthew 28:19), (2) personal evangelism, and (3) mercy ministry (medical and relief work).

For a free catalog of books and materials, contact:

YWAM Publishing
P.O. Box 55787, Seattle, WA 98155
(425) 771-1153 or (800) 922-2143
www.ywampublishing.com

Discipling Nations: The Power of Truth to Transform Cultures
Copyright © 1998 by Darrow L. Miller
Second Edition Copyright © 2001 by Darrow L. Miller

10 09 08 07 06   10 9 8 7 6 5 4

Published by YWAM Publishing
P.O. Box 55787, Seattle, WA 98155, USA

Unless otherwise noted, all Scripture quotations in this book are taken form the Holy Bible, New International Version®, Copyright© 1973, 1978, 1984 by the International Bible society. Used by permission of Zondervan Publishing House. The "NIV" and "New International Version" trademarks are registered in the United States Patent and Trademark Office by International Bible Society.

ISBN 1-57658-248-5

Printed in the United States of America.

This book is dedicated to those people of the world who are poor and hungry and who are longing for the blessing of Abraham to be extended and to those workers of compassion who invest their lives, time, talent, and treasure to bring the Good News of the Kingdom of God to those in need.

Contents

Preface

to the 2nd Edition

It has been a joy to see how this book on discipling nations has been blessed of the Lord. While it has not become a "best seller" by any sense of the imagination, it has been working its way around the world. Because my e-mail address—dmiller@fhi.net—has been published with the book, I have heard from both development professionals and missionaries. Routinely, both groups report that *Discipling Nations* has given them the wholistic framework they have been seeking for their work. May the Living God be praised for His grace in this way.

We have not made major changes in this second edition. But we have acknowledged and profited from the critique of those who have written with challenges, input and corrections. Thank you very much.

Since this book was written, a partnership has grown between The Harvest Foundation and Food for the Hungry International. This partnership, called the Samaritan Strategy, seeks to provide vision and "tools" to local church leaders and inspire them to use local resources to minister wholistically to meet local needs. If you would like to know more about this growing movement, please see the page on the Samaritan Strategy at the end of this book.

May the Lord bless you as you seek to minister His compassion to the poor and hungry, redeem culture and see nations discipled, that Christ would be glorified and the glory of the nations would be revealed.

Darrow L. Miller
January, 2001

Foreword
by George Grant

WHAT IS THE SINGLE MOST IMPORTANT ELEMENT of a successful relief and development project among the world's needy peoples? What is the most essential resource we can bring to any initiative to feed the hungry, clothe the naked, and succor the suffering? How do we mobilize our abundance on behalf of their lack? How can we best ensure justice? If discretion constitutes the better part of valor, what is it that constitutes the better part of mercy?

Answers to such questions invariably focus on mechanical or structural issues. We are prone to believe that care for the poor is a matter of logistics. We are inclined to believe that if we can put together the right projects, with the right support systems, with sufficient resources, and with the appropriate management efficiencies in place, we could solve almost any problem. If we could just raise awareness, heighten consciousness, and enlist government approval we could end the blight of lack around the globe.

In this remarkable book, however, Darrow Miller proposes something radically different. He argues that the most effective tool we can wield in our efforts on behalf of the needy is a biblical worldview. Not more money, greater manpower, or better mailing lists. Not more programs, greater efficiency, or better systems. Not more governmental involvement, greater grassroots participation, or better public exposure. Not more denominational unity, greater international cooperation, or better distribution channels.

Instead, he argues, it is ideas that have the most powerful consequences. When we have the right ideas driving our actions, everything else will come in its time. But when we are plagued by bad ideas, our best-laid plans will inevitably come to naught.

George Grant, PhD, DLit, is the director of the King's Meadow Study Center. Well known for his work on behalf of the homeless, for international relief and development, and for the sanctity of life, he is the author of some four dozen books in the areas of history, politics, biography, social issues, and theology, including *The Micah Mandate*, *Bringing in the Sheaves*, *Grand Illusions*, and *The Patriots Handbook*. In addition to teaching regular classes in history, literature, and the arts at the Franklin Classical School, he maintains an active speaking schedule in the United States and around the world.

Witness the deleterious results of many of the best-intentioned efforts to aid the poor in the twentieth century. Vast resources, brilliant strategies, and determined programs have been frustrated at nearly every turn by inadequate, inconsistent, or iniquitous philosophies. The best we have to offer is insufficient if compromised by bad ideas.

Ideas do indeed have consequences.

In 1917, when American troops were preparing to sail across the seas to take to the battlefields of France and Belgium in the First World War, the New York Bible Society asked Roosevelt to inscribe a message in the pocket New Testaments that each of the soldiers would be given. The great man happily complied. And he began by quoting a striking biblical call for a life of balance—what he called the "Micah Mandate."

> He has shown you, O man, what is good and what the Lord requires of you: but to do justice, and to love mercy, and to walk humbly with your God (Micah 6:8).

Saying that "The whole teaching of the New Testament" is actually "foreshadowed in Micah's verse," he exhorted the men to lead the world in "both word and deed" through unimpeachable moral uprightness.

In his brief message to the soldiers, he explained:

> Do justice; and therefore fight valiantly against those that stand for the reign of Moloch and Beelzebub on this earth. Love mercy; treat your enemies well; succor the afflicted; treat every woman as if she were your sister; care for the little children; and be tender with the old and helpless. Walk humbly; you will do so if you study the life and teachings of the Savior, walking in His steps.

He concluded by saying:

> Remember: the most perfect machinery of government will not keep us as a nation from destruction if there is not within us a soul. No abounding of material prosperity shall avail us if our spiritual senses atrophy. The foes of our own household will surely prevail

against us unless there be in our people an inner life which finds its outward expression in a morality like unto that preached by the seers and prophets of God when the grandeur that was Greece and the glory that was Rome still lay in the future.

Roosevelt believed that the ultimate security of men and nations depended on a faithful adherence to the venerable Old Testament prophet's threefold demonstration of moral and practical balance: a strident commitment to justice, a tangible concern for mercy, and a reverent humility before the Almighty. He was certain that even with the deployment of superior forces in superior numbers with superior armaments, the American armies would ultimately be defeated during the war if they took to the field bereft of this kind of worldview integrity.

The clarion call of this book is equally clear. It is one that we must hear and heed if we are to effectively carry out our mandate to exercise genuine compassion in this poor fallen world. In our struggle against poverty and depravation we must gird our concerns for "justice, mercy, and humility before Almighty God" with a consistent biblical worldview. After all, even with the deployment of superior forces in superior numbers with superior armaments, our relief and development forces will ultimately be defeated if we take to the field bereft of worldview integrity.

This is a vital book. It is vital precisely because ideas have consequences. It is my prayer that these ideas will have extraordinary consequences the world over. It is my prayer that *Discipling Nations* will transform the story of relief and development in our time.

George Grant
King's Meadow Study Center
P.O. Box 1601
Franklin, TN 37065
U.S.A.

Foreword

by Vishal Mangalwadi

GOD MEANT MAN TO LIVE IN A GARDEN; sin has sent him to the slums. The gospel is the power of God for salvation from sin...and its consequences as well.

Gautama Buddha, the pioneer of Oriental "enlightenment," saw human suffering to be a universal and awful reality. He summarized his philosophy in the famous Four Noble Truths. The first of these was "Life is suffering." It implied that life without suffering was not possible, and, therefore, the only way to escape suffering was to escape life itself. One sad result of this "enlightenment" has been that much of the energy of my culture has gone into pursuing religious techniques (e.g., meditation and asceticism) for finding Nirvana (escape) from life rather than escaping sin and fighting suffering.

The first noble truth of a development worker is that life need not be suffering. A great deal of suffering is avoidable if we know what life is and how it ought to be lived. Knowing the right story, therefore, as Darrow Miller says, is of paramount importance.

Not too long ago I met a young woman who went to an American university to study social work. She wanted her life to make a difference to the world. During her four years she discovered that none of her professors believed that an individual such as she could make any difference to the world. The secular mind in the West, of course, lacks Buddha's integrity to exalt its pessimism as a foundational philosophical principle. But then, neither could it give the woman a credible intellectual basis for affirming hope. In contrast, Darrow Miller's teaching gave her a radical enough optimism that inspired her to go to a war-torn country in Africa, at personal risk, to serve refugees and to teach the warring tribes the way to life. There are thousands of young

Vishal Mangalwadi, winner of the *Dr. Bhimrao Ambedkar Distinguished National Service Award*, founded the Association for Comprehensive Rural Assistance with his wife Ruth to serve India's poor. A well-known political activist and social reformer who lectures internationally and writes with prophetic passion, he has authored several books, including *The World of Gurus*, *Truth and Social Reform*, and *Missionary Conspiracy: Letters to a Postmodern Hindu*.

people today serving in all parts of the world, with groups such as Food for the Hungry and Youth With A Mission, who can similarly testify to the influence of Darrow Miller's teaching on their lives.

The current dark mood of the secular intelligentsia has resulted from the collapse of the Western Enlightenment. The logic of the Enlightenment asserted that because there was no God, man had to be his own messiah. It assumed that man was only a part of physical nature and, therefore, it was possible to discover laws that regulated human behavior. Those "scientific" laws could then be used to build utopia. This quasi-scientific, metaphysical "story" gave birth to the nineteenth-century notion of social engineering. It was imagined that just as the chemical or electrical engineers use physical laws to build fantastic goods and gadgets, the social engineers ought to be able to build perfect societies. Fascism (including Nazism) and communism (including some versions of socialism) were two of the most ambitious such attempts to build scientific utopia. The horrors they created in the twentieth century demolished the optimism of secular Enlightenment. Now we know that we are neither capable enough nor good enough to be our own saviors.

The European Enlightenment did not birth the traditional Western optimism. The Enlightenment only secularized the hope that the biblical worldview had given to the Western culture. One key source of this optimism was the unique view of the significance of man that developed during the Renaissance. The fourteenth-century theologians had been debating the issue: Who is greater, man or angels? The debate was settled in favor of man on the ground that God had come as man in Jesus the Messiah to save man—both male and female. God could become man, the theologians reasoned, because man was made in the image of God.

Obviously, the idea that man was greater than angels seemed *prima facie* ridiculous. Even today a society, a caste, a tribe, or a family discards one of its members to lie on the streets of Calcutta to beg and to be eaten by worms, maggots, or vultures precisely because it perceives him or her to be a worthless burden. How could such a useless, powerless human being possibly be greater than angels?

The theologians argued that he (including she) is greater because his (her) worth equals the blood of the Son of God. If that "useless" human being is important enough for God to leave His throne in heaven and come to this earth and die for him, then he is also valuable enough for a Mother Teresa to sacrifice her life for him. The Renaissance theologians also concluded that if man really is made in God's image, then it is reasonable to assume that he can take control over the forces of nature, harness their power for good, and (under God) help shape his own destiny.

Muslims, understandably, dismiss the account of God becoming man in Jesus Christ as a blasphemous myth—a historical untruth. What they don't seem to understand, tragically, is that in so doing they also undermine the most potent humanizing principle that history has ever seen. Islam affirms that man is significant enough for God to send prophets to tell him what to do and what not to do. But according to Islam, when man does what is wrong and is perishing, God does not consider him valuable enough to come down to this earth Himself to save him. Man, they imply, can have God's law but not His self-sacrificing love.

Suppose one of my daughters goes astray, gets caught in a hopeless mess, in a whirlpool of her own making, and is hurting. Would I merely send instructions, or would I run down myself to suffer with her and do whatever I can to help her put her life together again? If I believe the gospel and seek to be godly—godlike—then I have to be as loving towards my children as God has been towards me. After demonstrating that all of my children are valuable enough for me to suffer with them and for them, I earn the right to expect and demand that my children see each other as precious enough to be served at personal cost. Jesus was able to command us to love our neighbors as ourselves because in dying for us, He shows that He loves us as much as He loves His own life.

Darrow Miller is a popular teacher, much in demand on all the continents. All of us who have sat at his feet are grateful that he is now making his teaching available to a wider audience. I have no doubt that it will both inspire and equip many to practice biblical godliness.

I expect the strongest criticism of Darrow's teaching to come from some of our own peers in the "development industry."

Some would be critical because they have been misled by postmodernism to believe that tolerance means showing equal respect to all moral and metaphysical ideas. They think being tolerant towards people who disagree with us is a virtue. However, tolerating false ideas and evil social practices can be wickedness and cruelty. Surely the professors and writers who propagated Nazism, communism, and socialism deserved to be critiqued and condemned, just as we in India now condemn our leaders who shackled us by their socialism. Studies conducted by forums such as the World Bank have conceded that not all moral ideas and practices have the same consequences. The poor nations are often the "corrupt" nations. Not many people expect the World Bank to have the courage to publicly investigate the question whether or not religio-cultural beliefs are an important source of the moral corruption in some cultures. Yet, that is a fact that Plato had perceived ages ago. In *Republic*, his classic work, Plato says to his fellow Greeks that they cannot even begin to build a just society without getting rid of the foul stories of their gods and goddesses. A people cannot be better than their gods. Darrow Miller issues a similar call today.

Unfortunately, some others of our peers will critique Miller because, for many of us, community service has become a profitable commerce at public expense. They interpret poverty primarily in economic terms. This gives them the right to demand public money to "fight" poverty. The idea that the fight against poverty may mean battling ideas that cause poverty is to their disadvantage. Their quasi "anti-poverty programs" bring to them not only money but also honor. To challenge cherished cultural beliefs that cause suffering often results in one's rejection and crucifixion. That is a price not many are willing to pay. They are happy to be "public servants" as long as it brings no persecution. The following pages demonstrate that Darrow Miller has sufficient compassion for the poor to slaughter the holy cows (sacred beliefs) that cause much of our world's poverty. He truly follows a Savior who was willing to be crucified by the very people He came to save.

Vishal Mangalwadi
Ivy Cottage,
Landour,
Mussoorie (U.P.)
India 248 179

Acknowledgements

Thanks to Dr. Ted Yamamori, President Emeritus of Food for the Hungry, who told me it was time for me to write a book and encouraged me every time he saw me.

To Stan Guthrie who took my narratives and extensive lecture notes from the Development Ethic Workshop and transformed them into the quality chapters that make up this book.

To Chris Colby of Mercy Ships and David Boyd, Chancellor of the University of the Nations, who believed in this project and wanted to be identified with it.

To Scott Allen and Steve Corbett for helping with the content, Tom Steffen and Lisa Leff for producing the graphics, Linda Sibert, Sarah Luster, and Cindy Benn for data entry and word processing, and Karen Randau for her advice and editing.

Thanks last and foremost to my wife Marilyn and my four children Nathan, David, Jonathan, and Maryrose, who for a decade watched their father throw scraps of paper in a box—"the book in the box"—and who contributed with patience and encouragement.

Introduction

IT WAS GETTING COLD, and two-year-old Ntaganira stood barefoot and shivering against Gisenyi's night air, waiting. Ntaganira and his family had fled the genocide in their native Rwanda, along with more than a million other refugees. But men with guns had separated him and his four-year-old brother Niyo from their parents at the sprawling refugee camp in Goma, Zaire. Frightened, hungry, and confused, Ntaganira and Niyo were among dozens of "unaccompanied children" who had been forced back across the border to Rwanda, where their parents could expect to be killed if they returned.

In my work with Food for the Hungry, I had spent the day in Gisenyi with coworkers and staffers from other private voluntary organizations asking "big picture" questions. Under the auspices of the United Nations High Commissioner for Refugees, we were talking about people flows; supplies of food, water, and blankets; and a thousand and one other details for "processing" large numbers of people.

Then I made the mistake of looking over at Ntaganira. A series of disturbing questions slapped my face like the evening chill. Will "the system" handle him? Will someone care for him, or will he slip through the cracks? Suddenly the big picture had dissolved into the personal. With a knot in my stomach, I turned away.

Here, longing for the refuge of his mother's arms, stands a hungry two-year-old—not a number to be "processed." Who is going to care for him? No. That is the wrong question. Am *I* going to care for him? Will I pick him up, wrap my jacket around him, be his advocate with the Rwandan military, and find him food, water, and shelter?

This book is for all those who, out of compassion or altruism, principle or pity, ask the simple question, "Am I going to care?" It is for those who want to help all the Ntaganiras in their communities, in nearby slums, and around the world. It is for those who see the great masses of refugees, the countless faces of the hungry. It is for those who cry out, "Enough! Enough!" It is for the seasoned professional compassion worker* or social worker thirsting for a fresh look at a complex problem. This book is for the volunteer in the local soup kitchen, for the one who raises money for the poor. It is for all who care to care. It is for *you*.

The Question

Jesus said, "The poor you always have with you." A glance at today's world proves how right His observation was, even two millennia later. Despite the billions of dollars spent through the Great Society programs, the poverty rate in the United States, the richest nation in the world's history, has remained disturbingly high. Some advocates say that one in four American kids lives in poverty. And despite the global advance of free trade, hundreds of millions of people live hopelessly locked in a cycle of want and ignorance, sickness and fear.

The question is, Why? What are the causes of poverty? Are physical circumstances the prime reasons for deprivation, or must we look elsewhere?

Most compassion professionals examine the issue from a social, economic, or political point of view. Poverty and underdevelopment have many causes. These may be summarized by what some have called external and internal constraints. External constraints are systems and events which are outside the control of the individual or community which inhibit their ability to develop. There are two major external constraints—structural evil and natural evil.*

The social injustice—structural evil—that the prophets condemned is one of the prime causes of underdevelopment. Likewise, natural evil—earthquakes, droughts, floods, disease—are a major cause of poverty and hunger. To the former, the Cross of Christ not only means the salvation of individuals, but it provides a radical critique of unjust social, political and economic institutions of society. Regeneration and repentance of individuals, MUST lead to the reformation of culture* and the rebuilding of societies. The social, economic, and political institutions must function more justly. In response to natural evil, the truths of science* must be applied in technology* to fight against hunger and disease (see Chapter 5).

Most authors who write on this subject focus on the external causes for underdevelopment and poverty. Because there is ample analysis on this level, the focus of this book will be to go beyond the

---

*Words listed in the glossary are marked in the text with an asterisk at their first appearance.

external to the internal constraints, to the meta-physical roots. I will seek to respond to the question of why individuals, communities and nations are underdeveloped from the perspective of story*—not a work of fiction, but the metaphysical stories people tell about themselves. This book aims to provide answers you probably haven't seen on the evening news or heard discussed at a conference on relief and development,* even if it was a Christian one. I will explore the cultural values and religious beliefs that shapes not only the way people, communities, and nations *think* but also the way they *live*.

The Story

Does any story encourage human development? Yes, one; but it's not new. In fact, it's the "old, old story," but told in a new way, with emphases most Christians tragically have missed. The basic elements of this story include a King, His kingdom, His stewards, and a task.

The King is the personal, rational, and moral God of the universe. The kingdom is the entire created order, both physical and spiritual. This kingdom, with gates open to the King and His subjects, has a set of laws that govern the stewards and their task. The stewards, or servants, are all members of the human race, called to glorify the King by serving in His kingdom household. Yet these servants have rebelled against the Sovereign, thereby plunging themselves into poverty and death. But that is not the end of the story, for the King's subjects are all uniquely endowed and individually important. The servants are to steward the King's household, both preserving it and bringing forth the bounty* that the King has cached inside. Further, the servants are to spread the knowledge of the King, thus developing the world and advancing the kingdom.

As Bernard T. Adeney says, "God's revelation in history is a story to which we fuse our own story. By doing so we learn to make sense of our lives as a coherent narrative."[1]

The Greek word for house, *oikos*, and its family of words help us understand the metaphor of God's house, and our role in it, more clearly. English derivatives of *oikos* include ecology* (study of the house), economics* (stewardship,* administration of the house), and edification (building up the house). All three realms describe what God calls us to do as His representatives on earth. That call is God's ultimate purpose for us.

We all need stories, no matter how old we are. Stanley Hauerwas states:

> The metaphors that determine our vision must form a
> coherent story if our lives are to have duration and
> unity. Such stories create the context of meaning for
> the concrete moral rules and principles to which we
> adhere. There is no principled way to separate the "reli-
> gious" from the "moral" in such stories.
> We may discover that our account of our experience
> needs to be reinterpreted in light of the biblical story.[2]

Our story began in a garden (see Genesis 2) and will end in a city
(see Revelation 21). It is a story of glory, of corruption, of restoration, of
development. There is sweat and frustration, but also progress.* But as
the ancient Hebrew axiom says so well, "For as he thinketh in his heart,
so is he" (Proverbs 23:7 KJV). Development is more than working, even
working *hard*. It is about *thinking*, and about *what we think*. The attitudes of our hearts inevitably show up sooner or later in our behavior,
speech, writing, and handiwork. Further, our social institutions and
policies bear the unmistakable imprint of our thoughts. Few Christians
have grasped this simple fact down through history. George Grant
describes one "great man" who did—Augustine of Hippo.

> Augustine recognized that people's dominant world-
> view* inevitably shapes the world they have in view.
> And he also recognized that the church is the starting
> point for the development of that worldview as it ful-
> fills its calling to do justice, love mercy, and walk
> humbly with Almighty God.[3]

What does our worldview or story have to do with development?
Everything. Here's what two secular development writers said about the
matter:

> [A]ny development program that fails to take into con-
> sideration the prevailing belief system of a people and
> the possible influence of this belief system on the pro-
> posed development plan runs a serious risk of
> foundering before it gets off the ground.[4]

The development of people, communities, and nations doesn't just
happen, nor does it occur in a vacuum. Just as the soil in which a tree

is planted will play a decisive role in the growth of the tree, likewise the values, attitudes, culture, and *ethos** of a people will determine whether its development is healthy, stunted, or nonexistent. It is the thesis of this book that there is a story that can transform poverty to bounty; there is a set of principles, a development ethic,* that creates a fertile soil for development.

The War

We normally think of war in physical terms: bombs, guns, troops, deaths, bodies. But viewing war as a clash not just of armies but also of ideas allows us to better see what is going on around us. Many people say there is a culture war in the United States right now, a clash between competing liberal and conservative visions of the country. Anyone who reads the newspapers knows that this is more than a friendly debate. Besides seeing this clash of values, we see economic war when businesses attempt to destroy their competitors and when nations attempt to bend others to their will through trade or blackmail. No shots are fired, but the stakes are real in either case.

Christianity has revealed that for the time being, there is a war going on between life and death, good and evil, God and Satan. This spiritual conflict is not just something we read about in our Bibles. It intrudes into our everyday world of ideas and ideals, shaping our history, determining our future, and to a large extent controlling how we live. While it is sometimes possible to declare one's neutrality in a military conflict, it is not possible to do so in the overarching spiritual war engulfing this planet. As Bob Dylan said, "Everybody's gotta serve somebody."

When it comes to helping the poor, therefore, good intentions are not enough. Theologian Ronald Nash has pointed out that good intentions combined with bad theory have produced bad policies that have harmed the very people they were supposed to help.[5] Economist Walter Williams has called for dispassionate analysis letting the facts speak for themselves, saying:

> [W]e have to think with our brains instead of our hearts when we approach the problems of poverty.[6]

Too often the church, being motivated by Christ to help the poor, has bowed to secular analyses and strategies of poverty and relief.

Many within the Christian relief and development community have simply followed the latest trends in the poverty industry.

Other Christians, being more gnostic in their thinking, have concerned themselves only with "spiritual things" and have abandoned their heritage of compassion. Both, in different ways, have forgotten the Great Commission is to "disciple nations," teaching them to obey *all* that Christ has commanded.

True Charity

We will not end up where we want to be unless we start from the right place and head in the right direction. Man-centered and ethnocentric approaches will bring us up short or lead us off the path. We must take a theocentric approach: God must be the source, the means, and the end for all we do with and for the poor.

Of course, each of the great theocentric faiths*—Christianity, Islam,* and Judaism—recognizes that God exists, that there is a reality that transcends the five senses, that there are absolutes (both moral and metaphysical), that reality consists of both the physical universe and the supernatural realm. Further, the Christian theocentrist will (or ought to) recognize the existence of universal laws and principles that govern both physical and spiritual reality, and that all cultures— Western and non-Western, modern and ancient—must be judged by them.

Only in this framework can true charity exist and thrive. True charity distinguishes between, but never separates, heart and mind, method and content, style and substance.

Let's look for a moment at the last couplet, style and substance. In dealing with the poor, style has to do with our attitude, with the approach we take in dialogue with others over the issue, and with how we treat the poor whose paths we cross. We are to have compassion, which is not mere pity or sentimentality but is oriented to relationships. Another virtue of true charity is love, putting someone else ahead of yourself, even loving your enemies.

Civil discourse is part of it. Michael Novak reminds us that when we fight for our ideas we must fight with "the rules of ideas not the rules of war."[7]

> Thomas Aquinas observed that civilization (as opposed to barbarism) is constituted by civil argument in which citizens, convinced of each other's capacity for

understanding and free will, attempt to influence one another's judgments and to forge public choices by rational persuasion, never by coercion.[8]

Style deals with *how* we say and do things. Substance deals with *what* we say and do; it is about content, ideas, and truth.* Substance is far from an academic pursuit around an ivory tower. I will say it more than once in this volume: **Ideas have consequences.** Therefore, to make sure they are the right ideas, we must examine the assumptions behind them. We must evaluate the attitudes and behavior, policies and practice that flow from them. And we must critique them closely, always asking the question, **"Are they true?"** Substance will lead us to discover something I call the development ethic—but more on that later!

True charity will consider people's stories. We must examine a people's attitudes, a culture's values, to determine where they support development or poverty. Then we must articulate the universal principles that provide fertile soil for development. The material in this book is not new. It is a call to return to first principles, to restore our heritage, to revive the Reformation.*

My Bias

Before we jump in, I need to tell you a little bit about myself. Friends have called me a "passionate paradigm shifter." I am a social activist who has come to see the importance of ideas. Loren Cunningham, founder and chairman of Youth With A Mission has said of me:

> Darrow is not an intellectual; he is a Christian who is busy making a difference worldwide, and committed to seeing the minds of Christians renewed by God's truth in order to more correctly and effectively reflect and initiate His truth into every realm of society, and thereby "disciple the nations"—which is the key to solving the world's problems.

I am not a relativist. Development is not value-neutral. Readers who are will be disappointed with this book. But the truth is, God matters, not only in the hereafter but also in the here and now. I am a theist in general, a monotheist in particular. Certain conclusions flow from this bias, and I believe they are amply supportable. In this book I'll attempt to show this.

My desire is to pursue what I call the *radical middle*, to avoid the extremes of the right or the left, the liberal or the conservative. I have a hunch that committed liberals will find me too conservative, while conservatives will find me too liberal. My bias is theological, not political. I seek to be a progressive conservative in the best sense of both words. It is sometimes jokingly said that a conservative is a liberal who's been mugged, while a liberal is a conservative who's been accused of mugging! Actually, I hope to take the best from each camp, having ultimate allegiance to God and to His word.

I hope to be liberal (from the Latin *liber*, free) in the sense of being progressive and forward thinking, open to new ideas; generous and free-spirited, with a largeness of mind; able to respect and critically evaluate others' opinions. I do not mean to be a "liberal" in the sense of being libertine, without moral constraints. Nor am I a secularist, as many on the political left are perceived to be.

I also hope to be conservative (from Latin words *com* and *servare* meaning to keep or to guard) in the sense of conserving fundamental principles, celebrating the whole counsel of God, and guarding the fundamental truths of the faith (including the one that says that life is found only in Christ). I have said, with Peter:

> Lord, to whom shall we go? You have the words of eternal life (John 6:68).

I do not mean to be closed-minded or dogmatic about nonessentials. I don't want to major on the minors. This is about Truth. Paul said we should "Hold on to the good" (1 Thessalonians 5:21). There's no need to cling to anything less.

The message in this book is a work in progress. It has been growing and maturing for a decade now. Many friends have critiqued the content and encouraged the progress. Your comments and constructive criticism will promote my own learning. I can be contacted at **dmiller@fhi.net**.

Throughout the book are study questions on the material that should help you clarify your own thinking on the subjects we discuss. Taking the time to think them through should allow you to begin to transform your own worldview to more closely reflect the biblical story.

This story makes a profound difference when applied to development issues. The next few chapters will show why.

Study Questions

What is the basic thesis for this book?

What examples can you give, from development work you've seen or been involved in, of Nash's statement about "good intentions with bad theory"?

What is the basis of true charity?

What two things will true charity do?

In your own words, define

Development:

Ethic:

Your own assumptions will affect how you interact with this book. It would be good for you to consciously express them. I've stated my bias; please identify yours.

What questions, challenges, or further examples do you have concerning the ideas presented in this introduction?

The Story

If you hold to my teaching, you are really my disciples. Then you will know the truth, and the truth will set you free.

John 8:31b, 32

These two world views [Judeo-Christian theism* and secular humanism] stand as totals in complete antithesis to each other in content and also in their natural results—including sociological and governmental results, and specifically including law.

It is not that these two world views are different only in how they understand the nature of reality and existence. They also inevitably produce totally different results. The operative word here is inevitably. It is not just that they happen to bring forth different results, but it is absolutely inevitable that they will bring forth different results.

Francis Schaeffer
A Christian Manifesto

CHAPTER ONE

Everyone Has a Story
Worldview and Development

JOSIE KORNEGAY WORKED AS a Peace Corps nurse for the Serabu Mission Hospital in the Bo District of Sierra Leone, West Africa. She had just finished teaching a microbiology course for 10 local nursing students. All of them had worked hard, mastered the information, and demonstrated knowledge of the viruses, bacteria, and other microscopic organisms that cause disease. After the final exam, one student raised her hand and said, "Miss, I know that you taught us about polio, but do you want to know how people *really* get it?"

Her heart sinking, Josie asked, "How?"

"It's *the witches!*" her student said. "They are invisible. They fly around at night and bite people's backs!"

Josie told me later, "At that moment, with a heaviness of heart, I realized that as far as the Sierra Leonean students were concerned, I didn't know what I was talking about. Their grandmothers had taught them that witches were real and microorganisms were what white people believed in."[1]

Josie learned the hard way that worldview dominates how a person thinks about health. Members of animistic cultures see the fates or spirits (often demonic) as all-powerful. In Islamic culture the common phrase "it is written" creates a crushing framework of fatalism. In

Thailand peasants are labeled *jaak-con*: "destined to poverty." Hinduism* sees perfection as a state of resignation. Better to withdraw from the world than attack its evils. Secularism,* for its part, sees man[2] as little more than a complex machine, just one more component of the physical universe. There is little motivation to fight hunger and poverty or protect the preborn, disabled, and elderly.

Preponderance of Belief

Every culture holds many beliefs. Yet despite the common societal tension between a dominant culture and its subcultures, which have different worldviews and values, some beliefs turn up more often and are held more strongly than others. This creates a preponderance of belief toward certain positions.

To see this concept in action, let's observe how three distinct cultures view man's relationship to nature: the United States, with its classical Western perspective; Japan, reflecting an Asian perspective; and the animistic or folk perspective of Colombia's Mestizo Indians (see Figure 1.1).

Every culture has its own set of blinders that prohibit people from seeing all of reality. The nursing students in Sierra Leone, coming from an animistic culture, were blind to the "germ theory" and the physical causes of disease. Josie, on the other hand, educated in a materialistic, Western perspective, was blind to the personal nature of evil and the impact of the demonic on health.

Ideas Have Consequences

All people and cultures have a particular model of the universe, or worldview. Their worldview docs more to shape their development, their prosperity or poverty, than does their physical environment or other circumstances. We will concern ourselves with three worldview archetypes: **biblical theism**,* **secularism**, and **animism**.* Each worldview creates different cultural stories and produces different values. Ideas produce behaviors and lifestyles that affect people, cultures, nations, and history.

Biblical theism[3], the biblical worldview, holds that because God exists, an objective reality exists that is known and has been established by God. Reality is *ultimately personal* because it has been established by the ultimate Person.

In contrast, secularism sees reality as *ultimately physical*. By definition, this model denies the existence of a spiritual or transcendent reality.

Preponderance of Belief

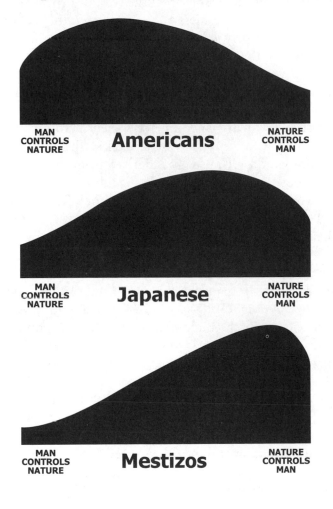

Figure 1.1[2]

Animism[4] views reality as essentially spiritual. The physical world is *maya*, illusion. It is "animated" by spirits.

If animism and secularism were absolutely self-consistent internally, they would have nothing in common and would not touch theism at any point. Yet no person or culture can live consistently within either of these two philosophies. All people live in the reality God has created. The more closely we conform to reality as it is, and not to the way we imagine it, the closer we are to life and prosperity. The more closely we adhere to a nontheistic worldview, the farther we are from objective reality, and the closer we are to death and destruction. As God has said, "All who hate me love death" (Proverbs 8:36).

Those seeking to live and impact society across cultures must examine worldview in three critical areas. First, they must know their personal worldview, which usually is derived from their nation's dominant culture or their own minority's subculture. Second, they must study the worldview of the people with whom they are living and working. Third, Christians must become *consciously Christian*, repenting[5] of their false views of reality and embracing God's reality.

Historical Roots

The philosopher Immanuel Kant* (1724–1804) coined the German term *Weltanschauung* (*Welt*—meaning world and *Anschauung*— German for view).[6] By the middle of the nineteenth century, the term had become part of the German vocabulary. German social economist Max Weber* used the word in his analysis of the relationship between a people's belief system and their prosperity or poverty.[7]

While Weber was raised in a Protestant (Lutheran) tradition and consciously wrote from that tradition, he did not personally believe in Jesus Christ. Weber stood at the threshold of a new world, with one foot in the Reformation and the other in secular science.

Weber shared his German heritage and a passion for social and economic philosophy with a contemporary, Karl Marx.* But the similarities ended there. Marx was a thoroughgoing materialist. He believed that matter is all that matters. In contrast, Weber's key thesis, that ideas have consequences, rooted the creation of wealth in the metaphysical realm. Weber believed that mind governs matter, not the other way around. Religion shapes character and daily behavior. It establishes the social, economic, and political structures that provide life's framework.

Weber is probably best known for his phrase "the Protestant work ethic,"* which described the ethos that empowered the countries of northern Europe to lift themselves out of poverty. For Weber, the *Weltanschauung* of Protestantism stood in contrast to the world and life systems of the coming secularists, the East, and animism. It established an ethos, or set of values, that transformed how whole nations saw the world.

Abraham Kuyper* (1837–1920), the Dutch prime minister, theologian, and founder of the Free University, described the concept of worldview from within the Christian tradition. Kuyper, a devout believer in Jesus Christ, understood that whole cultures were transformed during the Reformation as people were given access to God's worldview via the Bible. Christianity's worldview is consistent with reality and thus useful on a pragmatic level. Paul admonished believers to bring "every thought captive to Christ" (2 Corinthians 10:5). Every area of human life is to be under Christ's lordship, and every aspect of culture is to be redeemed for God's glory, the advancement of His kingdom, and the development of nations.

Synonyms

A number of modern writers have grappled with the worldview concept. Writing in *Future Shock*, Alvin Toffler has said, "Every person carries in his head a mental model of the world, a subjective representation of external reality."[8] Economist Thomas Sowell has said, "A vision is our sense of how the world works…the foundations on which theories are built…a sense of *causation*."[9] Writing in *Worldviews in Conflict*, Ronald H. Nash has observed, "A worldview is a *conceptual scheme*, by which we, consciously or unconsciously place or fit everything we believe and by which we interpret and judge reality."[10] German sociologist Niels Mulder, writing in *Inside Thai Society*, defines *Weltanschauung* as "Those core concepts that share the culture's *basic cognitive orientation*."[11]

Other loose synonyms of worldview include "sacred belief system," "religious assumptions," "presupposition,"* "mental infrastructure," "pre-analytical cognitive act," "meta-story," or "cultural story." The Marxist would call it an ideology, while a scientist would label it a paradigm.

Our Working Definition

With all these different labels representing what is essentially the same idea, it is important for us to be clear about what we mean. I use this one-sentence definition in lectures and training workshops around the world. It will also serve our purposes in this book:

> **A worldview is a set of assumptions held consciously or unconsciously in faith about the basic makeup of the world and how the world works.**[12]

Phrase by phrase this definition means:

a set of assumptions: Those presuppositions or axioms one considers to be true.

held consciously or unconsciously: Worldview is deeply seated in the recesses of the mind. Every person and culture has one. If it is held unconsciously, it has been received through enculturation or socialization. If consciously held, a person has critically examined his assumptions and their consequences. Ideally, all people would be "critically conscious" of their belief systems.

in faith: To the extent that a worldview is examined, it is a rational faith statement. To the extent that it is unexamined, it is nonrational. Because everyone believes something, everyone is religious. There is no neutral ground. Even modern science makes metaphysical claims about reality that cannot be empirically tested. Secularism has been called the prevailing religious philosophy of the West.[13]

about the basic makeup of the world and how the world works: A worldview deals with all aspects of reality—the epistemological,* metaphysical, and moral. It interprets, explains, and defines the world. It not only establishes our vision of "what is" but also tells us what "ought to be." In the sense that everyone has a worldview, everyone is a philosopher.

Man's Basic Questions

Epistemological questions concern themselves with the nature, limits, and validity of knowledge. "Is there truth?" "What can I know?" and "How can I know?" are examples of the kinds of fundamental questions from which all others spring.

Metaphysical questions concern themselves with the fundamental nature of reality and being. Metaphysical questions include "What is ultimate reality?" "Is there a God?" "What is the essence of nature and of time?" The disciplines of metaphysics* include *ontology** (the study of being), *cosmology** (the study of the nature of the universe), and *teleology** (the study of purposes).

Moral questions cover values, ethics, and morals in general and the problem of evil in particular. "Is there right and wrong?" "What is good?" "What is beautiful?" and "Where did evil come from?" are examples. This field of study is known as *axiology,** from the Greek words αξιος, meaning "worth," and λογος, "the study of."

It is not enough to ask the right questions. All people ask basically the same questions. The answers they give, however, are radically different, depending on their worldviews. The way people and societies answer these questions determines the types of cultures and societies they create. Some answers to these questions lead to poverty and barbarism; others, to development and civilization.

How Does a Worldview Work?

Jesus told His listeners, "He who has ears to hear, let him hear." Changing the metaphor, a worldview affects what we see, not what there is to be seen. Rose-colored glasses portray a different world than amber-tinted spectacles. In the dark, night vision goggles will reveal more than sunglasses. All of us wear a set of lenses in our minds, but few of us are aware of their presence.

What Do You See?

Figure 1.2

To test your own glasses, look at this well-known picture. What do you see?

Some people see an old woman, some see a young woman. Actually, the picture contains both, but your individual mental spectacles will predispose you toward seeing one over the other.

What Do You See?

Figure 1.3

How would you categorize the objects in this picture?

Typically, analytical, mathematically inclined Westerners will categorize the objects as tools and food. But people who are storytellers, those with narrative minds, will see a story about eating; that is, the hammer cracks open the nuts, and the knife cuts or peels the orange and the apple. Two viewpoints lead to two interpretations of the same data.

A worldview, like a road map, sets our direction and guides us through life. Like wind blowing through the trees, it cannot be seen, yet it enlivens and animates. Worldview infuses a community with life and establishes its dynamic. It says, "This is who we are."

The Three Major Worldviews

All worldviews can be found somewhere along a continuum, with secularism and animism at either end and theism in the middle.

While secularism goes back to the ancients, its modern roots were planted in nineteenth- and twentieth-century Europe. Secularism sees

The Worldview Continuum

Animism	Theism	Secularism
Ultimate Reality Is Spiritual	Ultimate Reality Is Personal	Ultimate Reality Is Physical

Figure 1.4

reality as ultimately physical and thus focuses on the unity of nature. Darwin,* one of the great high priests of secularism, believed that life is the result of the interactions of matter and energy, time and chance. Secularists affirm that truth is empirical. Truth is what the senses can perceive. Morals are relative. Values emerge from social consensus. As a religion, secularism is pantheistic, since it equates god with the laws of the universe. The cry of the secularist might be, "Everything is God!" This is philosophical materialism. Matter is the only and fundamental reality; all being, processes, and phenomena are explained as manifestations of matter. During the Enlightenment* these ideas received the label "secular humanism."

Theism is rooted in the ancient Near East. It sees ultimate reality as personal and relational. God exists. He created a universe of physical and spiritual dimensions, seen and unseen worlds. Truth, as revealed by God, is objective and can be known by man. God's character establishes absolute morals. Theism holds to one personal-infinite God, the great "I AM" of Scripture. Philosophical theism believes that the one God created man and the world. God transcends the world yet is immanent in it.

Animism (including its modern form, the New Age*) is rooted in the Far East and the world's folk religions. Spirits animate everything, and everything moves toward oneness of spirit. The real world is unseen, truth is hidden and irrational, all is mystery. While filled with evil, the universe is basically amoral. Monistic, animism asserts that there is only one kind of ultimate substance. The animist might cry, "All is one!" This is philosophical idealism, which maintains that ultimate reality lies in a realm that transcends worldly phenomena; essentially, reality is consciousness.

How Worldviews Spread

Worldviews do not stay in the dusty pages of the obscure tomes of a professor's library. They are diffused across oceans, through societies, and over the centuries, shaping individuals, cultures, nations, and the flow of history.

Worldviews *spread horizontally.* Geographically, they begin with an individual and spread to his disciples, who take the message to the community, to the nation, and, ultimately, to the world. For example, after His resurrection, Christ told His disciples, "[Y]ou will be my witnesses in Jerusalem, and in all Judea and Samaria, and to the ends of the earth" (Acts 1:8). In the first century the gospel spread across the map from Palestine: east as far as India (possibly even into southern China), south into Mediterranean Africa, west as far as Spain, and perhaps as far north as the British Isles. After this initial missions thrust, ships carried the gospel along the coasts to the world's port cities. In the modern missionary era, the gospel moved inland from the coasts through societies such as the China Inland Mission and the Sudan Interior Mission. Now, at the end of the twentieth century, the Good News is being preached to ethnic or tribal people who are often poor, illiterate, and heretofore unreached.

Ideas also *penetrate vertically* into every sphere of life, shaping the values, social structures, and institutions of a culture (see Figure 1.5). Ideas usually develop as religious doctrine, philosophical abstractions, or scientific theories and then are transmitted downward via music and the arts. (It has been said that if you want to know how members of the next generation will order their lives, listen to contemporary music and go to a museum of modern art.) The ideas then become institutionalized in a society's laws, politics, and social and economic structures, before flowing to pop culture and affecting the behavior and lifestyle of the average citizen.

Ideas begin with the intellectuals and spread to the educated or professional classes: teachers, lawyers, pastors, journalists, writers, entertainers, and politicians. They then become life's context for the common man. History pivots on the debates of individuals. In the 1930s, Robert Hutchins* (1899–1977) and John Dewey* (1859–1952) debated the proper philosophy of education. Hutchins, president of the University of Chicago, upheld the classic position that education's purpose was to "prepare people for life." Dewey, a philosopher and signer of the Humanist Manifesto, took the modern, secular position that education's purpose was to "prepare people for a job." Dewey won the debate, and his pedagogy has impacted not only education in America and in much of the rest of the world (see Figure 1.6) but also how all of us live and work in our culture. How different the world would have been had Hutchins prevailed! Imagine what could have happened if a Christian educator had been involved in the debate.

Ideas also *diffuse through time*. It has always taken time for ideas to travel around the world and penetrate cultures. But today, with the advent of modern information technologies, ideas require less and less time to spread—for good and ill.

Worldview Impact on Popular Culture

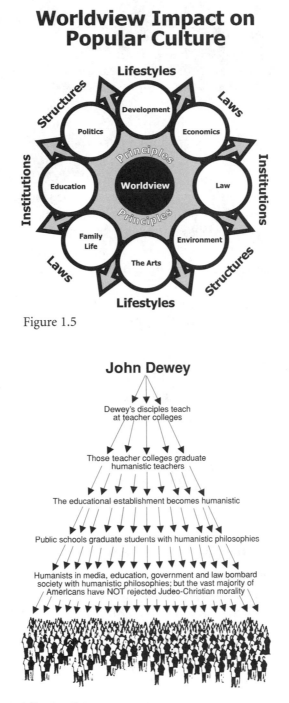

Figure 1.5

Figure 1.6[14]

Developmental economist E.F. Schumacher stated in his classic text *Small Is Beautiful*:

> Those that bring forth new ideas are seldom ruled by them. But their ideas obtain power over men's lives in the third and fourth generations when they have become a part of that great mass of ideas, including language, which seeps into a person's mind during his "Dark Ages."[15]

In 1883, in his short essay *The Madman*, German philosopher Friedrich Nietzsche* (1844–1900) pronounced the death of God. For Nietzsche, to deny God was not merely to cease being religious. It was to jettison everything based on His existence. If God is dead, man is dead. Truth and morals, communion and community are dead as well. Life is absurd!

But Nietzsche knew it would take time for the common man to experience the consequences of his actions. The philosopher wrote:

> At last he [the madman] threw the lantern on the ground, so that it broke in pieces and was extinguished. "I come too early," he then said, "I am not yet at the right time. This prodigious event is still on its way, and is traveling—it has not yet reached men's ears. Lightning and thunder need time, the light of the stars needs time, deeds need time, even after they are done, to be seen and heard. This deed is as yet further from them than the furthest star—and yet they have done it."[16]

The Changing of a Worldview: An Example

Prior to modernism, the predominant worldview of the West, the overarching story, assumed a transcendent, infinite, personal God who existed before all else. God created the universe both animate and inanimate, spiritual and physical, separate from Himself but not independent of Him. God is both transcendent (outside of his creation) and immanent (present within it). He is everywhere present and involved, immanent in history. The universe is not a closed system; it is open to God's purpose and intervention.

This worldview, **theism**, allows communication and interaction between the physical and spiritual realms. God has revealed Himself through special revelation*—first through the written Word, the Bible, and then through the living Word, Jesus Christ. At the same time, man can use his God-given reason* to discover truth about God and the universe. Through general revelation,* including man's nature and the design of creation, all people can know certain facts about God and the universe.

Theism's view

Figure 1.7[17]

The consensus for this worldview began crumbling in Europe and England during the Age of Enlightenment. Intellectuals of the time were seeking to free man *from* God's authority and established dogmas and free man *for* his own autonomy. One manifestation of this shift was the advent of **deism**, in which God was seen as transcendent but not immanent. The deist's God created the universe and founded it on natural law. Like a clock maker, God wound up the universe and allowed it to run its course. Not surprisingly, the Age of Enlightenment saw the birth of rationalism. The universe was viewed as a machine with man at the center. Because God is not immanent in this model, special revelation is excluded, and man cannot know Him personally. However, people can use their rationality to grasp the existence of God, along with the natural laws God has built into the universe.

Deism's view

Figure 1.8

Atheistic materialism, or secularism, brought the process one more step. If God does not communicate with man and is not immanent, why do we need a god at all? The revolt of autonomous man was nearly complete by the end of the nineteenth and

Secularism's view

Figure 1.9

beginning of the twentieth centuries. Man was alone in an impersonal, mechanical universe. Secularism was unfolded in every area of life, and materialism came to dominate the West. Man was now free from all absolutes, able to decide what is true and false, right and wrong. Without God, there was no revelation. While man may reason, there is nothing transcendent to discover.

As secularism began sweeping the academy, seminaries were faced with seeping theological liberalism. Unfortunately, with few exceptions, fundamentalist and evangelical leaders opted out of the debate. In effect, they abandoned reason and called the church to "just believe." Faith was removed from the public square and privatized. Instead of defending the eminently defensible Judeo-Christian world-

Evangelical Gnosticism's view

Figure 1.10

Animism's view

Figure 1.12

view, the church disengaged from all that it considered "secular" as it retreated to a constricted place called the "sacred."

Unwittingly, Christians had fallen into the ancient Greek dichotomy dividing the universe into the spiritual realm, which was considered sacred, and the physical, viewed as profane. Faith, theology,* ethics, missions, the devotional life, and evangelism were placed in the spiritual realm and considered of first importance. Reason, science, business, politics, art, music, and meeting people's physical needs occupied the lower, physical realm. In expressing a desire to serve in missions or the pastorate, Christians often betray their dichotomized thinking when they declare that they want to go into "full-time Christian service," implying that all other Christians engaged in "secular" pursuits are part-time Christians.

Thus many Christians today suffer from "split personalities." Their lives are divided into compartments: the "religious," what they do when attending church or a Bible study; and the "secular," their jobs, recreation, and education. Millions of believers operate from this worldview, which I call evangelical gnosticism* (see Figure 1.11). Never hearing the challenge to be *consciously* Christian in their daily lives, they are conformed to the pattern of this world and have secular minds.

Yet secularism and liberal Christianity have not had the last word. The "end of history," as Francis Fukuyama put it, has not come. Worldviews continue to develop because secularism cannot meet man's deepest needs. In reaction against the deadness and decay of secularism, many people in the West are turning to the New Age (see Figure 1.12) for answers. So we are seeing a revival of Eastern animistic religion, which teaches people to escape from this physical world and concentrate on the ultimate goal—spiritual enlightenment.

Worldview's Impact on Development

What does all this have to do with development work? Nearly everything. The fundamental principles of a culture, the story it accepts as true, its people's dreams, ideals, and vision, provide the foundation for its development.

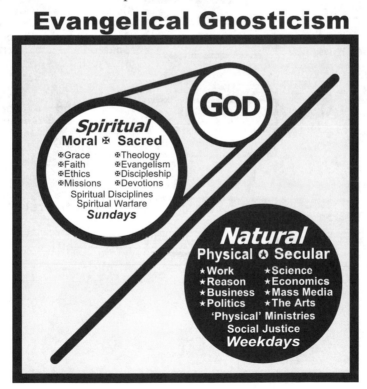

Figure 1.11

Worldview Impact on Development

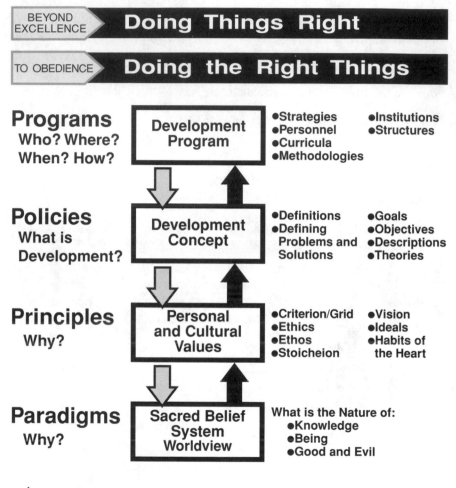

BEYOND EXCELLENCE ▶ Doing Things Right

TO OBEDIENCE ▶ Doing the Right Things

Programs
Who? Where? When? How?

Development Program
- Strategies
- Personnel
- Curricula
- Methodologies
- Institutions
- Structures

Policies
What is Development?

Development Concept
- Definitions
- Defining Problems and Solutions
- Goals
- Objectives
- Descriptions
- Theories

Principles
Why?

Personal and Cultural Values
- Criterion/Grid
- Ethics
- Ethos
- Stoicheion
- Vision
- Ideals
- Habits of the Heart

Paradigms
Why?

Sacred Belief System Worldview

What is the Nature of:
- Knowledge
- Being
- Good and Evil

↑ Kingdom Fruit

⇓ Worldview penetration

*It is **not** only important to do a program audit to insure that the program is well-run and achieves its goals; it is also important to do a "metaphysical audit" to insure that the program is reflective of the principles and paradigm that the organization holds. If a metaphysical audit is not done, an organization may find itself doing the "wrong things" professionally.*

Figure 1.13

Aid workers need to examine their own worldviews, too. Most people involved in compassion ministries are activists who focus on programs with physical goals. They want to know *who, where, when,* and *how.* They care about strategies, methods, personnel, resources, curricula, and institutions. Yet they often forget that their practices stem from policies that are derived from a particular concept of development—rooted in a worldview (see Figure 1.13).

What is development? What makes *Christian* development work *Christian?* The story a development worker holds will determine the kind of program he or she implements. Ideas have consequences, especially those centering on worldview.

Study Questions

In your own words, define worldview.

List and explain the three major categories for man's basic questions.

In what ways is a worldview like a pair of eyeglasses?

Can you give any other analogies for how a worldview operates?

Explain three ways a worldview can spread.

How did the Western church respond to the shift in predominant worldview?

How do you see this affecting your congregation?

How do you see the effects in modern missions?

What questions or challenges do you have in response to the ideas
presented in this chapter?

· CHAPTER TWO ·

Poor Stories
Worldview and Poverty

"WHY ARE PEOPLE POOR AND HUNGRY?" While on the surface this seems to be a simple question, how you answer it depends on your worldview. Your answer, in turn, will lead you to propose different solutions to the problem. In this chapter we will look at how secularists and animists answer the question, and where their answers lead. Chapter 3 will examine the answers and results offered by theism.

Secularism's Story

Secularism says that the roots of hunger are outside of man in the physical world. Secularism's story has two major positions: the evolutionary perspective and the revolutionary perspective. An evolutionary secularist will tell you that there are too many people in the world, that there is not enough food to go around, that the natural resources or infrastructure of a place is insufficient for adequate food production.

A revolutionary secularist, on the other hand, will emphasize that people are poor and hungry because of the exploitation of colonialism or Western consumerism. Again, the roots of hunger are seen as *extrinsic* to man. The bottom line for both the evolutionary secularist and his revolutionary counterpart is that people are poor and hungry because of some imbalance in the physical world.

Malthus' Population Problem

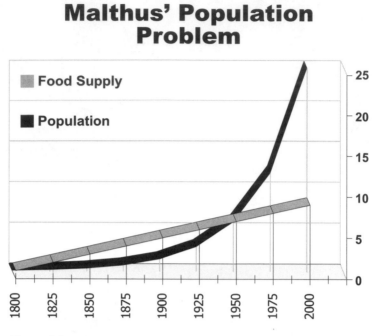

Figure 2.1

The evolutionary secularist blames hunger on factors *inside* a country or region. One example is overpopulation.* Two hundred years ago Thomas Malthus* (1766–1834) wrote a paper called "The Principle of Population,"[1] which is still the Magna Carta of overpopulation advocates such as Paul Ehrlich and worldwide agencies like Zero Population Growth and Planned Parenthood. Malthus said that population, when unchecked, increases in a geometric ratio, while the food supply increases only in an arithmetic ratio. In other words, resources grow by addition, but population grows by multiplication. Malthus, an English minister, feared that population growth would outstrip food supply, leading to mass starvation.[2]

A corollary of this story focuses not on a lack of food but on a lack of natural resources. When I was in Somalia during the 1982–83 famine, I heard some relief workers poor-mouthing Somalia as a "basket case." (True, it is one of the five or six poorest countries in the world.) Reflecting their secular mindset, these workers said Somalia would never develop because it lacks natural resources. Its greatest export is camels. "What is the market for camels in Japan, the United States, or Korea?" they asked. So in their minds, Somalia was hopeless.

They relegated an entire nation to poverty because of a shortage of natural resources.

Sometimes evolutionary secularists say the problem is not inadequate resources but a lack of infrastructure. Exhibit A for them is India, which for years has been a net food exporter. India, they say, has produced more than enough food to feed its people, yet they remain hungry. These secularists pinpoint the problem as a lack of infrastructure, that there are not enough roads, bridges, and storage facilities.

Exhibit B might be Africa, which is home to a thousand language groups. A hundred languages are spoken just in Ethiopia, and the national language, Amharic, is spoken by only 30 percent of the people. This multiplicity of languages makes it difficult for commerce, education, and communication to take place. Hence, people go hungry.

When the problem is stated this way, "There are too many people," the solution is as obvious as it is deadly. Get rid of people (see Figure 2.2). Garrett Hardin, a professor of biology at the University of California at Santa Barbara, came up with the "lifeboat ethics" concept.

Evolutionary Secularism's Answer:
" Get rid of people"

Figure 2.2

It goes like this: A big ocean liner, synonymous with the world, is sinking. There is one lifeboat, and it will not hold all the passengers. So we need to get rid of some people (exactly who is left on the ship is a matter of interesting debate). The idea is to "let nature take its course." Hardin has said that when a famine kills people, it is a tragedy for the starving people, but it is a good thing for their nation and the world. Nature is simply taking care of the overpopulation problem.[3]

Of course, some evolutionists refuse to be this cold-blooded about it. They say that we can solve this problem through science and technology. They want to stop the "rabbits" of the world from reproducing in the first place. How? Through population control. The major focus of the much criticized United Nations Conference on Population and Development in Cairo was this question: "How do we stop the people of color, the people in the Third World, from having children?"[4] Planned Parenthood strongly advocates this approach,[5] called eugenics, the movement to control human reproduction, to bring "...no more individuals into the world than can be properly cared for and those only of the best stock,"[6] to breed a superior human by weeding out the weak.

The first approach of the secular worldview, then, is evolutionary. The second is revolutionary. Here the problem does not originate from inside a country or region because of too many people or too few resources. It comes from *outside*, through imperialism or other forms of exploitation. Underdevelopment and hunger are a direct result of the oppression of the poor through complex, unjust social and economic structures. People are poor and hungry because of things totally outside their control. Those who hold this perspective say that wherever colonialism went, resources were raped, loaded onto trucks and trains, transported to the coast, and shipped to Europe, where they were consumed.[7]

Of course, for the past 40 years, colonialism has been dying around the world. Hong Kong's reversion to mainland China is just one example of the end of an era. So while political colonialism is little more than an anachronism, economic colonialism is alive and well, it is said. In this scenario, people are controlled not by governments but by multinational corporations such as Coca-Cola and Toyota. The economic power of some of these companies does in fact dwarf that of some Third World nations.

Another form of colonialism comes courtesy of quasi-governmental organizations such as the World Bank and the United Nations. These bureaucracies make decisions that have a profound impact on entire regions. For example, the World Bank has sought to encourage the development of the Amazon Basin, pumping untold millions of dollars into this ecosystem. Unfortunately, the bank's intervention has accelerated the destruction of the rain forest.

Blaming multinational agencies doesn't actually identify the root cause, the revolutionists assert; the real cause of poverty is the mass consumption lifestyle of Westerners. It has been commonly said that the United States has 6 percent of the world's population but consumes 40 percent of the world's resources. It takes 16 pounds of edible grain to produce one pound of edible beef. So every time you eat a Big Mac you are consuming four pounds of grain.[8] In much of the Third World, the argument goes, poor farmers who have been growing vegetables for their families are being enticed to start growing grain—a cash crop. These farmers grow the grain, which is shipped to "feed lots" to fatten cows that will be ground into hamburger for Big Macs. Proponents of this view see a direct correlation between our lifestyles in the West and Third World poverty. The problem, they say, comes from outside the afflicted region.

So how do you solve the problem? By redistributing scarce resources (see Figure 2.3). If 6 percent of the world's people are consuming 40 percent of its resources, the resources of the wealthy countries must be confiscated through taxation. That money must be "given back" to the poor so that everybody has equal shares. Unlike the evolutionary secularists, those who hold revolutionary views don't want to get rid of people; they want to be "fair," which means that we must slice the pie thinner and thinner and create local and global systems to redistribute resources to the poor. Ultimately, if you can't create the structures peacefully, you start a revolution.

Answering the Secularist's Evolutionary Tale

For the evolutionary secularist, Somalia is a classic example of too many people and too few resources. Somalia has no resources to speak of. 9.9 million people, or 16 per square kilometer, live in this destitute country on the horn of Africa. This is a good test of the secular stories. Japan, with about the same land mass and the same lack of natural resources, is rich. Even more damning to the evolutionist's argument is that Japan has 335 people per square kilometer–or *21 times* as many as Somalia. Or compare the former Zaire and Holland, both with abundant

Revolutionary Secularism's Answer:
"Redistribute Resources"

Figure 2.3

resources. The Congo, with 21 people per square kilometer, is ever on the verge of chaos. (Indeed, during the editing of the first edition of this book, Mobutu was overthrown and Zaire was renamed the Congo.) Holland, with 461 people per square kilometer, is stable and prosperous. China, another example, containing one fifth of the world's people, is supposed to have a great overpopulation problem. To combat it, Chinese authorities have decreed a harsh limit of one child per family. Yet China has only 131 people per square kilometer. Meanwhile, the "other China," Taiwan, has more than 670 people per square kilometer. Where would you rather live in terms of the quality of life, health care, education, and freedom?[9]

Now let's examine the revolutionary story. Are colonialism and neocolonialism really determining factors in wealth or poverty? Some very wealthy countries, such as Switzerland and Sweden, were never part of the colonial system, while a lot of current or former colonies are wealthy. Australia, the United States, and Hong Kong are a few.

Population, Resources, and Wealth

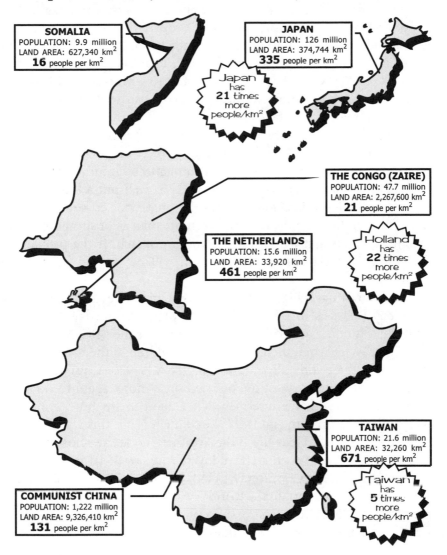

SOMALIA
POPULATION: 9.9 million
LAND AREA: 627,340 km^2
16 people per km^2

JAPAN
POPULATION: 126 million
LAND AREA: 374,744 km^2
335 people per km^2

Japan has **21** times more people/km^2

THE CONGO (ZAIRE)
POPULATION: 47.7 million
LAND AREA: 2,267,600 km^2
21 people per km^2

THE NETHERLANDS
POPULATION: 15.6 million
LAND AREA: 33,920 km^2
461 people per km^2

Holland has **22** times more people/km^2

TAIWAN
POPULATION: 21.6 million
LAND AREA: 32,260 km^2
671 people per km^2

Taiwan has **5** times more people/km^2

COMMUNIST CHINA
POPULATION: 1,222 million
LAND AREA: 9,326,410 km^2
131 people per km^2

Figure 2.4

Also, some very poor countries—Nepal and Afghanistan among them—were never part of the colonial system in the first place. Of course, in some countries, colonialism has had a negative impact, but there is no deterministic relationship between poverty and colonialism.

Saying, as revolutionists do, that the source of a country's poverty is some other system or country makes the people who actually live in the country appear helpless and impotent. They bear no responsibility for their poverty. Changing the situation from within, short of revolution, is hopeless. Is it any wonder that people so written off become dependent on others to take care of them?

Both the evolutionary and revolutionary positions stem from a materialistic point of view. Hunger and poverty are seen primarily in physical terms: in nature, in the environment, in circumstances. Both view nature as a closed system. You might as well put a titanium box around it. By definition, matter is all that matters. Resources are limited. Thus, in this scheme, man is little more than a consumer of scarce resources, an animal with a mouth and a stomach. If the problem is defined in material terms, the solution will be framed in material terms.

Malcolm Muggeridge was one of the leading television journalists of his day. He was also a third-generation Marxist. One day in Calcutta while he was doing a piece on Mother Teresa for the BBC, Muggeridge asked her, "Why, when there are so many children in the world, do you try to keep these kids alive?" Her only answer was a quizzical look. Thinking this a basic question, he tried once more, again to no avail. So he went on with his interview. That night in his hotel room, an insight dawned on him suddenly (he said later that this was his spiritual turning point). He realized that Mother Teresa saw those children in a totally different way than he did. While he saw them as consumers, she saw them as image bearers of God. To ask Mother Teresa, "Aren't there too many children in the world?" was like saying, "Mother Teresa, aren't there too many stars in the sky and too many flowers in the field?" For her it was an absurd question.

The Animistic Response

Secularism is one nonbiblical story about why people are poor and hungry. Another is animism—the amorphous religious system held to by millions of folk religionists, Buddhists, and Hindus, as well as syncrytized Muslims and Christians around the world. To the animist, the causes of hunger and poverty lie outside the physical world. Animists often believe in millions of gods, who are capricious and unpredictable. Floods and earthquakes, droughts and diseases are the physical manifestations of ultimately irrational forces. Bad things happen when the gods are angry or inattentive to man's needs. The solution? Constant appeasement.

In this worldview, man must live in harmony with the gods. Ultimately, the world we see is illusion. Man's goal is to survive the endless cycle of existence and escape the world. The spiritual world consumes the physical, because only the spiritual is real. The physical is transitory. What is man? A spirit.

Animism posits that events come solely from the outside, from the spiritual realm, as do the solutions. To solve a problem, one must appease the spirits. Other than that, nothing can be done. People are trapped. The most they can do is try to escape their lot in the next life or wait for a new golden age.

As different as these animistic and secularistic viewpoints appear to be, they still hold important common ground. All three views insist that the causes of hunger and poverty are "out there," external to man. Both revolutionary and evolutionary secularism locate the problem out in the physical environment. Animism locates the problem out in some spiritual realm.

A Qualification

Before we consider the biblical theist's radically different analysis of this problem, I want to address a common objection field workers have made about my "broad brush strokes."

Each of these three systems have an element of truth. For the sake of profit and "tolerance," multinational corporations do turn a blind eye toward terrible crimes against humanity. Brutal, tyrannical regimes exist. Unjust landowners don't allow their tenant farmers enough land to feed their families. I know corruption. I know greed. These things are real and have an impact on people's lives. Colonialism has had an impact. Neocolonialism does have an impact. There really are spirits that affect our lives. These facts are evident. But each of the three views we've briefly examined is fundamentally flawed in its assessments. It doesn't look deep enough because of its assumptions. When we look at the same problem through the story of the Bible, our biblical worldview leads us to a much broader and deeper analysis and to radically different solutions.

Study Questions

Why is it important to examine different answers to the question
   "Why are people poor and hungry?"

Describe how the following perspectives define *the problem of* and
   the solution to poverty and hunger.

   Evolutionary secularism

   Revolutionary secularism

   Animism

What are the strengths and weaknesses of each view?

Give an example of a story, accepted by the community where you
minister, that contributes to poverty.

What questions or challenges do you have in response to the ideas
presented in this chapter?

CHAPTER THREE

The Transforming Story
The Story That Develops

AS WE ENTER A NEW MILLENNIUM, missions researchers have increasingly focused on what it will take to fulfill Christ's Great Commission. Despite the incredible progress that has been made in bringing the Good News to the unevangelized and making Christianity the truly global faith that it has become this century,[1] huge swathes of the earth are still largely untouched by the gospel.

To help people in the pews get a picture of the prime area of need, Luis Bush, international director of the AD2000 and Beyond Movement,[2] advances the term *The 10/40 Window*. The "window" refers to a geographical box from 10 degrees to 40 degrees north of the Equator, stretching from North Africa in the West to Asia in the east. While in some respects the window is a simplification of complex spiritual realities on the ground, it has helped many people visualize an area of tremendous need. The need is not just "spiritual." The lands in the 10/40 Window are among the poorest on earth. Many have noticed, perhaps for the first time, that the lands with the least access to the gospel are also among the neediest.

This is no coincidence. While the two manifestations of secularism plus animism assert that the problem comes from the "outside," biblical theism correctly holds that hunger and poverty begin inside of

The 10/40 Window

The Poor, The Unevangelized, & The 10/40 Window

99% of the unevangelized poorest of the poor live in the 10/40 Window

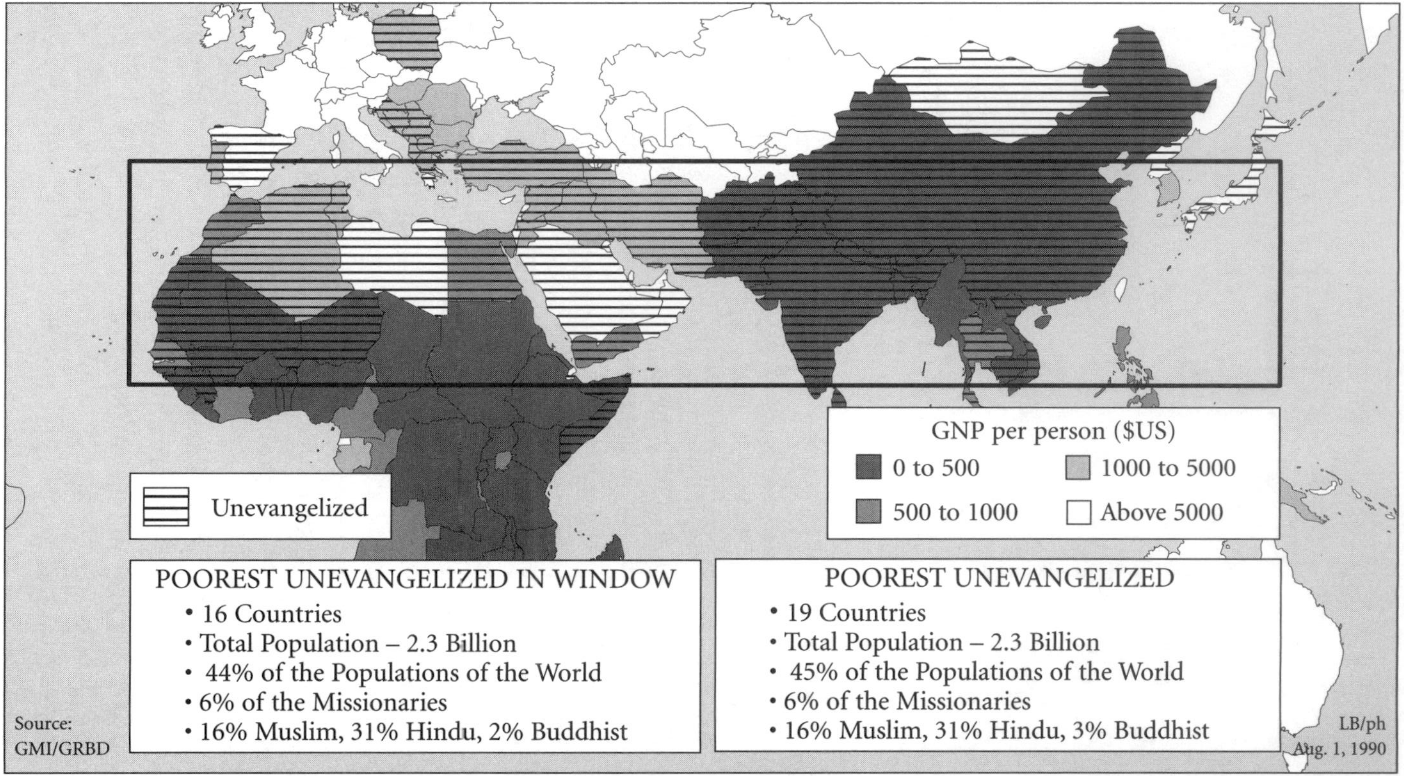

GNP per person ($US)
- 0 to 500
- 500 to 1000
- 1000 to 5000
- Above 5000

Unevangelized

POOREST UNEVANGELIZED IN WINDOW
- 16 Countries
- Total Population – 2.3 Billion
- 44% of the Populations of the World
- 6% of the Missionaries
- 16% Muslim, 31% Hindu, 2% Buddhist

POOREST UNEVANGELIZED
- 19 Countries
- Total Population – 2.3 Billion
- 45% of the Populations of the World
- 6% of the Missionaries
- 16% Muslim, 31% Hindu, 3% Buddhist

Source:
GMI/GRBD

LB/ph
Aug. 1, 1990

Figure 3.1

man. Generally, any strategy to reach those unreached with the gospel must also be a strategy to reach the poor.[3]

The Root of Poverty

So why are people poor and hungry? Except for catastrophic events such as war, drought, or flood, physical poverty doesn't "just happen." It is the logical result of the way people look at themselves and the world, the stories that they tell to make sense of their world. Physical poverty is rooted in a mindset of poverty, a set of ideas held corporately that produce certain behaviors. These behaviors can be institutionalized into the laws and structures of society. The consequence of these behaviors and structures is poverty. In the West we used to call it pauperism.* While the word has been largely abandoned as old-fashioned, the concept, *poverty of mind*, endures. Those with a poverty of mind see the world through glasses of poverty. They say, or their actions say for them, "I am poor. I will always be poor, and there is nothing I can do about it" (fatalism). Or, as many say today, "I am poor because others made me poor. They are going to have to solve my problem. I cannot."

As with all false worldviews, this kind of thinking is rooted in man's sin and rebellion against his Creator, who created a world of abundance and blessing. Man's alienation from God (and God's principles) produces a mindset of poverty that further poisons the mind, spirit, and heart. This pauper mentality has consequences in the physical world, leaving people poor and hungry—and unable to even imagine a way of escape.

The Bible is clear enough that being poor is not in itself a sin, that God has a special concern for the poor, and that being rich is not necessarily a sign of God's spiritual favor. Jesus warned repeatedly about the spiritual dangers of wealth. Yet God did not create poverty; man did. The problem is usually rooted in mindsets that retard and resist development, trapping people in destitution.

The Role of Satan

These values are lies, and they ultimately come from the devil. Jesus said of him, "He was a murderer from the beginning, not holding to the truth, for there is no truth in him. When he lies, he speaks his native language, for he is a liar and the father of lies" (John 8:44). Aiding and abetting Satan in his deceptions are other malevolent spiritual beings, referred to in the Bible as principalities and powers. The apostle Paul admonished the wayward first-century church in Galatia: "Formerly, when you did not know God, you were slaves to those who by nature are not gods. But now that you know God—or rather are known by God—how is it that you are turning back to those weak and miserable principles? Do you wish to be enslaved by them all over again?" (Galatians 4:8–9).

The spiritual principalities and powers use these "weak and miserable principles" (the Greek word is *stoicheion*[4]) to enslave people who, until they know Christ, have no alternative but to follow worldly principles that lead to death. At another point in his ministry, Paul stated, "See to it that no one takes you captive through hollow and deceptive philosophy, which depends on human tradition and the basic principles of this world rather than on Christ." (Colossians 2:8) Satan uses false *stoicheion* to enslave whole cultures in webs of lies. These deceptions impact people not only on the moral and spiritual levels but also on the social, economic, and political planes.[5] Let's look at a few of them.

Webs of Lies

One lie told in our materialistic society is "There is no tomorrow." If this is true, the hedonism of the Old World in antiquity and the rampant consumerism of the New World become logical approaches to life. If there is no future, then "eat, drink, and be merry, for tomorrow we die." Fun is one of the highest values, which at least partly explains the West's all-consuming fascination with sports, entertainment, and recreation.

Another lie is "Truth, if it exists at all, is unknowable." Secularism denies the existence of absolute truth, while animism often says that it is unknowable. In Hinduism the principle of *aviya* means "to worship the gods in ignorance." Hindu society actually values ignorance. Imag-ine you are a development worker who wants to teach poor people in India how to read and write. After all, you reason, illiterate people have little chance of improving their lives. Yet when you get there and begin to grasp the Hindu culture, it slowly dawns on you: In the Hindu system, encouraging the poor to learn is asking them to sin.

Another lie, found in both secularism and animism, is that human life has no value. Is it any surprise, as secularism has overtaken Western culture, that abortion has become so common and is cherished as a right? Few speak out for the millions of unborn children sacrificed on the altar of "choice." Hinduism, for its part, has no rationale for why people should be helped. This system asserts that the poor are poor because of what they did in their past lives, and their quickest way out of poverty in the next life is to suffer in this one. Unlike Christianity, Hinduism does not value the individual or see people as "fearfully and wonderfully made" in the image of God.

Of course, Hinduism is not the only system with a low view of man. During Ethiopia's monstrous famine in the mid-1980s, Ted Yamamori, the president of Food for the Hungry, visited a refugee camp that was home to tens of thousands. From one hut he heard a baby cry and decided to investigate. He went in and saw a baby all alone, gasping for air. Ted quickly scooped the baby into his arms and went looking for its parents. Soon he found the mother and offered her the child. "Put it back," she told him coldly. "It was meant to die." Looking her in the eye, Ted replied firmly, "No! This baby was born to live!" Not only did their statements reveal two totally different world-views, their actions produced immediately different results for that little one—because Ted Yamamori took the infant to a health center. Different worldviews, different outcomes.

The lie behind the mother's inaction was fatalism. When I first came to Food for the Hungry, I visited some friends who were working in a beautiful, almost alpine valley called Costanza in the Dominican Republic. It has many farms and a temperate climate year-round. As we drove in, I remarked, "This almost looks like paradise." The people we were working among were some of the poorest in the country, yet I saw some beautiful villas on a hill with a majestic view of the countryside. "Who owns those houses?" I asked. My companions replied, "There are some Japanese families here." It turned out that these Japanese had come to the Dominican Republic right after the war, with *nothing*. Like the locals, they labored as poor farmers. Yet after just a few decades they were prosperous, while the Dominicans still struggled to eke out a living in the midst of a breathtaking setting. The difference was not physical; it was worldview. The Japanese settlers have a social value called *gambare*, which roughly translates, "Try harder, don't give up, never give up!" (Churchill would have loved it.) The local farmers were fatalistic, believing "whatever will be, will be." A lie. Ideas have consequences. As the Bible says, "For as he thinketh in his heart, so is he" (Proverbs 23:7 KJV).

Breaking the Web of Lies

Physical conditions alone do not dictate poverty. Poverty comes from a web of lies that binds people on both personal and cultural levels. Man's sin and rebellion against God and His created order cause him to believe these lies. Since the problem begins inside of man, the solution must, too. The web must be broken in three ways—preaching the gospel, renewing minds, and discipling nations.

Proclaiming the gospel

Proclaiming the gospel breaks the power of sin and death. Paul stated boldly:

> I am not ashamed of the gospel, because it is the power of God for the salvation of everyone who believes: first for the Jew, then for the Gentile (Romans 1:16).

At another point, Paul stated:

> As for you, you were dead in your transgressions and sins, in which you used to live when you followed the ways of this world and of the ruler of the kingdom of the air, the spirit who is now at work in those who are disobedient. All of us also lived among them at one time, gratifying the cravings of our sinful nature and following its desires and thoughts. Like the rest, we were by nature objects of wrath. But because of his great love for us, God, who is rich in mercy, made us alive with Christ even when we were dead in transgressions—it is by grace you have been saved. And God raised us up with Christ and seated us with him in the heavenly realms in Christ Jesus (Ephesians 2:1–6).

Joanne Shetler, formerly a missionary among the animistic Balangao people in the Philippines, tells the story of how one friend named Tekla began experiencing her new position in Christ. "Suddenly Tekla radiated joy. 'I can actually talk to God in Balangao, my own language,' she said. 'I can even tell Him my fears. He's my protector; He's more powerful than the spirits. And He isn't like them: He doesn't lie and He doesn't need my pigs and chickens like they do. I actually matter to Him!'"[6]

Renewing the Mind

The second way to break the web of lies is to renew (or instill) the Christian mind. It's not enough to simply put our trust in Jesus Christ, although this is the indispensable first step. Because both Christians and non-Christians have fallen for Satan's propaganda, we who follow Christ must learn to think God's thoughts after Him. We live in an anti-intellectual age in which both secularism and animism dominate. We must learn to *think Christianly* in every area of life. This excludes secularizing approaches, since secularism by definition denies absolute truth, demanding its followers to live by what remains, subjective emotion. It also excludes animistic approaches, since animism is by nature mystical and anti-intellectual. We already have enough unthinking secular evangelicals and evangelical animists. Sadly, most people don't even realize that they have given up their birthright—a sound mind.

A true Christian intellectualism* is amply supported in the Bible. (In the following selections the emphasis is mine.) One day a teacher of the Old Testament law asked Jesus which commandment was most important.

> The most important one, answered Jesus, is this: "Hear, O Israel, the Lord our God, the Lord is one. Love the Lord your God with all your heart and with all your soul and *with all your mind* and with all your strength" (Mark 12:29–30).

Paul urged believers:

> Do not conform any longer to the pattern of this world, but be transformed by *the renewing of your mind.* Then you will be able to *test* and *approve* what *God's will is*— his good, pleasing and perfect will (Romans 12:2).

Elsewhere, the apostle said of his own ministry:

> We demolish *arguments* and every *pretension* that sets itself up against the *knowledge* of God, and we take captive *every thought* to make it obedient to Christ (2 Corinthians 10:5, emphasis added).

Paul never "dumbed down" the gospel to make it more palatable. God's Word commends the believers in Berea (see Acts 17:10–15), because they used their minds to discover whether the gospel was true. The apostle Peter urged Christians:

> Therefore, prepare your *minds* for action; be self-controlled; set your hope fully on the grace to be given you when Jesus Christ is revealed (1 Peter 1:13).

If we are grounded in the biblical worldview, we will be able to expose Satan's lies by knowing the truth.

> Then you will *know* the truth, and *the truth* will set you free (John 8:32).

Discipling Nations

So what did Christ mean when he told us to "disciple all nations"?

This is far from an academic exercise. Our answer to this question shows how well we know our God. He has been working at this same project since He covenanted with Abraham to make him a blessing *to all nations* (see Genesis 12:3). In Christ we have become Abraham's spiritual offspring (see Galatians 3:7). The responsibility to be a blessing is now ours. Jesus commanded His followers to

> make disciples of all nations, baptizing them in the name of the Father and of the Son and of the Holy Spirit, and teaching them to obey everything I have commanded you (Matthew 28:19,20).

Today Christians hold one of four basic mental models regarding missions and development, only one of which best reflects God's heart as revealed in Scripture. One is the *secular-evolutionary* approach, which we looked at in Chapter 2. Unfortunately, this is the view of the typical Christian relief and development agency. A second view, held by *liberation theologians*, was also discussed in the previous chapter (secular-revolutionary) and relies heavily on a Marxist analysis. The third view, *animistic-cosmological*, is an example of what I call "last-days evangelicalism." Because we are said to be in the final days before the return of Christ, these Christians mostly emphasize "saving souls" and, in some cases, providing relief supplies to the hungry. There is no long-term perspective at all. After all, if Jesus is coming back next week (or if the world will soon be destroyed by the Great Tribulation), why bother building for the future?

While both feeding and preaching are excellent, they fall short of the full-orbed biblical approach that I call *theistic-transformation*. For much of the twentieth century, an intellectual war has raged within Christendom between those who would give priority to either evangelism or social action. Both sides are right, and both are wrong. Transformation means nothing less than radical change, in all spheres of life, as when a caterpillar turns into a butterfly. It is not merely a change in religious sentiments but a radical reorientation of a person's life. The one so transformed can then go from being softheaded and susceptible to believing the world's lies to a tough-minded pursuer of truth. He goes from having a hard heart to a warm heart, unrighteous behavior to righteousness, and death to life. This transformation begins on the inside, at the level of beliefs and values, and moves outward to embrace behavior and its consequences. The gospel is so much more than evangelism. Many Christians have accepted a diluted, pietistic version of Christ's command to disciple all nations; but the gospel is God's total response to man's total need.[7]

The Bible declares, "[T]he earth will be full of the knowledge of the Lord as the waters cover the sea" (Isaiah 11:9). This is God's will, and it does not end with evangelism. We are to bring the life and wisdom* of God to bear in *all* of life, not just (as naturalists insist) in a privatized "religious" sphere. This means our goal must be nothing short of transformational development, which impacts both man's spirit and body. God intends for cultures to be redeemed. Discipling nations (εϑνος) means "laying" kingdom principles and a biblical worldview as the founding order or ethos (εϑυς) of a people. This is our historic Christian heritage, and the subject of this book.[8]

Everybody Has a Worldview

Despite the current fascination with diversity and pluralism, there are really only three major worldviews: secularism, animism, and theism. These three establish a continuum upon which all religious systems can be placed. However, along this continuum, worldviews come in a multitude of mixtures and variations. Nonetheless, each person and society can be located somewhere along the continuum.

Everybody has a worldview. If you haven't examined your own, it is probably secular or animistic, since these are the prevailing cultural tides of our day. It is essential that you examine your worldview because it affects everything you do, even how you obey Christ. Our values and behavior (and their consequences) all flow from our assumptions about reality. Those of us who want to work effectively with the poor need to learn three distinct worldviews: our own, that of the culture we're try-ing to disciple (our host culture), and biblical theism.

As long as a man holds to a mindset of poverty, changing his envi-ronment will not help him. Societies change as individuals change. Nations are discipled one person at a time. Transformational develop-ment is a dynamic process. It begins through the proclamation of the gospel and involves the exchange of lies for the truth (repentance) and death for life (regeneration). But contrary to the incomplete paradigm of so many Bible-believing Christians today, that is *just the beginning*. God intends that whole cultures be reformed to reflect His goodness and glory. To get there, individual Christians must begin thinking about worldviews and laying a kingdom foundation for cultures. Next, we will look at one crucial stone in that foundation.

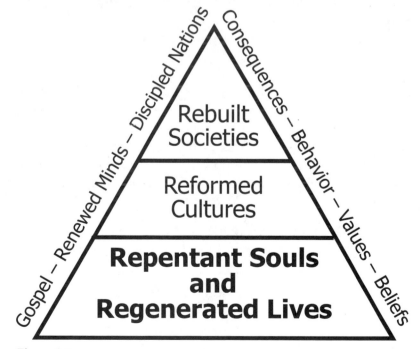

Figure 3.2

Study Questions

What is the 10/40 Window?

What is the relationship between the 10/40 Window and the world of poverty?

What are the implications of this relationship for missions? For development?

What is the root cause of poverty?

What is meant by the term *web of lies*? Give three or four examples.

What must be done to break this web of lies?

Describe each of the four basic mental models Christians use when thinking about missions and development.

What practical steps can you take to better understand the worldview of

Your home culture

Your host culture (NOTE: your host and home cultures may be different even if you minister/serve in your own country. For example: a middle-class Peruvian from Lima working in an Indian community or a rural pastor ministering in an urban center.)

Yourself

The Bible

Summarize the meaning of "transformational development."

What questions or challenges do you have in response to the ideas presented in this chapter?

The King

Praise the LORD, O my soul; all my inmost being, praise his holy
    name.
The LORD has established his throne in heaven,
        and his kingdom rules over all. Praise the LORD, you his
        angels, you mighty ones who do his bidding, who obey his
        word.
Praise the LORD, all his heavenly hosts, you his servants who do
        his will. Praise the LORD, all his works everywhere in his
        dominion.
Praise the LORD, O my soul.

Psalm 103:1, 19–22

Praise to the Lord, the Almighty, the King of creation!
O my soul, praise Him, for He is thy health and salvation:
Come, ye who hear,
Brothers and sisters, draw near,
Praise Him in glad adoration!

Praise to the Lord, who o'er all things so wondrously reigneth!
Shelters thee under His wings, yea, so gently sustaineth:
Hast thou not seen?
All that is needful has been
Granted in what He ordaineth.

Praise to the Lord, who doth prosper thy work and defend thee!
Surely His goodness and mercy here daily attend thee:
Ponder anew
What the Almighty can do,
He who with love doth befriend thee.

Praise to the Lord! O let all that is in me adore Him!
All that hath life and breath come now with praises before Him!
Let the amen
Sound from His people again:
Gladly for aye we adore Him!

Joachim Neander (1650–80)
Translated by: Catherine Winkworth (1829–78) and others

· CHAPTER FOUR ·

God Is a Person
The Universe Is Relational

IN HIS PBS TELEVISION SERIES and his book *Cosmos*, the late Carl Sagan stated with "scientific" certitude, "The Cosmos is all that is or ever was or ever will be."[1] This statement was not science. It was metaphysics. Yet few people challenged this Cornell astronomer and popularizer of science to back up his creed. In our culture's grab-bag mix of modernism and post-modernism, many people simply accepted Sagan's worldview at face value. After all, it fit nicely with the prevailing secular and animistic interpretations. If you believed that "matter is all that matters," then you could agree that only the universe, not God, is eternal. But if you were more animistic, you could take comfort in Sagan's mystical musings about our oneness with the universe. Either way, Sagan's syncretistic worldview was in opposition to the traditional Judeo-Christian position, which unabashedly holds that "In the beginning God...."

That's where the development story begins—with God, who is the chief writer, actor, producer, and critic. Only biblical theism has a correct understanding of God as king of the universe. Shakespeare said, "All the world's a stage." Let's examine the character of this king.

THE UNIVERSE

Secularism's view

Figure 4.1

THE UNIVERSE

Animism's view

Figure 4.2

THE UNIVERSE

Theism's view

Figure 4.3

Same Data, Different Stories

Each worldview, whether it is biblical theism, animism, or secularism, has a story about beginnings, a plot line, and a vision for the future. For Sagan, the key to past, present, and future was evolution. Secularism's story begins with "In the beginning Nature…." Through evolution, man develops from lower forms of life, becomes aware of himself, and eventually escapes the "superstition" of God through science, using technology to make himself more comfortable in a life that has no purpose. Evolution, at least the scientifically respectable kind, leaves no room for God. All that is comes from an impersonal mix of matter, energy, time, and chance. There is neither purpose in the universe nor future.

Animism, for its part, says, "In the beginning was an undivided spirit: a Oneness." Rather than believe evolution, the animist believes in a kind of *devolution*, a process of *de-creation* in which a myriad of gods, individual spirits, and mankind emerge from "the one." Life is a series of struggles to be mastered through the manipulation and appeasement of the gods, who are capricious and unpredictable. Man's goal is to be set free from the physical bondage of this world and to return to the unity of spirit.

Theism, by contrast, begins with a personal and infinite Creator who has made man in His image and likeness. He calls man, His vice-regent, to care for and develop the *creation* (not an impersonal "nature"). Yet man has rebelled against God and broken His everlasting laws. Man needs redemption, which God graciously provides through Jesus Christ. God's ultimate purpose for the universe, intimate fellowship with mankind, *must* be fulfilled.

Worldviews, at their roots, are either personal or impersonal. Impersonal worldviews come in two varieties. In one, Eastern *monism*, reality is seen as an organic whole. To the monist, "All is one." Hinduism, Transcendental Meditation, and Buddhism* are examples. The New Age movement, which is basically Hinduism in a business suit, is an example of the "crossover appeal" of Eastern monism in the West. The Western version of the impersonal, of course, is secularism; it is also known as *pantheism,* because the combined forces and laws of the universe are seen as "god(s)." There is no transcendent reality.

Monotheism* is only one option for those who believe the first cause of the universe is personal. The other is *polytheism.** Greek and Roman mythology, Shintoism, Mormonism, and folk animism, are all forms of this belief that there are many personal (but limited) deities. In contrast, although monotheists usually acknowledge the existence of lesser created spiritual beings, *monotheism* proposes a single infinite yet personal God. (There is yet another division. In their pure forms, Islam, Judaism, Jehovah's Witnesses and the Unity sect are all *unitarian* [God is one], while historic Christianity is *trinitarian** [the one God has revealed Himself in three Persons].)

Of these four starting points, only one—monotheism—provides an adequate foundation for life and development. The other three, each in its own way, produce cultures of poverty and death. It's only logical.

Different Starting Points

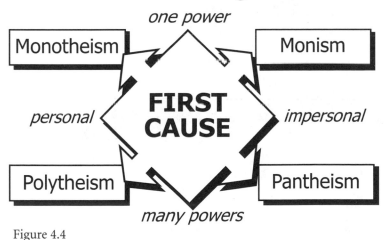

Figure 4.4

In secularism, the universe is ultimately impersonal and mechanical—a machine. Man is a biological machine as well, unable to escape his materialistic box. Nietzsche realized that if the infinite personal God of classical Christianity was dead, then man, the image bearer of God, is also dead. It was not enough for Nietzsche to cease worshiping a God who was not there. All things that come from belief in this God and that give human life meaning and beauty are also dead. Out Nietzsche's door went love, compassion, holiness, justice, truth, reason, communion, and communication, all buried with God.

In animism, the universe is ultimately spiritual. Yes, it is also "polypersonal," with many small gods. But these gods are ultimately controlled by the forces of the universe. While man's spirit is important, his rational, moral, volitional, and physical attributes have no significance.

God—A Person!

The universe is ultimately personal, in the sense that it was created by the ultimate Person. In Genesis 1 we witness a distinct Being creating with the power of His voice. God says:

> Let *us* make man
> in *our* image
> in *our* likeness
> (Genesis 1:26).

This brief quote reveals volumes about the theistic worldview. Relationship, communication, and personality are all more essential to the universe than light, time, energy, or matter! God is knowable, and by learning about Him we can learn something about His creation, about ourselves, and about how to help the poor who live among us.

A key characteristic of God is His presence. On one hand, He is transcendent, standing outside of space and time, sovereign over His creation, separate from it in both His being and His holiness. "For you, O LORD, are the Most High over all the earth; you are exalted far above all gods" (Psalm 97:9). On the other hand, God is *immanent*, near, as close at hand as a loving Father. The Bible has always shown God's desire to have a personal relationship with man, as He walks in the garden (Genesis 3:8) and lives among His people Israel (see Exodus 25:8–9; 29:42–46; and Numbers 2:1–2; 35:34). He is a father to the fatherless (Psalm 68:3–6) and the source of our life (Acts 17:27–28).

While He is transcendent, He is also immanent, wishing to dwell in the midst of the camp and in the midst of a person's life.

God expresses His nearness in four primary ways. First, by His omnipresence. Since He is everywhere, He is here now. Second, by His providence. God controls history (Hebrews 1:1–3). Historian Daniel Boorstin captured the Jewish understanding of God's control of history when he wrote:

> The tradition remained that God had not ceased His creative activity when the world had been made. Or, as a modern commentator observes, God kept on talking after His Book had gone to press. At this very moment He is creating the events of our time.[2]

God's intimate involvement in history can be seen in the Old Testament record. Examples include His making the covenant with Abraham, His deliverance of the Hebrew people from Egypt, His giving of the Ten Commandments to Moses, and His intervention in the lives of the poor and forgotten (see 1 Kings 17:9–16).

Third, the Incarnation of Christ, in which God became man, proves God's nearness to and intimate care for His creation. As Frank Houghton described it in his lovely Christmas carol:

> Thou who wast rich beyond all splendour,
> All for love's sake becamest poor.
> Thou who art God beyond all praising,
> All for love's sake becamest Man.[3]

Fourth, God proves His nearness by sending the Holy Spirit to be an indwelling Helper to Jesus' disciples (see John 14:26; 16:5–11). The Holy Spirit, the third Person of the Trinity, indwells believers, counseling them, encouraging them, praying for them, and teaching them. Our God is an intimate, personal Presence. In addition, He, the ultimate Person, made people in His image.

The universe's basic starting point, therefore, is not matter, nor energy, nor millions of spirits. No, the universe was spoken into existence by the Triune God—Father, Son, and Holy Spirit—who has let us know in unmistakable terms that He graciously wants to live among us. Yes, our God is transcendent, existing before and outside our universe.

But He is also immanent, condescending to bring us into fellowship with Himself.

God's Attributes

Another way to understand His attributes is by dividing them into two categories, the infinite and the personal. God's infinite characteristics are His and His alone, being part of His absolute being for which there are no adequate analogies in the created order. God's personal characteristics, on the other hand, are those He imparts to His image bearer, man. These are archetypal in that they provide the blueprint or standard for human beings.

Unlike many modern theologians, Christian apologist Francis Schaeffer understood the difference between God's infinite and personal attributes:

> I am as separated from God in the area of His being the Creator and infinite and I being the creature and finite, as is the atom or energy particle. I am no closer to God on this side than the machine.
> However, on the side of God's *personality*, the break comes between man and the rest of creation.... Schweitzer identified himself with the hippopotamus, for he did not understand that man's relationship is upward; and therefore he looked downward to a creature which does many of the same things as himself.[4]

Secular man says that if you want to understand man, you must study the "other" animals, apes in particular. God is irrelevant to the argument and is said to be made in the image of man. Theism, however, says that if you want to understand man, you must first study God, because man is made in the image of God, and his primary identity comes from God. Since man's humanity (what Schaeffer called his "mannishness") and all else come from God, the ultimate Person, ultimate reality is personal. God has many personal roles we can infer from the design of the universe. God is Creator, Designer, Artist, Mathematician, Architect, Composer, Poet, Lover, Communicator, Developer, and so on.

God's infinite attributes reflect the fact that He is the first cause of all that exists. No one else possesses these marks of deity. God is infinite, without limits and standing outside of space; eternal, without beginning or end, standing outside of time; omnipresent, fully and simultaneously present everywhere; omnipotent; omniscient; and immutable. God also has personal characteristics. These he has shared with man, and they are the pattern for human life. They may be divided into four areas: spiritual, intellectual, moral, and volitional.

Spiritual

God's spiritual attributes refer to the fact that He is a spirit, a living Being. As Jesus stated so majestically, "God is spirit, and his worshipers must worship in spirit and in truth" (John 4:24). Because the Creator is a Spirit, we can directly deduce that spiritual realities shape and impact the physical realm. "The Spirit of God has made me; the breath of the Almighty gives me life" (Job 33:4).[5]

Intellectual

God's intellectual attributes reflect the fact that God has a mind. God's intellect is the perfect pattern for man's limited (and now fallen) ability to reason. While man's mind is woefully limited when compared to God's boundless fountainhead of intellect, still we can learn something about the world and our place in it by pondering the mind of the Almighty, even though we will never comprehend all its awesome majesty. God's mind, as we have noted, is perfect and absolute. God sees things not only as they are but also as they ought to be. God's knowledge is comprehensive and extends to Himself, to all of creation, and to man's past, present, and future. Unlike man, who knows only in part and who tends to focus on the externals, God knows it all, including the human heart (see 1 Samuel 16:7).

For decades scientists have been searching feverishly for a unified theory of knowledge that would explain all the phenomena of the universe.[6] God already knows how everything fits together. He has known all this from eternity past and will know it just as well in eternity future. Thus, we have a sure foundation for a unified field of knowledge, because He has told us the beginning and the end. That foundation is found in the story that states with certitude beyond that of empiricism, "In the beginning God created the heavens and the earth" (Genesis 1:1). Every culture, of course, has a story that purports to explain all of life. Only God's story, which is unique among those of the nations, lays a foundation for development. It does so because it is completely true to what *is*.

Included among God's intellectual attributes is His wisdom. While knowledge is conceptual, wisdom is practical. Wisdom understands the perfect ends (*telos*) of God and appropriates the perfect means to achieve them. Wisdom's source is found in God (see Proverbs 1:7). The apostle Paul, in his letter to the church in Rome, rightly noted how much higher God's wisdom is than man's:

> Oh the depth of the riches of the wisdom and knowledge of God! How unsearchable his judgments, and his paths beyond tracing out! "Who has known the mind of the Lord? Or who has been his counselor?" (Romans 11:33–34).

God's intellect is also inextricably linked to His truthfulness (see Psalm 31:5; John 14:6). God has built the foundation for truth in three intellect-related areas. First, *logically*. God's truth is internally consistent and true to itself. It is rational. Second, *empirically*. Truth is self-evident. It can be demonstrated and is true to what is. It conforms to reality. Third, *morally*. God's truth is true to "the way things ought to be."

Consistent with His intellectual attributes, the Lord communicates His truth plainly (manifestly, demonstrably, presuppositionally); that is, He appeals to man's intellect and rationality. God discloses Himself through creation and through man. God also reveals Himself through Jesus Christ (the living Word), and through the Bible (the written Word). With two kinds of creative general revelation and two methods of communicative special revelation we see that God discloses Himself to man in four ways.

CAN GOD BE KNOWN?

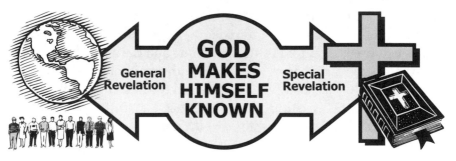

Figure 4.5

While God's revealed truth is both objective and absolute (as opposed to subjective and relative), it is not exhaustive. God has not told us all there is to know about Him. For one thing, man is a finite creature and could not absorb all there is to know anyway. It would quite literally "blow our minds." Yet the data the Lord has provided is, to borrow the words of Francis Schaeffer, "true truth." It provides a unified field of knowledge about all there is: God (the transcendent), space (the cosmos), time (history), and man (made in the image of God).

Moral

The Scriptures witness to God's goodness in many ways. God is, in Himself, absolute perfection, and His moral nature is the very definition of goodness. This is no impersonal, theoretical goodness, for we are assured that God is love (1 John 4:8). God deals bountifully and kindly toward His creation, overflowing with love and mercy. These traits are so essential to God's nature that He includes them when He reveals His name.[7] We have heard the words of John 3:16 so often that we sometimes overlook their breathtaking force: "For God so loved the world that he gave his one and only Son, that whoever believes in him shall not perish but have eternal life."

In both testaments we read of God's mercy and compassion. In the Old Testament the word is *chesed*; in the New Testament, *eleos*.[8] Both point to a God who, astonishingly, draws near to people in need.

In the world God's goodness is sometimes hard to find. During a recent refugee crisis in Sudan, relief worker Bruce Lawson was overwhelmed by the devastation and suffering. People were being brutally killed. Food, of all things, was being used as a weapon, and whole portions of the population were being starved as a matter of policy in the Muslim government's merciless *jihad*. Month after month all he could think of was the accusing question, "How can God allow this?" Lawson was faced with a terrible crisis of faith. Then one day he remembered Christ on the cross, experiencing the ultimate suffering for us. Suddenly it dawned on Lawson: God was there in the midst of this suffering, too.

Love is more than an abstract concept for God. The same *should* be said for man. Sometimes, it is. Emperor Julian was forced to admit that he had found a new breed of man among the early followers of Christ who were smeared as "atheists" because they did not worship the Roman pantheon.

Atheism has been specially advanced through the loving service rendered to strangers, and through their
care for the burial of the dead. It is a scandal that there
is not a single Jew who is a beggar, and that the godless
Galileans care not only for their own poor but for ours
as well; while those who belong to us look in vain for
the help that we should render them.[9]

This kind of love is founded not on syrupy sentimentality but on
God's righteousness. "For God is light," the New Testament informs
us; "in him there is no darkness at all" (1 John 1:5). Jesus reminds us
that His Father's name is holy (see Matthew 6:9) and that He is holy
(see Revelation 4:8). God's holiness is synonymous with His moral
perfection and the purity of His being. God's justice means He does
what is right in every circumstance. This justice was made manifest
on the cross when God refused to overlook sin, pouring out His
wrath on Jesus, who paid the penalty we deserved. As a result, the
righteousness of Christ is credited to all who believe. This transac-
tion was anything but easy, but it satisfied God's strict standard of
justice.

Volitional

Finally, the last personal attribute of God we will examine is His
will, or sovereignty. Rather than being a term of theological dispute,
God's sovereignty provides the pattern for man's vocation. As the
Creator and Sustainer of all things, visible and invisible, God is the
undisputed sovereign of the universe. As Deuteronomy 10: 14, 17 says,
"To the LORD your God belong the heavens, even the highest heavens,
the earth and everything in it…. For the LORD your God is God of gods
and Lord of lords, the great God, mighty and awesome, who shows no
partiality and accepts no bribes."

God's sovereignty is expressed in two ways—His legal will (de jure)
and His power (de facto). God rules over the universe as His kingdom
and receives glory in it because He created it. He has a legal, sovereign
right over His creation. God's de facto sovereignty means that by His
omnipotence He does whatever He pleases. God carries out His divine
will, and there is no one to stay His hand. God is sovereign. In his book
Miracles C.S. Lewis noted:

The fitness of the Christian miracles, and their difference from…mythological miracles, lies in the fact that they show invasion by a Power which is not alien. They are what might be expected to happen when she [Nature] is invaded not simply by a god, but by the God of Nature: by a Power which is outside her jurisdiction not as a foreigner but as a sovereign. They proclaim that He who has come is not merely a king, but *the* King, her King and ours.[10]

As the psalmist writes,

Lift up your heads, O you gates; be lifted up, you ancient doors, that the King of glory may come in. Who is this King of glory? The LORD strong and mighty, the LORD mighty in battle (Psalm 24:7–8).

Solomon understood nearly 3,000 years ago that God's sovereignty is uncontested.

There is no wisdom, no insight, no plan
that can succeed against the LORD (Proverbs 21:30).

The Universe Is Relational

So what? What difference does it make that the universe God crafted is fundamentally personal? As the saying goes, "No man is an island." Personality demands community. Even the one God exists as three Persons. Relationships are critical to life and health and are a primary measure of wealth. To be a person is to be in relationship. The "kinship triangle" in Figure 4.6 illustrates the different ways God and man have of relating in the context of creation.

Man is to worship and serve his Creator. God has the right of ownership over creation, while man is given the task of stewardship over all that God has made. Man is God's steward (servant) or vice-regent, in submission to God but in authority over the world and its resources. Thus, man's primary relationship, his relationship with God, is outward and vertical. This is why theology (the study of God) has been called the queen of the sciences.

The Kinship Triangle

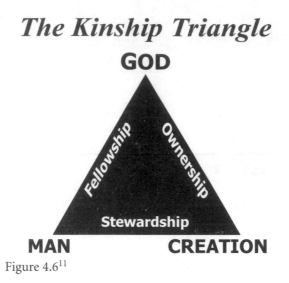

Figure 4.6[11]

The kinship triangle also points the way to man's secondary relationships. These relationships deal with what man does as God's vice-regent in creation and encompass four spheres (see Figure 4.7). The first, **psychology**,* is inward, as man studies his soul, spirit, or inner self. The second, **sociology**,* is outward, as man studies human beings in community. The third, **ecology**, the study of "the house" (*oikos*), involves man's interaction with the physical world. Ecology is related to economics, which focuses on stewardship in God's "house."[12] The fourth area, **metaphysics**, has several facets: *epistemology*, the study of knowledge and truth; *axiology*, the study of good and evil, ethics and morals; and *teleology*, the study of "ends," purpose and design—from which man gets his sense of purpose in serving his Creator.

All of life is to be lived in relationship. Human beings cannot be understood apart from their kinship with God, others, and themselves. Man's primary relationship is toward the living God. To fully experience his humanity, man must be "before the face of God," living *coram Deo*.* Man's "mannishness"—spiritual, rational, moral, and volitional—is fully esteemed when he is at home with his Creator. His humanness atrophies, however, when he is separated from God. We are to live each day *coram Deo*. The apostle Paul wrote:

> And whatever you do, whether in word or deed, do it
> all in the name of the Lord Jesus, giving thanks to God
> the Father through him (Colossians 3:17).

Man and His Relationships

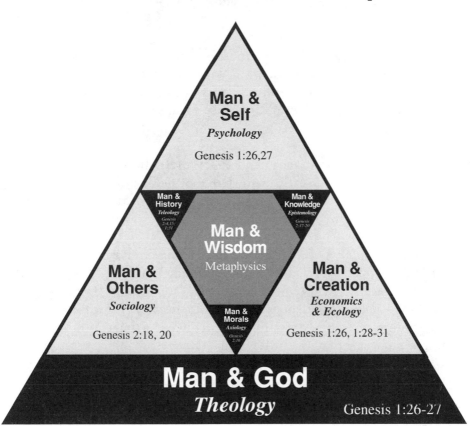

Figure 4.7

So whether you eat or drink or whatever you do, do it all for the glory of God (1 Corinthians 10:31).

[C]ontinue to work out your salvation with fear and trembling, for it is God who works in you to will and to act according to his good purpose (Philippians 2:12–13).

All of man's secondary relationships are defined in the context of this primary relationship with his Creator. If our understanding of wisdom, creation, ourselves, and others is not based upon our foundational relationship, then everything else collapses (see Figure 4.7). Paul asserted that we are to

demolish arguments and every pretension that sets itself up against the knowledge of God, and we take captive every thought to make it obedient to Christ (2 Corinthians 10:5).

Wealth and bounty, therefore, come in relationship. Poverty comes not from a lack of resources but from separating our secondary relationships from our primary one. The nature of wealth is relationships.

While naturalism defines wealth in exclusively physical terms, the consuming of things, and animism defines it primarily in spiritual terms, biblical theism overrides both. It defines wealth in terms of the wholeness of relationships, first with God, then with man, and finally with the rest of creation. Man's relationship with God is his highest form of wealth. As Paul reminded the church at Corinth:

For you know the grace of our Lord Jesus Christ, that though he was rich, yet for your sakes he became poor, so that you through his poverty might become rich (2 Corinthians 8:9).

To love God and enjoy Him forever is not only the chief end of man; it is man's supreme treasure. Material wealth, "stuff," despite what our culture intimates, is actually one of the lowest forms of wealth. He who dies with the most toys does *not* win. Material wealth is a weak substitute for bounty, which comes from God.

Worth flows down from the Creator to His creation: to man, animals, plants, and inanimate things. God created all things good, but things actually gain in value as they serve what is above them. God created a hierarchy of value, not a cosmic democracy. We are not "brothers" with the animals, much less their inferiors, contrary to what some radical environmentalists claim today. A man is more valuable than an animal, and an animal is more valuable than a rock. Minerals "serve" plants as food and man as raw materials for a multitude of products. Plants "serve" animals as food. They provide man with beauty, medicines, food, clothing, and shelter. Animals offer man power, transportation, beauty, and companionship. Man serves God with his worship and with his stewardship of creation.

Finally, the Creator is glorified by *serving the lower*. The highest expression of this, of course, came when God redeemed man through His self-sacrificial love. Man, as God's vice-regent on the earth, receives glory by serving others and stewarding creation in God's stead.

Because ideas have consequences, we need to make sure that our ideas, our stories, match reality. Thus, we must grasp our responsibility to think clearly and logically. Thankfully, the universe is intelligible, open to the probing of our minds. That is the subject of the next chapter.

Study Questions

What is significant about God wanting to dwell *with* us?

In what four ways has God revealed Himself to man?

How do people in your culture recognize God in creation?

In the fourth century, Emperor Julian commented on the impact that God's love had on the behavior and lifestyle of the early Christians. How can you extend this love more to the people you are working with?

If wealth is found primarily in relationships, use Figure 4.7 to identify places of wealth and poverty in the community where you work.

In your own words, what does it mean to live *coram Deo*?

What questions or challenges do you have in response to the ideas presented in this chapter?

CHAPTER FIVE

God Is Rational:
The Universe Is Intelligible

WHEN WILLIAM CAREY BROUGHT the gospel to late eighteenth-century India, like many visitors, he was immediately confronted with the stark poverty of this ancient society's people. But to Carey, revered by many as "the father of modern missions," the key to their poverty was found not in their lack of physical resources but in their minds, in their stories.

> "Their minds resembled their mud homesteads, devoid of pictures, ornaments and books," Carey later wrote. "Harmless, indifferent, vacant, they plod on in the path of their forefathers; and even truths in geography, astronomy, or any other science, if out of their beaten track, make no more impression on them than sublimer truths of religion."[1]

Life flows from how we think, just as the universe was fashioned by the ultimate Mind. The universe is rational, understandable, and orderly, because its Source built into it natural laws that reflect Him. Truth—objective truth—exists because He exists (see Figure 5.1). We can know truth because God has revealed it by His works and His

KNOWLEDGE

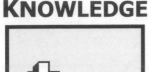

Theism's view

Figure 5.1

words. Man, because of his finiteness, cannot know this truth exhaustively; but, since he is made in the image of God he can know it objectively and to a degree. That is, man can investigate the world and draw certain conclusions that correspond to the way things really are, although man cannot know everything (see Figure 5.2).

Lest we be tempted to shrug our shoulders and yawn, it would be good to remember that only the story of biblical theism provides an adequate foundation for such an understanding. Like a tree, the roots (ideas) ultimately produce the fruit (actions). The way we answer the question "How do we know?" will determine what we consider "real," and this in turn will shape our concept of good and evil.

In its secular form, the ethic of poverty* says that truth is relative; in its animistic form, that truth is hidden, unknowable. The one leads to moral bankruptcy; the other, to ignorance.

Secularism's starting premise, that there is no God, leads inexorably to the rejection of objective standards for truth. Information replaces the formation of mind and character. Truth is relative, since the foundation for knowledge is man himself (rationalism). As Nietzsche said, "There are many eyes, therefore there are many truths, therefore there is no truth."[2] Truth, for the secularist, is in the eye of the beholder (see Figure 5.4). Something is true not because it corresponds with reality or an objective standard but because a person believes it. As Allan Bloom reminded us in *The Closing of the American Mind*, modern man's ultimate value is not truth but an openness that is open to everything except absolutes. Such "tolerance," as it is sometimes called, leaves people ill-equipped to forsake evil and choose good.

Animism, for its part, sees the universe as mysterious, unknowable, and irrational, a cosmic lottery driven by randomness, luck, or fate (see Figure 5.6). In animism, ignorance is

HOW CAN I KNOW?

Theism's answer:
Revelation and
Observation

Figure 5.2

a virtue. Very little development can take place when such thinking predominates, as Carey understood. In the context of secularism and animism, revealed reason is a radical idea with vast implications for science, economics, and education. Absolute truth, true wisdom, and real freedom depend upon and find their basis in God's revealed character.

Our Firm Foundation

God is rational. He has a reason for all that He does. As we've seen, He communicates truth about who He is and what He does in two ways—via special revelation and general revelation. Man, made in God's image, is a reasonable creature and has the capacity for an orderly mind that can grasp God's message, God's story to us. Special revelation is God's message encapsulated in Scripture. The Bible teaches us that while God is transcendent, He is nonetheless involved in His creation, governing the universe by His providence.

"In the beginning God created the heavens and the earth," the first verse of Genesis informs us in a statement that is majestic in its sweep, simple in its economy. The psalmist stated similarly, "For he spoke, and it was done; he commanded, and it stood fast" (Psalm 33:9). John the apostle said of the Son of God:

> In the beginning was the Word, and the Word was with God, and the Word was God. He was with God in the beginning. Through Him all things were made that have been made. In Him was life, and that life was the light of men (John 1:1–4).

Secularism's view

Figure 5.3

HOW CAN I KNOW?

Secularism's answer: Rationalism

Figure 5.4

KNOWLEDGE

Animism's view

Figure 5.5

HOW CAN I KNOW?

Animism's answer:
Mysticism

Figure 5.6

These verses affirm three important truths: that God existed before all else, that He created all that is, out of nothing, and that He willed creation into existence by speaking.

General revelation, the message revealed in what God has made, while not so specific, tells mankind other vital truths about God. The apostle Paul told the church at Rome:

> For the wrath of God is revealed from heaven against all ungodliness and unrighteousness of men, who suppress the truth of God in unrighteousness, for what may be known of God is manifest in them, for God has shown it to them. For since the creation of the world His invisible attributes are clearly seen, being understood by the things that are made, even His eternal power and Godhead, so that they are without excuse (Romans 1:18–20 NKJV).

Upon seeing a beautiful sunrise from atop Mount Snowden, Wordsworth wrote:

> Reflected, it appeared to me the type
> Of a majestic *intellect,*
> .... There I beheld the *emblem of a mind.*[3]

French biologist Jacques Monod (1910–1976) wrote:

> Objectivity nevertheless obliges us to recognize the teleonomic character of living organisms, to admit that in their structure and performance they act projectively—realize and pursue a purpose.[4]

When they are honest, both poet and scientist recognize creation's beauty and purposefulness. The creation reveals a Creator. As Paul affirmed, "For since the creation of the world his invisible attributes are clearly seen, being understood by the things that are made...."

Truth and beauty, science and art, order and spontaneity all reveal the Mind of the consummate Mathematician-Artist. As Schaeffer noted, life is bordered by both form and freedom, which in their own ways point back to God. We have noted that He reveals His divine order to mankind via general revelation in two ways: by the witness man has in himself, as a being in the image of God with an orderly mind, and by the external universe.

God stewards and cares for His creation actively. "He is before all things," Paul tells us about Christ, "and in him all things hold together" (Colossians 1:17). The writer to the Hebrews affirms that Christ is "sustaining all things by his powerful word" (Hebrews 1:3). The Bible says God created all that is for a purpose. The universe had a definite beginning. It also is unfolding toward a certain end. While the naturalist envisions the ultimate "heat death of the universe," and the animist is trapped in endless cycles, the biblical theist knows that history is going somewhere. God controls all of it, past, present, and future. As Creator, He started the process. As the ultimate Steward, He kindly sustains and preserves the creation, which without Him would collapse into nothingness. As sovereign King, God governs the unfolding story to its appointed end.

Orderliness of the Universe (Providence)

To borrow once more from Schaeffer, we live in a universe characterized by a uniformity of natural causes in an open system. That is, we can count on certain physical processes—gravity, for example—to continue, giving us a basis for action in a cause-and-effect world. In such a world there are consequences—good and bad—for our actions. So if we walk off a cliff in this world, we can be assured we will plunge to the ground. Nevertheless, it is an *open* system, because God is always free to act and supersede the laws by which He usually governs.

Secularism, by contrast, sees us living in a universe where there is a uniformity of natural causes in a *closed* system. The difference is crucial. For despite insisting that man is a marvelously complex being at the top of the evolutionary ladder, the secularist locks himself in a purposeless universe. History is going nowhere, except to mass extinction. To the secularist, man is just a product of chance, a cog in the machine. Freedom is an illusion, because man is only an animal. The secular scientist, having rejected reason and objective truth (the foundations for science), is like the cartoon character Wile E. Coyote. He has run headlong off a cliff. For a second it seems his momentum will carry him across the chasm. But he has left the solid ground, and it is only a moment before he comes crashing down. Sooner or later reality imposes itself upon illusion, and so the secularist must examine the assumptions he holds dear or abandon his reason.

The animist is in no better position to hold onto rationality. To the animist, the universe is ruled by gods or fates that act totally unpredictably. Natural law is unknown. The universe has no underlying order (or, in the case of Hinduism, the universe itself is an illusion). The gods bring calamity, disasters, and disease, either out of pure malevolence or because man has somehow transgressed. Therefore, instead of trying to master creation as God's vice-regent, man is reduced to wasting his life and resources attempting to appease the spirits through sacrifice. Joanne Shetler wrote of the Balangao people:

> Balangaos struggled to produce enough food for themselves and to raise enough pigs and chickens to keep the spirits pacified so they would let their children live. Sometimes an entire extended family's resources were tapped to satisfy the spirits' demands.[5]

Orderliness of the Mind

Biblical theism makes clear that there is order and that it comes from a mind. John 1:1 asserts, "In the beginning was the Word." Referring to Jesus Christ, John uses the Greek term *logos*,* which means "the expression of thought." Logos is sometimes translated "word," "speech," "reason," or "wisdom." It's no wonder that the word *logic* is derived from *logos*. Applied to Christ, we can immediately agree that this Mind, the divine reason, a preexisting intelligence, lived before human beings and provides the foundation for human reason. This *logos* is thus personal, intelligent, eternal, transcendent—indeed, life itself. C.S. Lewis said in this regard:

> He is the source from which all your reasoning power comes: you could not be right and He wrong any more than a stream can rise higher than its own source. When you are arguing against Him you are arguing against the very power that makes you able to argue at all...[6]

What is more, this Mind is not an isolated intellectual abstraction. The material world—matter—was created by this Mind and is subject to it. Man, as God's representative on earth, shares some of that authority. George Gilder writes, "Made in the image of its creator, human mind wields the power of knowledge against the power of decay."[7]

The mind of man does this through its ability to reason, which brings order to the mind. Just as natural law is to nature, so reason is to the mind. A definition for reason is "the laws of thought." Reason provides the common ground for communication, allowing analytical thinking the way intuition allows creative thinking. Judging our feelings and guiding our actions, reason allows us to commune with the mind of God, explore the world, discover and apply natural law, and bring order and civilization to the world. As Lewis stated in admiration:

> The order of the Divine mind, embodied in the Divine Law, is beautiful. What should man do but try to reproduce it, as far as possible, in his daily life?[8]

In contrast, secularism's ethic of poverty begins with the impersonal and unintelligible, throws out the foundation for objective truth, and sets in place arbitrary absolutes. Instead of the beauty of reason, it admires anti-intellectualism, subjectivism, and, indeed, irrationalism. It is said that nature abhors a vacuum. If people cease believing in God, they do not therefore believe in nothing. They will instead believe in anything, as the bloody tyranny of the twentieth century makes clear. U.C. Berkeley law professor Phillip Johnson notes:

> [T]hose who turn away from God and toward naturalistic philosophy give up their minds in the process and end up endorsing sophisticated nonsense and nature worship.[9]

Animism's ethic of poverty leads to a similar dead end. It assumes a nonrational mind (remember Hinduism's belief that ignorance is a virtue?) and a nonrational universe (think of the capriciousness of the "gods").

Principles

Without an intelligible universe, we have no truth, wisdom, or freedom. These three virtues are impossible in an irrational world.

Of course, the fountainhead of truth is Jesus Christ, who stated, "I am the way and *the truth* and the life" (John 14:6, emphasis added). Before His coming, the Greeks believed that truth was something hidden, shrouded in mystery. The New Testament writers, however, created a new word that transformed the Greek concept. To them, truth is revealed, and it corresponds with reality.[10]

Truth, moreover, is defined by God's own being, not man's. God has revealed Himself generally, as we have seen, via natural law, which is *outside of* man, and via the law of reason, which is *in* man. He has also graciously revealed Himself to the elect through His Word, both the living Word (Christ) and the written Word (the Bible). I personally learned this lesson in February of 1969.

It was a crisp, cold winter night in the Swiss Alps. Snow gently fell. My wife Marilyn and I were guests in the home of Debbie and Udo Middelmann. Sunday evenings always included time for high tea. Ten of us sat around the coffee table drinking real English tea from real china. The candle on the table danced in time with the classical music, accentuating the conversation. In the midst of this beautiful setting Udo, a German lawyer, spoke.

"Darrow, you know that Christianity is true even if you don't believe it!"

"What?"

"Christianity is true even if you don't believe it," he repeated.

This statement contradicted everything inside of me. I had been taught as a young Christian that Christianity was true *precisely* **because** *I believed it.*

For two nights I could not sleep. Finally, I realized what Udo was saying. Christianity is true even if no one in the world believes. Christianity is true because God exists. It is true because it matches reality. Christianity is true with a capital T.

With this revelation I came to understand how secular my own thinking was. Secularism says there is no God; therefore, there is no truth; everyone has an opinion; therefore, whatever you believe is true. If you believe in Buddha, that is truth *for you*. If you believe there is no God, that is truth *for you*. If you believe in Islam, that is truth *for you*. If you believe in Christianity, that is truth *for you*. I realized that I had accepted Christianity as defined by my secular set of glasses. I had a circumcised heart but an uncircumcised mind.

I also realized that if Christianity is *absolutely* true, God wants to speak into *every* area of life. My own heart had been burdened for people who were poor and needy. I realized that in addition to wanting me to be *motivated by* Christ, God wanted me to *have the mind of* Christ in my response to the problems of poverty and hunger.

Because truth is grounded in God, it is universal, applicable to and binding on all cultures. It is enduring, absolute, propositional (reasonable and rational), and knowable, at least in part. And truth is objective rather than subjective. That is, it is not based on feelings but is true whether anyone believes it or not. The objective perspective asks questions such as "Is it reasonable?" and "Does it match reality?"

Reality, of course, is an integration of the physical and the spiritual. God exists outside of nature, but nonetheless nature is real and is His creation. Truth, therefore, is found in God and in creation. It is outside of us, independent of our limited perceptions, which include our five senses plus our reason. There is a consistency between reality and worldview, and thus between the empirical and the metaphysical. Because of this, science and technology, a moral philosophy for economics, civil society, and a comprehensive philosophy for education are all possible, waiting to be discovered by man. Ideas have consequences.

Unfortunately, subjective approaches seem to have gained the upper hand at the dawn of the new millennium. Instead of asking the questions "Is it reasonable?" and "Does it match reality?"—the subjective perspective asks, "How does it feel?" and "Does it work for me?" So instead of standing on a solid foundation for development, we are mired in the quicksand of emotionalism and pragmatism.

While biblical theism understands that truth is outside of man, the subjectivist (whether he be an animist or a secularist) sees it as coming from inside of man, either through intuition (animism) or sensory-based insight (secularism). This makes sense because the animist says the natural is absorbed by the spiritual, while the secularist says that nature is all there is. Thus, for both, truth is personally "discovered." Anyone can claim to have an experience or insight by which he has come to know the truth. There is no objective standard by which we can measure the claims of those who have become enlightened or aware. For us simple-minded, mundane folks, truth is more than hidden; it is an illusion. Everything is a matter of opinion. Conveniently, this personalized approach to truth excludes any need for consistency between the physical and the spiritual.

Only biblical theism makes sense and gives proper respect to both the physical and the spiritual. Only theism offers a unified field of knowledge. All of life is unified; all knowledge is related and integrated. All the "pieces" fit together in a coherent pattern to serve God's unfolding kingdom. That is why theology was appreciated for so long as the "queen of the sciences." It is foundational to all other fields of study. Everything gets its meaning as it relates to its Creator. Everything receives its value as it relates to the higher.

Author and educator George Grant writes of Augustine:

> According to Augustine, culture is not a reflection of a people's race, ethnicity, politics, language, or heritage. Rather, it is an outworking of a people's creed. In other words, culture is the temporal manifestation of a people's faith....
> The reason he spent so much of his life and ministry critiquing the pagan philosophies of the world, and exposing the aberrant theologies of the church, was that Augustine understood only too well that those things matter not only in the realm of eternity, determining the spiritual destiny of masses of humanity, but in the realm of the here and now—determining the temporal destiny of whole civilizations.[11]

Building on Augustine's work, the Reformers knew that all of life is to be lived *coram Deo*. Secularists, however, compartmentalize or fragment life and privatize truth. Without God holding all things together, their world splinters into a billion pieces. Like centrifugal force, everything flies away from the center. Animists have a different problem. They fuse all of life and mystify truth. All of life is pulled centripetally into a collapsing star, imploding all of life into a black hole of ignorance.

Wisdom Workers: Applying the Truth

To avoid the poverty of secularism and animism, we must not simply know the truth; we must apply it. We need wisdom, which is a lens we use to both discover and apply truth. Simply put, wisdom is the moral application of truth, requiring both reflection and action. Action without reflection is mere activism,* while reflection without action is, according to Paulo Freire,[12] a powerless intellectualism. Wisdom is not something we work up or magically produce. Wisdom begins with the fear of God (see Proverbs 1:7).

Moreover, wisdom leads to life; its opposite, folly, leads to death. Wisdom personified says in Proverbs 8:35–36, "For whoever finds me finds life and receives favor from the LORD. But whoever fails to find me harms himself; all who hate me love death." There is an organic relationship between keeping God's laws and enjoying life and prosperity and between violating God's laws and experiencing death and destruction.

However, these are not a mechanical relationship. I am not preaching a "health and wealth" prosperity gospel. God is sovereign in His grace and judgment, causing the rain to fall on the just and the unjust (see Matthew 5:43–48). In this fallen world, the godly are often persecuted, and the guilty often go free. Nevertheless, as a general rule, life and prosperity follow those who live out God's principles, while those who flout God often end up paying the price. Think of all the drug addicts, the sexually promiscuous, and those who live by violence. Not many see their "threescore years and ten" (Psalm 90:10 KJV). This is to be expected. While the Old Testament is replete with God's promises of blessing for the obedient, the New Testament embraces this concept as well. Jesus said, "Therefore everyone who hears these words of mine is like a wise man who built his house on the rock" (Matthew 7:24). James exhorts:

> Do not merely listen to the word, and so deceive yourselves. Do what it says…. the man who looks intently into the perfect law that gives freedom, and continues to do this, not forgetting what he has heard, but doing it—he will be blessed in what he does (James 1:22–25).

Wisdom, the moral application of knowledge, is at the apex of the epistemological pyramid (see Figure 5.8). It is trailed by (in order) understanding, which is the dynamic perception of knowledge; knowledge, which is the apprehending of information; information, which is an assemblage of facts or data; data, which are bits of information; bits, which are pieces of data; and bytes, the smallest units of bits. So it's easy to see the mountain one has to climb to acquire wisdom, and why it is so rare. Few make it to the peak.

It's much easier to simply deny God and embrace a secular or animistic philosophy. Of course, this leads to empty minds, bereft of wisdom, and darkened hearts, destitute of compassion and understanding.

Epistemological Pyramid

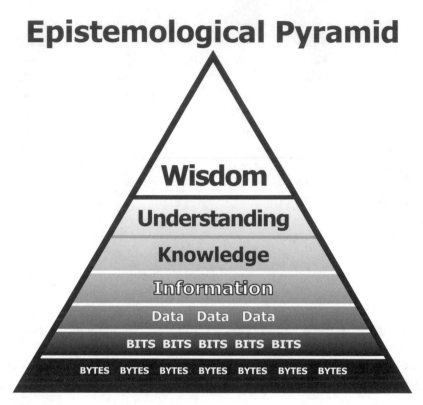

Wisdom

Understanding

Knowledge

Information

Data Data Data

BITS BITS BITS BITS BITS

BYTES BYTES BYTES BYTES BYTES BYTES BYTES

Figure 5.8

This closing of the mind and hardening of the heart leads to God's judgment and everlasting contempt. As Paul says, "For although they knew God, they neither glorified him as God nor gave thanks to him, but their thinking became futile and their foolish hearts were darkened" (Romans 1:21). Truly, as Paul says, they are "without excuse."

Yet the gospel is all about grace. Jeremiah records God's willingness to save a whole city if he can find just one wise man to work through. "Go up and down the streets of Jerusalem, look around and consider, search through her squares," God told the prophet. "If you can find but one person who deals honestly and seeks the truth, I will forgive this city" (Jeremiah 5:1). The supreme example that I can give, of course, is Jesus Christ: "For God did not send his Son into the world to condemn the world, but to save the world through him" (John 3:17). What a difference one person can make!

Today we hear much talk about "knowledge workers," even in the field of development. While good as far as it goes, this concept fails to scale the pyramid. By adding the truth and morals God has revealed, "knowledge workers" can become "wisdom workers."* These people share not only what's in their heads but also what's in their hearts. By their life, words, and work, they share their relationship to the living God. Consciously Christian (as if there is any other kind of Christian), they seek to integrate their Judeo-Christian worldview into their professional lives, helping people see God and the universe the way He made it. To do so, they encourage people to think new thoughts. They promote analytical thinking and problem solving, since these flower from the soil of biblical theism. They are uniquely equipped to move from principle to practice, from the theoretical to the practical. They help people not only understand the framework of reality but also live within it.

Wisdom workers fulfill our God-given mission; they extend God's blessing. They are the fruit of a healthy church, their deeds the flower that comes from roots in good soil. But there are other options. If we go back to tier one or two and assume different foundational issues or principles, we will inevitably build a very different society. So what are the options? In human history, what are the counterpoints to biblical liberty? What are the results when secularism wins the day on the level of ideas?

Anarchy

Integral to the work of the development worker is the concept of freedom. There can be no progress without it. The moral foundation for freedom springs from the progression that there is absolute truth, that it can be known, and that it can be applied.

While many secularists wax poetic about freedom, their system provides for anarchy, not liberty. Why? Because they have jettisoned truth. Without God, there is no absolute standard for truth. Therefore, all "truths" are subjective. The only absolute statement allowed is the one that says, "There are no absolutes." Allan Bloom summarized their position:

> There are no absolutes; freedom is absolute...The danger they have been taught to fear from absolutism is not error but intolerance.[13]

The secularist aims to counter what he sees as intolerance by openness, but this instrument is far too blunt for the delicate task of truth detecting. Lewis wrote sagely:

An open mind, in questions that are not ultimate, is
useful. But an open mind about ultimate foundations
either of Theoretical or Practical Reason is idiocy.[14]

Despotism

Besides anarchy, secularists also pave the way for uniformity. How
can this be, since anarchy seemingly allows for a limitless number of
"truths"? Because man searches for order in his world, ever seeking
control. If reality-based absolutes are jettisoned, he will cling to arbitrary ones. For example, the 1960s were the heyday of the so-called free
speech movement. Proponents espoused an anarchy of the mind,
based on this sequence: no God, therefore no truth, therefore believe in
anything. Today, however, we are inundated with what's known as
political correctness. People are told they may think only the way the
PC establishment thinks. This habit of mind comes complete with its
own "thought police," who rigorously try to enforce its rules.

More seriously, the twentieth century's sorry record of despotism
can be traced to the decline in the acceptance of moral absolutes,
nursed by Charles Darwin's theory of evolution, which by definition
excludes God. John Whitehead writes:

> Darwin spawned a philosophy of intellectual, moral,
> and ethical relativity that accompanied the amazing
> development of *totalitarian absolutism* (or uncondi-
> tional certainty of Darwinian "laws") during the twen-
> tieth century. *Relativism* (the limitation of certainty) in
> theology and morality* inevitably brings with it a
> *political absolutism*.[15]

The Bible will have none of this. Over and over it commends those
who seek truth—truth that corresponds with reality. "Now the Bereans
were of more noble character than the Thessalonians, for they received
the message with great eagerness and examined the Scriptures every
day to see if what Paul said was true" (Acts 17:11). In Isaiah 1:18, God
says to His people, "Come now, let us reason together." Paul tells us to
forsake conformity with the world and obey God.

> Do not conform any longer to the pattern of this
> world, but be transformed by the renewing of your

mind. Then you will be able to test and approve what God's will is—his good, pleasing and perfect will (Romans 12:2).

Schaeffer writes:

> Truth demands confrontation. It must be loving confrontation, but there must be confrontation nonetheless...Most of the evangelical world has not been active in the battle...Here is the great evangelical disaster— the failure of the evangelical world to stand for truth as truth...the evangelical church has accommodated to the world spirit of the age.[16]

What Schaeffer calls for is a rarity in today's politically correct world: the ability to think independently, governed not by today's current fad or trend but by reason. The individual who can do this has, with God's grace, the ability to discover the truth God has revealed in creation, in history, and in the Scriptures. As theologian J. Gresham Machen noted:

> It is a great mistake...to suppose that we who are called "conservatives" hold desperately to certain beliefs merely because they are old, and are opposed to the discovery of new facts. On the contrary, we welcome new discoveries with all our hearts, and we believe that our cause will come to its rights again only when youth throws off its present intellectual lethargy, refuses to go thoughtlessly with the anti-intellectual current of the age, and recovers some genuine independence of mind.[17]

Four crucial tests are available for the independent-minded person to weigh the truth in any claim. (1) *Reason*. The metaphysical or philosophical approach asks, "Is it reasonable?" (2) *Reality*. The empirical or scientific approach asks, "Does it match reality? (3) *Breadth*. The emphasis on scope or a unified field of knowledge asks, "Does it explain all of life?" (4) *Practice*. The personal or subjective approach asks, "Is it livable?" This final standard is considered only after the former tests have been applied.

Application

An intelligible universe has practical implications for every area of life. Let's consider three of the classical disciplines: science, economics, and education.

Science: Thinking God's Thoughts

Once we start asking these questions, we are well on our way to reading God's blueprints for the universe. We will be in position as God's vice-regents to unlock the universe's potential, helping our fellow human beings to also learn how to rule over and care for creation. Key weapons in our arsenal are science and technology. Far from being simply "Western constructs," they help us see, in part, how God has designed the world. To a point, they give us mastery over the physical universe as God's stewards. In a sense, science and technology allow us to think God's thoughts after Him.

This is not simply a perspective born in the technological twentieth century. William Carey, who blows apart most modern conceptions of what a "missionary" is supposed to do, thought the same thing in the eighteenth century.

> Carey wanted to introduce India to the scientific culture of astronomy. He did not believe that the heavenly bodies were "deities that governed our lives." He knew that human beings are created to govern nature, and the sun, moon, and planets are created to assist us in our task of governing. Carey thought that the heavenly bodies ought to be carefully studied since the Creator had made them to be signs or markers. They help divide the monotony of the universe of *space* into directions—East, West, North and South—and of *time* into days, years, and seasons. They make it possible for us to devise calendars; to study geography and history; to plan our lives, our work and our societies. The culture of astronomy sets us free to be rulers, whereas, the culture of astrology had made us the ruled ones—determined by our stars.[18]

Only a biblical theist such as Carey could embrace science. It is well known that science was born out of a Judeo-Christian worldview and that many of the men and women who founded today's scientific disciplines were believers.[19] Ever wonder why you have never seen an animistic scientist? The term is an oxymoron, like a square circle. The animist deifies and worships nature; he or she doesn't study it. Likewise, the Hindu says that the visible world is *maya*, or illusion. Why would a Hindu who is consistent with his philosophy seek to study what is not real?

In contrast, the Christian accepts nature as really there, since it is God's handiwork. He also sees it as inherently good, and thus worthy of study and care. And because it was spoken into existence by the Supreme Lawgiver, the universe is an orderly place, governed by natural law. Man can have dominion over nature by understanding the laws that govern it. Once man has discovered creation's order through science, he can improve his life through technology.

As discussed earlier, creation is characterized by the uniformity of natural causes in an open system. Uniformity means that physical laws* do not change throughout creation. The atomic weight of hydrogen is the same here as on the far edge of the Andromeda galaxy. We can count on mathematical precision because God created the universe precisely as He desired it to be. This is not to discount the challenges inherent in quantum physics, which describes the universe at the subatomic level that seems less orderly and neat than the one we observe directly; we know that the universe is orderly because it was created by an orderly God. It is this orderliness and precision that gives the scientist confidence in his empirical observations. Such confidence is not possible apart from a Judeo-Christian worldview. The physicist C.F. Von Weizsacker has stated:

> Matter in the Platonic sense, which must be "prevailed upon" by reason, will not obey mathematical laws exactly: matter which God has created from nothing may well strictly follow the rules which its Creator has laid down for it. In this sense I called modern science a legacy, I might even have said a child, of Christianity.[20]

Yet physical laws do not control. We live in an open system, open to God, angels, and man. God created natural law, but He is not bound by it. As the physical chemist Charles Thaxton noted:

The world does not have its own inherent rationality, but it is intelligible because it reflects God's rationality.[21]

Elsewhere, discussing a theological system known as voluntarism, Thaxton noted:

> Voluntarism insisted that the structure of the universe—indeed its very existence—is not rationally necessary but is contingent upon (the) free and transcendent will of God.[22]

The obvious implication is that the universe must be observed, which leads in turn to the scientific method. As Paul Davies, professor of mathematical physics at Australia's University of Adelaide, said while accepting the Templeton Prize on May 3, 1995:

> All the early scientists, like Newton, were religious in one way or another. They saw their science as a means for uncovering traces of God's handiwork in the universe. What we now call the laws of physics they regarded as God's abstract creation: thoughts, so to speak, in the mind of God. So in doing science, they supposed, one might be able to glimpse the mind of God—an exhilarating and audacious claim.[23]

Audacious, perhaps, but also solidly biblical. Solomon wrote:

> It is the glory of God to conceal a matter;
> to search out a matter is the glory of kings
> (Proverbs 25:2).

Man is made in God's image. With a mind patterned after God's, he can, in the words of Johann Kepler, "think God's thoughts after him." Historian Daniel Boorstin captured the adventure in all this in his 1985 book *The Discoverers*:

> My hero is Man the Discoverer. The world we now view from the literate West—the vistas of time, the land and seas, the heavenly bodies and our own bodies, the

plants and animals, history and human societies past and present—had to be opened for us by countless Columbuses. In the deep recesses of the past, they remain anonymous. As we come closer to the present, they emerge into the light of history, a cast of characters as varied as human nature. Discoveries become episodes of biography, unpredictable as the new worlds the discoverers opened to us.[24]

In contrast, the laws of nature lay unseen before the eyes of animist man, whose rational mind has not been trained to "see" because his concept of a capricious universe does not lend itself to scientific inquiry. Even the Greeks had a concept of science that was a dead end as far as modern science is concerned. The rationalist, Aristotelian concept of science was deductive, moving from the general to the particular:

> For the Aristotelian, nature consists of matter structured by purpose, essence, forms. The scientist best understands a natural object by asking what it is for.[25]

Such an approach flies in the face of modern science, which is inductive, moving from the particular to the general. Such an approach, as noted, springs from voluntarist theology.

> For if God created freely rather than by logical necessity, then we cannot gain knowledge of it by logical deduction (which traces necessary connections). Instead, we have to go out and look, to observe and experiment.[26]

The empirical method of science and other studies assumes that the universe is ordered by the Creator and that, like a book, it is God's "natural" revelation to be read and studied, and that by so doing one can learn about His power, divine nature, and laws. Once man discovers those laws by science, he is ready to use them in his technology to develop the earth. As David proclaimed:

> The heavens declare the glory of God;
> the skies proclaim the work of his hands (Psalm 19:1).

Francis Schaeffer pointed out that man is both different from and higher than nature. Created in God's image, man is to have dominion over nature and to be responsible for it. But as a created being, man in another sense is on the same level as nature. Man is a steward, told to tend the garden (Genesis) and build the city (Revelation). Again, Thaxton is instructive:

> Dominion was understood not as license to exploit nature ruthlessly, but as a responsibility to cultivate it, care for it, and harness its forces for human benefit.[27]

Science historian P.M. Rattansi notes:

> Protestant principles…imposed a religious obligation to make such study serve the twin ends of glorifying God and benefiting fellow men.[28]

Science, ideally, is the fulfillment of man's moral obligation to inquire into the nature of creation for God's glory. Technology is (or should be) the moral application of scientific knowledge for the benefit of mankind. You can spot secular applications of technology a mile away. A case in point would be the use of fetal tissue in medical research. Secular technology asks the question "Can we do it?" Theistic technology asks the additional, essential question "Ought we to do it?" Theism-based technology does not concern itself with following scientific trends wherever they may lead us into a "brave new world" shorn of morality and compassion. It is concerned with applying science to reverse the suffering and ravages of the fall: removing disease and death, increasing food production and supplies, and building machines to reduce man's toilsome, back-breaking labor.

Economics: The Economy of Mind

In a theistic perspective, economics (oikonomia[29]) is a moral philosophy. The "house" we are stewarding belongs to God. Economics is an intelligent stewardship, not mindless, menial servitude. In his book Wealth and Poverty, George Gilder states:

> Because economies are governed by thoughts, they reflect not the laws of matter but the laws of mind. One crucial law of mind is that belief precedes knowledge.[30]

Belief also precedes resources. Former Israeli Prime Minister Shimon Peres said, "This year Israel will make out of [its] brains more than the Saudis will make out of their oil wells."[31]

Solomon noted:

> Blessed is the man who finds wisdom, the man who gains understanding, for she is more profitable than silver and yields better returns than gold. She is more precious than rubies; nothing you desire can compare with her (Proverbs 3:13–15).

Discussing Judeo-Christian principles, economic journalist Warren T. Brookes states that

> wealth is not physical, but metaphysical; that it is to be found not in matter, but in mind; and that being in mind it is at once individually liberating and expansive, universally available and unifying.[32]

Wealth is not found in material things. Brookes also observes:

> We are going to have to reorient totally our thinking about the true nature of wealth. This floppy disc in my word processor is made up of ten cents worth of plastic and paper. But the program it contains is worth over $300 on the market, and the work it can do in terms of informational output displaces thousands of hours of manual clerical labor. Because it translates the physical energy into informational bits, it expands our wealth, while taking nothing from our resources.[33]

Michael Novak reminds us that the real source of wealth is *mind*, literally *caput*,* from which we derive the word *capitalism*.* Gilder points out:

> Matter is subordinate to mind and spirit and can only be comprehended by free men.... Made in the image of its creator, human mind wields the power of knowledge against the power of decay.[34]

Rational resources dominate natural resources. Again, Gilder writes:

> Gone is the view of a thermodynamic world economy, dominated by "natural resources" being turned to entropy and waste by human extraction and use. Once seen as a physical system tending toward exhaustion and decline, the world economy has clearly emerged as an intellectual system driven by knowledge. The key fact of knowledge is that it is anti-entropic; it accumulates and compounds as it is used.[35]

But none of this happens without good, old-fashioned vision.

> Where there is no vision the people perish:
> but he that keepeth the law, happy is he
> (Proverbs 29:18 KJV).

When the apostle Peter saw a disabled beggar, one thing he gave him, in addition to healing in the name of Christ, was vision: the vision that despite being crippled from birth, the man *could* in fact walk—in the name of Jesus Christ (see Acts 3:6). The Mangalwadis said of William Carey:

> Where Carey saw barren wilderness, he did not revert to lamenting, but began to plan forests. He studied trees, planted them, and then taught forestry. Where he saw weeds, he imagined gardens, cultivated them, published books and established forums…to help give sustained support to his initiatives.[36]

During a field trip when I was a student in Israel, I observed a forest-bedecked hill in the middle of what was otherwise a desert. As I looked, I realized that the trees were all the same size, which was unlike any forest I had ever seen or explored. Then I saw that the trees were not randomly distributed but were in neat rows. I asked my professor about the forest. He told me the Israelis had planted it.

"Darrow, there were two different visions for the land," he told me. "The Israelis, worshiping Jehovah, believed God when He said that this was a land flowing with milk and honey. The Palestinians believe that

Allah has cursed the land. You have two different people with two different visions for the same land." Same land, different visions—different results.

Standing above Lake Tiberias in Galilee, I again saw the Israeli vision at work: beautiful farmland stretching along the shore, a front-end loader lifting volcanic rock and thistles into dump trucks to prepare new fields for planting. The Israelis saw things not only as they were but also as they ought to be.

Vision really has two levels. On the macro level, our job is to help people see the big picture of what God is doing in history to restore the world, end hunger, and build His kingdom. On the micro level, it is to help people see His vision for the community. We want people to visualize God's good intentions for them and their communities.

Education: The Theistic Purpose of Learning

The highest purpose of education is theistic. We want people to know God. As John Milton said, "The end of all learning is to know God, and out of that knowledge to love and imitate Him."[37]

Because, as we have seen, a unified field of knowledge exists, true education should give us an integrated, comprehensive view of reality. Unlike the truncated and fragmented systems so prevalent today, learners informed by biblical theism should be able to find the relationships between God, man, and creation. They should think broadly and across disciplines. A real education examines both the physical and the transcendent, the eternal and the temporal.

We live in an intelligible universe. Because truth is both real and knowable (at least in part), we are fully justified in developing our God-given spirit of exploration, discovery, and learning. When relativism is king, knowledge is important only insofar as it is utilitarian. The drive to actually learn is shattered, replaced, at best with the method of observation, at worst with a lust to occupy one's mind and be entertained. A passion for learning exists only when truth can be known.

How different is biblical theism when it comes to education! Remember the debate between the secular humanist Dewey and the defender of a classical education, Hutchins? The former wanted merely to prepare people for a job, while the latter wanted to prepare them for life. The contrast is equally startling with animism, which imprisons the mind by prizing ignorance.

The problem with Africa is that the African mind is imprisoned. If Africa is to develop, the African mind must be set free.[38]

In Thai Buddhist culture, another expression of animism, *Ya kit mak*, is a popular phrase. It means, "Don't think too much!"

I once heard Francis Schaeffer say, "Never let a child's schooling get in the way of their education!" While his expression was grammatically inelegant, Schaeffer recognized something that most of our secularized "education establishment" has failed to grasp—that man was created to think and create throughout his life. Sixteen years of formal schooling, the new standard, is *just the beginning*. Confucius said:

> If you plan for a year, plant a seed;
> If for 10 years, plant a tree;
> If for a hundred years, teach the people.

To "get ahead," one must be educated. One must do more than work *hard*. One must also work *smart*. The wife of a former Rwandan ambassador mentioned to me that African women work extremely hard, sometimes 14 to 16 hours a day. But they make no progress because there is no order in their lives. They have no orderly foundation on which to build because the African educational system, by and large, does not encourage this. With much of the continent still steeped in animistic modes of thinking, it is no wonder that

> [M]ost of the people of the world live and die without ever achieving membership in a community larger than the family or tribe....
> Except as people create and maintain corporate organization, they cannot have a modern economy. To put the matter positively: the higher the level of living to be attained, the greater the need for organization.
> ....People live and think in very different ways, and some of these ways are radically inconsistent with the requirements of formal organizations.[39]

Civil Society: Building Order out of Chaos

The knowledge that God exists, and that He has created and maintains an orderly universe, creates a context for order in society. For a society to prosper, it must have a just legal system, political associations bound by charter relationships, civic administration based on order, and stable, rational public policy. Public servants must be and do what their name specifies. They must *serve the public*, not themselves. In the public and private sectors, hiring must be based on character and competence, not on social, family, or caste relationships. Business and government will not function for the benefit of all if truth and honesty are not esteemed. The "values" of a society must also be transformed.

These things, of course, are well nigh impossible if the worldview of Christianity is absent. The Mangalwadis point out that William Carey's "religious spirit of gentleness" and "missionary spirit of service" did much to transform the British administrators of India.

Of course, without what some call the "mediating institutions,"* none of this would make a difference. All good government and accurate scales can do is lay the groundwork. Every society needs free and responsible individuals; strong families; small, free associations of individuals; religious communities; and social, civic, and service clubs. As Francis Fukuyama so deftly pointed out, societies need a level of *trust* between members to properly function.[40]

All this, however, is not a blanket endorsement of Western democratic capitalism which is riddled with flaws. The Bible does not mandate a specific form of government and economy. We do not wish to repeat the mistakes of some of the colonial-era missionaries who thought they must "civilize the savages" before they could "Christianize" them. The Bible critiques all cultures, including Western democratic capitalism. Winston Churchill once said that democratic capitalism is "the worst form of Government, except all those other forms that have been tried from time to time."[41] Even so, societies will not be measured by the U.S. Constitution or any other, but they will be measured by the standard of God's Word.

The universe is intelligible. "The God who is there"[42] is rational. He created an orderly universe and made man in His image. Because of these facts, truth, wisdom, and freedom not only are possible but also are to be treasured. These spiritual values have a direct impact on the material world in science, economics, education, and the "civilizing" of society. Those who wish to help the poor and disciple the nations must be "wisdom workers," helping the poor to rewrite their stories—and their lives.

Study Questions

Summarize in your own words how each worldview answers these
questions about knowledge.

Concerning **Science: Thinking God's Thoughts**, describe the scientific method in your own words.

What consequences would animistic concepts of the universe
have on science and technology?

Give a real-life illustration from your own experience.

Concerning **Economics: The Economy of Mind**, what is the source of
wealth and resources?

How does this compare with your concept?

According to the story of the people you work with, where do
resources come from?

Do the people you are working with have a vision for their future? If so, what is it?

What might God's vision be for the community?

How might you facilitate their catching a better glimpse of God's vision for their future?

Concerning **Education: The Theistic Purpose of Learning**, in what ways do you see an imprisoned or disorderly mind among the people you are working with?

What is one thing you can do to set their minds free to know God?

Concerning **Civil Society: Building Order out of Chaos**, where do you see disorder in the communities where you work?

How does this contribute to poverty?

What is one way you can facilitate bringing order to a specific area of public life?

As a development worker, you are a wisdom worker. Develop a plan for consistently studying God's Word from the viewpoint of development. What biblical principles apply to the problems we need to solve? To the relationships we build? How could Christ's parables bring transformation of thinking? Share your commitment with a fellow worker.

What questions or challenges do you have in response to the ideas presented in this chapter?

CHAPTER SIX

God Is Good
The Universe Is Moral

RICHARD HAUSKNECHT IS A New York City gynecologist. His specialty is high-risk pregnancies. *The New York Times* asked him to comment about partial-birth abortions, during which a late-term "fetus" is partially extracted from its mother's birth canal, its head left inside, its skull opened with a pair of scissors, its brains sucked out with a machine, and its skull crushed (abortionists say "collapsed"), before the body is finally disposed of. Dr. Hausknecht told the *Times*:

> Any procedure at this stage is pretty gruesome. When I did second-trimester abortions, I did them late in the day, and when I'd get home, my wife would say, "You did one today, didn't you?" It would be all over my face.

Richard Hausknecht no longer does late-term abortions.[1]

Reality Check

We live in a moral universe, no matter how hard we try to deny or forget it. Our story has a moral theme. C.S. Lewis stated it most succinctly:

> First,…human beings, all over the earth, have the curi-
> ous idea that they ought to behave in a certain way, and
> cannot really get rid of it. Secondly,…they do not in
> fact behave in that way. They know the Law of Nature;
> they break it.
> These two facts are the foundation of all clear thinking
> about ourselves and the universe we live in.[2]

As we can see in the controversy over abortion, the person who defines the terms controls the debate, shapes the discussion, and influences public opinion and policy. Before the U.S. House of Representatives voted once again to outlaw partial-birth abortions (which the *Times* inaccurately called simply "late abortions"), supporters of abortion rights attempted to focus on issues such as constitutional rights, not the medical facts about what happens to the unborn infant. A memorandum from a Democratic Party pollster advised fellow campaigners:

> Don't talk about the health and condition of the fetus.
> Voters believe that this procedure, no matter what we
> call it, kills an infant.[3]

So we hear terms such as *pro-choice* and *anti-choice, pro-life* and *anti-life*, depending on the views of the person doing the defining. As the U.S. becomes increasingly pagan, a "traditional family" no longer means what it used to: a husband, a wife, and children. Today, homosexuals are routinely allowed to adopt children. Large corporations grant homosexual workers the same benefits as heterosexual couples. In fact, the traditional husband-wife relationship is being replaced in the vernacular by terms such as *domestic partners* and *significant others.*

Defining Terms

As worldview changes, so do the words that mark it. Sometimes the words stay the same, but their meanings are changed. The word *compassion* used to signify "suffering together with another." Today it has been morphed into a flabby "feeling of pity." The words *sin, holiness,* and *truth*—while still in the dictionary—have virtually disappeared from the modern vocabulary.

Having no foundation of absolutes, the modern world uses language reflecting its relativism. Instead of morals, we have values, which describe what individuals and societies deem to be valuable—not, mind you, what might actually *be* valuable. Some of the key values prized in our "tolerant" and "open" society are comfort, personal peace and affluence, and avoidance of suffering.

We also have norms, which describe what a society deems to be normal. Members are expected to conform to these standards. Among today's norms are the use of politically correct language, an openness to all ideas (even those that contradict one another), and the avoidance of concepts that "divide" us (such as truth and morality).

Of course, morality used to be the norm, when Western society operated under a different worldview. Let's look at some of the classic definitions. *Moral* comes from the Latin *moralis*, meaning "manner or custom." It refers to the practice, manners, or conduct of men as social beings in relationship to each other. The word is applied to actions that are right or wrong, virtuous or vicious. The law of God is the standard by which all acts are judged.[4] Thus, moral law is the law of God, which prescribes one's moral and social duties while prohibiting their transgression.

In the modern sense, of course, *moral* describes a society's manners and customs. It describes what *is*. The classic use of the word, however, describes what is eternal (transcendent and universal) and thus prescriptive of what *ought to be*.

Another key classical term is *ethics*. It comes from the Greek *ethos*, or "character." An ethical system is a collection of moral principles, a system of rules for regulating the manners of men in society.[5] It describes the universal and eternal standard for right and wrong. Corresponding to the classic understanding of morals, it prescribes what ought to be. There is no room for syrupy sentimentality here. *Ethos* stands in stark contrast to *pathos*, or feeling and emotions. We are to be guided by *ethos*, not *pathos*. Morality is based on an objective standard. It comes from God.

God: The Source of Morality

The Bible is clear that God is different from the gods of the nations. And because He is different, we also must be different. God told Moses:

> Speak to the entire assembly of Israel and say to them:
> "Be holy because I, the LORD your God, am holy"
> (Leviticus 19:2).

Isaiah saw an awesome vision of God in His angel-filled temple, and
the prophet was never the same again.

> And they were calling to one another: "Holy, holy, holy
> is the LORD Almighty; the whole earth is full of his
> glory." At the sound of their voices the door posts and
> thresholds shook and the whole temple was filled with
> smoke. "Woe to me!" I cried. "I am ruined! For I am a
> man of unclean lips, and I live among a people of
> unclean lips, and my eyes have seen the King, the LORD
> Almighty" (Isaiah 6:3–5).

Even the names of this God reveal His moral perfection.

> And he passed in front of Moses, proclaiming, "The
> LORD, the LORD, the compassionate and gracious God,
> slow to anger, abounding in love and faithfulness, main-
> taining love to thousands, and forgiving wickedness,
> rebellion and sin. Yet he does not leave the guilty unpun-
> ished; he punishes the children and their children for the
> sin of the fathers to the third and fourth generation"
> (Exodus 34:6–7).

Thus, the universe—created "good" by God—has a moral foundation. Morality is not a human and therefore fallible construct. It is
based on nothing less than the character of God. It is eternal, unchanging. More than this, morals establish what is the good versus evil, right
versus wrong, beautiful versus vulgar, just versus unjust, and civil versus wild. They affirm God's original design for creation and call us to
uphold that design.

Therefore, relativity is wrong. We know there really are answers to
questions such as "Is there right and wrong?" "Is there beauty?" "What
is beautiful?" So Christians can be more destructive to what is good
and beautiful than secularists—when those Christians pursue the vulgar and act unethically. Religion without goodness is, at best, anemic.

At worst, it is tyrannical. Christ calls us to rebel against what is evil and vulgar, to serve what is holy and beautiful:

> But seek first his kingdom and his righteousness, and all these things will be given to you as well (Matthew 6:33).

Theism's view

Figure 6.1

God has revealed His moral laws the same two ways we saw Him reveal His personal nature. The first is by special revelation, exemplified by the Ten Commandments, which sum up the law written on tablets of stone. The second is general revelation, in this case natural law, which is the law written on the hearts of all men.

God spoke the Ten Commandments around 1,400 B.C. to Moses, a Hebrew-born Egyptian prince on the Sinai peninsula, shortly after the exodus. These words were spoken into an animistic world where the fates ruled arbitrarily, where man constantly sought to survive the ravages of nature, where law and justice were no more than figments of the imagination. The great conservative thinker Russell Kirk aptly describes the liberating order found in God's law.

> The terror of existence without object or rule was dissipated by the revelation that man is not alone in the universe; that an Other exists; and that Other is the One God, who makes it possible for human beings to be something better than the beasts that perish. Through the revelation of order in the universe, men and women are given the possibility of becoming fully human—of finding pattern and purpose in existence, unlike dogs that live from day to day only.
>
> So the Ten Commandments, the Decalogue, are not a set of harsh prohibitions imposed by an arbitrary tribal deity. Instead, they are liberating rules that enable a people to diminish the tyranny of sin; that teach a people how to live with one another and in relation with God, how to restrain violence and fraud,

how to know justice and to raise themselves above the
level of predatory animals.[6]

This Decalogue, or "ten words," parallels the ten words God used in
creation. The Ten Commandments bring order to society, much as the
ten words in Genesis (see Genesis 1:3–29) brought order to the external universe. The Ten Commandments (see Exodus 20:1–17) create a
foundation for civil society.

The first four commandments establish man's relationship to God
in communion. That is, we are now to have a personal relationship with
Him as His people. We are to (1) worship the one true God, (2) honor
only God (and not create idols), (3) keep God's name holy, and (4) keep
the Sabbath day holy by following God's pattern of work and rest.

The last six commandments establish how we are to relate to one
another in community. We are to (5) respect authority, especially our
parents, (6) respect human life as sacred, (7) keep marriage sacred, (8)
refrain from theft (and, indeed, give to others), (9) be truthful, and
(10) be content with what we have (and refrain from coveting).

The Decalogue, then, establishes the first principles for society which
create a civil order, which we mistakenly assume to be a modern invention. They provide for equality before the law (social justice), democratic
institutions (political justice), and free markets (economic justice).

Natural law, the other way God has revealed His ways to us, is the
law written into the hearts of man. Paul said that all people, whether
they have God's specially revealed law or not, have access to God's natural law. Made in God's image, man is a moral being.

> For when the Gentiles, who do not have the law, by
> nature do the things in the law, these, although not
> having the law, are a law unto themselves, who show
> the work of the law written in their hearts, their con-
> science also bearing witness, and between themselves
> their thoughts accusing or else excusing them...
> (Romans 2:14–15).

Using more contemporary language, we might say that man is
morally programmed: He has a moral memory of right and wrong.
Using what we call his common sense, man has a capacity, to an extent,
for moral reasoning and decision making.

Natural law is real. It is God's general revelation of His moral order to all people, seen in the good that human beings do "by nature"; it is built into the very structure of human nature. It is also a means whereby we understand God's good purposes.

The human conscience is a critical part of natural law. Conscience is the ability of our hearts and minds to pass moral judgments on ourselves. It involves both the awareness of right and wrong and the ability to apply the standard to specific life situations. The conscience judges by the highest standard it knows.

However, the conscience, through repeated actions a person knows are violations of that standard, can be seared, and the heart hardened. Referring to collapsing standards in society, Senator Daniel Patrick Moynihan referred to "the defining down of deviancy." I remember one summer when I worked as a lifeguard at a beach in California. A number of times I was partnered with a guy who told me of a contest he had with another guard to see which one could have intercourse with the most women. Two months into the summer he told me that he had had sex with 26 women. This guy's seared conscience would have profound consequences for dozens of women for many years, not to mention the damage he had done to himself.

The conscience is God's voice to man's soul. Obeying this voice leads to life and health, while disobedience leads to death and destruction. The apostle Paul said of such people:

> They are darkened in their understanding and separated from the life of God because of the ignorance that is in them due to the hardening of their hearts. Having lost all sensitivity, they have given themselves over to sensuality, so as to indulge in every kind of impurity, with a continual lust for more (Ephesians 4:18–19).

Natural law has been acknowledged down through history. Not only Christian writings but also Hindu, Chinese, and Greek literature support this concept. Augustine, Aquinas, and Calvin all wrote about it. The great Christian theorist John Locke influenced the deist Thomas Jefferson to refer to natural law in the Declaration of Independence.

In his book *The Abolition of Man,* Lewis provides examples[7] of natural law from ancient Chinese sources, Cicero, classical Egypt, ancient Greece, Babylon, and Hindu culture. He points to common themes from these varied cultures on duties to children, conceptions of justice, and veracity. Echoing Christ's Golden Rule, the Hindus said:

> Utter not a word by which anyone could be wounded.

The ancient Chinese urged:

> Never do to others what you would not like them to do to you.

Cicero of Rome said:

> Men were brought into existence for the sake of men that they might do one another good.

Because human beings are made in the image of God, and because the law has been written on our hearts, we are free and responsible beings who can make real moral choices.

Moral Freedom

> The LORD God took the man and put him in the Garden of Eden to work it and take care of it. And the LORD God commanded the man, "You are free to eat from any tree in the garden; but you must not eat from the tree of the knowledge of good and evil, for when you eat of it you will surely die" (Genesis 2:15–17).

Man was given moral freedom to make choices—significant choices. The secularists believe that man is a machine, an automaton. Animists, for their part, believe that man is dominated by outside forces. The truth is, we have real freedom. This means we face both real choices and genuine consequences. Man is the proactive creator of history, not an inactive fatalist or a reactive responder. In contrast to Hinduism and Buddhism, which hold that "man enters the water and makes no ripples," theism teaches that "man enters the water and makes ripples that go on forever." Lewis stated:

> Good and evil both increase at compound interest. That is why the little decisions you and I make every day are of such infinite importance.[8]

Theism encourages forbearance. In contrast to the common extremes of intolerance and openness, theists (because they know they do not know it all) are more likely to respect the decisions of others. At the same time, they flourish in a climate that allows them to vigorously pursue the truth. While, sadly, this has not always been the case within Christendom, we can see this approach clearly in the founding of modern science.

In Genesis 3:1–7, we are confronted by the tragic story of the fall of humanity, when man chose not to accept his dignified role as man but instead attempted to become "like God." Instead of being content as God's creature, man chose to challenge the Creator, breaking his primary relationship with God. This in turn poisoned all his secondary relationships—psychological, social, even ecological.

The ultimate consequence of man's attempted usurpation is death. First and foremost is spiritual death (see Genesis 2:17). Adam and Eve died spiritually on the day they ate the forbidden fruit. Paul says that before we were saved by Christ, we were "dead in [our] transgressions and sins" (Ephesians 2:1). But there is also physical death. Man was denied the tree of life because of his disobedience (Genesis 3:24). In addition we see the insidious advent of moral evil in man, "for all have sinned and fall short of the glory of God" (Romans 3:23).

Natural evil, yet another effect, entered the world. God pronounces a curse on childbirth, on male-female relationships, and on the ground (see Genesis 3:16–19). Personal evil also engages the world. Thrust out from heaven because of his own disobedience, Satan spends his limited time attacking humanity wherever he can (see Revelation 12:7–8). When God asks Satan where he has come from, Satan replies, "From roaming through the earth and going back and forth in it" (Job 1:7).

Evil is not just "the absence of good," as secularists believe. It exists in the world on the personal, natural, and moral levels because man invited it here. Secularism is ill-equipped to deal with the challenge of evil. Commenting on the evil unleashed on Cambodia during the Khmer Rouge's reign of terror, David Aikman of *Time* magazine stated:

> In the West today, there is a pervasive consent to the notion of moral relativism, a reluctance to admit that absolute evil can and does exist. This makes it especially difficult for some to accept the fact that the Cambodian experience is something far worse than a revolutionary aberration. Rather, it is the deadly logical consequence

of an atheistic, man-centered system of values, enforced by fallible human beings with total power…By no coincidence the most humane Marxist societies in Europe today are those that, like Poland or Hungary, permit the dilution of their doctrine by what Solzhenitsyn has called "the great reserves of mercy and sacrifice" from a Christian tradition.[9]

During the debriefing of an International Hunger Corps staff person who had just returned from serving with Food for the Hungry in Rwanda, I asked:

How do you explain the recent slaughter of over a million Rwandans?

This person, who had volunteered in the refugee camps, answered:

It was hell bubbling up to the surface.

Since man invited evil into the world, in a very real sense, evil is abnormal. God did not create an evil world; He hates evil and stands against it. Man, although he brought evil into the world, is to fight against it as well. He is to obey God and rebel against Satan, who is the temporary "god of this world." Man is to discipline his personal life against moral evil, challenge the dominion of personal evil, and fight against the ravages of physical evil by feeding the hungry, clothing the naked, setting the oppressed free, and so on. How unlike animism, which sees evil as normal, as something to be accepted.

Man is significant. His choices matter. God says:

See, I set before you today life and prosperity, death and destruction…. Now choose life, that you and your children may live (Deuteronomy 30:15, 19b).

So while the fall did in fact occur, we need not be mired in pessimism. We have God with us in fighting the evil. Because Christ conquered death, as shown in His resurrection from the grave, the final victory is assured. We can thus be cultural optimists, both realistic and idealistic at the same time.

Consequences of the Fall

Without this perspective and God's power shielding us, the fall crushes us with an irresistible weight. Rebelling against God's moral law leads to moral poverty, societal breakdown, and destitution. In its secular form, the ethic of poverty starts with a disbelief in God which leads to the relativistic rejection of absolutes. People are left to make up their own rights and wrongs, according to their own subjective or cultural criteria. Instead of morality, we have situational ethics.

MORALITY

Secularism's view

Figure 6.2

Is stealing or murder wrong? In an amoral system, it depends on the situation. If there is no God, everything is permitted. An immoral world assumes a moral standard that has been violated, but an amoral world is one without a moral standard. Here slavery is not wrong, abortion is just a "choice" (without consequences), Auschwitz was a misunderstanding, and Mao really "meant well" during the Cultural Revolution.

It's easy to see that few secularists have the courage of their convictions. Most cannot live logically within their own system. Still, few bother asking the question "Is it right?" Instead, they get lost in the thickets of hedonism, asking, "Is it fun? Does it feel good?" Or pragmatism: "Does it work?" Or utilitarianism: "Is it efficient?" Or plain old egoism: "Is it convenient? Is it comfortable?" We have reduced ourselves to small men pursuing small things, our eyes trained on the ground, oblivious to heaven or hell. In *No Place for Truth,* David Wells notes:

> Modernity has emptied life of serious moral purpose. Indeed, it emptied people of the capacity to see the world in moral terms, and this in turn, closes access to reality, for reality is fundamentally moral.[10]

Not only is life stripped of its sacredness, it is decidedly less safe. Secularism means the eventual end of moral man and civil society, once its full effects are played out. Instead of civilization, we get anarchy. We have seen so many stories of gangs brutalizing joggers, mothers killing their babies, doctors killing their patients (with or without their consent) that we have been inoculated to the shock we should feel. In the face of the relentless advance of "anti-civilization," is it any wonder that the "good people" of society and the church are apathetic?

We also face consumer nihilism,* the glorifying and merchandising of death. While the most precious pearls of life—time, love, relationships, the creation—are trampled underfoot, the masses eagerly snap up the most degrading filth purveyed by pop idols. The West is suffering from a kind of moral AIDS. It is slowly dying because it does not know that its moral immune system has been neutralized, leading to infection, decay, and certain death. Personal discipline is passé. The lack of inner constraints leads to anarchy and forces the government to set up more external constraints in the form of laws, police, and prisons.

Animism's ethic of poverty similarly rejects the moral order of the universe. Animists have fled from the righteous and holy Creator to a multitude of gods who act arbitrarily, on their own inscrutable whims—the perfect models of corrupt power. In this context, the Decalogue is a radical thing. Having justice linked to the unchanging nature of a holy God undermines the power structures of animistic society. Kirk writes:

> Such faith in God's ultimate justice, a true perception coming down to the Children of Israel from the dawn of conscience, distinguished the Hebrews from the other peoples of the ancient world. The gods of Israel's neighbors were many, and they had little to do with justice. The "Baals" of Syria and Mesopotamia were local deities, propitiated sometimes by human sacrifice; they were arbitrary gods, in no kinship with human beings; no universal sovereignty was claimed for them. The gods of Assyria and Phoenicia and other nations were voracious and dreadful. The gods of Egypt were strange to the point of lunacy. The gods of the Greeks were mere personified forces of nature, whose passions and caprices no man would think of emulating.[11]

Not only were there no moral absolutes, the "absolutes" in force were purely arbitrary. In such a situation legalism flourished. Codes of conduct had nothing to do with right and wrong (except incidentally) and everything to do with tradition. They were held rigidly and without question.

Hinduism and other pantheist religions today fuse good and evil. Indira Gandhi is quoted as saying, "This is the secret of India—the acceptance of life in all its fullness, the good and the evil."[12] Instead of fighting against evil, Hindus advance their notion of a law of recompense, in which evil is almost mechanically returned for evil, and good for good. Known as karma,* all suffering is seen as deserved payment for one's sins in a former life. To fight against this law is to only invite more suffering. Karma certainly encourages a callousness of heart among the

MORALITY

Animism's view

Figure 6.3

well-off members of society, since the poor must "deserve" their wretched lot in life. Harmony in this system is sought not by aligning oneself with moral absolutes but by seeking to control or appease other people and the gods. Hinduism is ultimately a religion of power. Therefore, corruption is actually a virtue. Bribery is perfectly fine. Doctors may need an inducement to finish operating on your wife; the clerk may need a perk before he or she can give you your driver's license or business permit; the police officer is only too happy to accept a bribe to release you from jail.

Without a moral code, immorality has a free reign—with devastating consequences. The entire population of 250,000 Garifuna people in Honduras risk extinction because of the AIDS virus.[13] In other situations, the lack of monogamous marriages imprisons women in poverty. With her husband not husbanding, the woman is obliged not only to run the household but also to provide food for the family. To add insult to injury, she must live in fear of sexually transmitted diseases. American women have found the sexual revolution anything but liberating.

> The sexual revolution in the United States has been a disaster for women.
> Why is it that the sexual freedom of the last twenty years hasn't produced hordes of impoverished single fathers? The answer is that in the absence of strong cultural pressures to the contrary men, as a group, do not find it impossible to abandon their children when the

task of supporting them becomes very difficult or very unpleasant. This comes as a particular shock to a generation of women raised by men who were dependable, at a time when reliable husbands and fathers were the norm.[14]

Moral Development

A society's structure comes ultimately not from written laws or constitutions but from the moral choices of its members. For a culture to develop, its social fabric must be woven one person, one family, and one community at a time. You cannot have development in the physical realm without development in the moral realm, because the universe is ultimately moral.

Christ summarized the moral development needed by calling us to love God with all our heart (passion), soul (life), mind (intellect), and strength (physical ability), and to love our neighbor as ourselves (Mark 12:29–31). Loving God is the vertical component; loving our neighbor, the horizontal. The second flows from the first and is its direct result. Our love for God is manifested in our love for our neighbor.

As the pop song asks, "What's love got to do with it?" Why discuss love when this chapter is about morality? Because love is moral law in action. The biblical words for love and compassion are stripped of their meaning when divorced from moral law. The word for love in Hebrew is *hesed*; in Greek, *agape*. Both refer to self-sacrificing, other-serving love. The word *compassion*, meanwhile, means "to companion in suffering," to "suffer together with another." True compassion is no mere sentiment or pity. Separated from moral law, love and compassion are reduced to "doing what feels good," which might be the opposite of what *is* good.

> God wants to remind us that loving our neighbor is the essential, principal and practical way we demonstrate our love for Him. This is the irreducible minimum of God's Law, His intentions.[15]

Mangalwadi calls the practice of moral law the "culture of the cross," for it requires an active determination to expend oneself for the welfare of others. It seeks first God's kingdom and righteousness, despite the cost. It is the moral pursuit of good and an implacable rebellion against evil.

The Cross is a symbol not of compromise but of conflict. The Cross is not a passive submission before
evil. It is an active refusal to bow before evil. It is a
willingness to take the consequences of our refusal to
compromise.[16]

As people begin to apply the moral law in their lives they begin laying a moral foundation for society. Mangalwadi describes this kind of
nation building in a moral framework as "moral nationalism."* Gary
Hipp aptly noted that this is the wedding of the Great Commandment
(love of God and neighbor) and the Great Commission (making disciples of all nations). Jesus summarized, "Thy kingdom come, thy will be
done on earth as it is in heaven." God's kingdom is governed by a moral
philosophy: *oikonomia*, "the stewardship of the house." The Lord is the
King, the household is His creation, the servants are all people who
serve the King, and the task of stewardship is to extend His kingdom.
We are to tend the garden, build the city, fill the earth with the knowledge of the Lord, and bless and disciple all the nations. Nothing is so
small and insignificant that it is outside the scope of God's kingdom.
Even the common is redeemed. The prophet Zechariah saw this clearly
when he wrote:

> On that day HOLY TO THE LORD will be inscribed
> on the bells of the horses, and the cooking pots…
> (Zechariah 14:20).

Justice means freedom under laws established by government.
Despite all the antigovernment rhetoric we hear these days, the Bible
says that government is ordained by God.

> Everyone must submit himself to the governing author-
> ities, for there is no authority except that which God has
> established. The authorities that exist have been estab-
> lished by God. Consequently, he who rebels against the
> authority is rebelling against what God has instituted,
> and those who do so will bring judgment on them-
> selves…. Give everyone what you owe him: If you owe
> taxes, pay taxes; if revenue, then revenue; if respect, the
> respect; if honor, then honor (Romans 13:1–7).

As already noted, God's moral law creates the foundation for three critical areas in civil society—justice, economics, and politics.

Justice

The laws of the state are to be founded upon the law of God. Because all people are equal, justice is to be "colorblind." In Lausanne the statue called Lady Justice wears a blindfold. In one hand she holds a sword of truth, which points toward the Word of God. In the other she holds the scales of justice. In a moral order, justice is to serve the truth. Without truth and moral accountability, there is no justice. Instead of asking what is true, right, or just, the secularist asks, "What can I get away with?" In today's legal system, lawyers are charged with giving their clients the most vigorous defense they can. "Smart" lawyers, in fact, never ask their clients about their guilt or innocence.

Secularism opens the door for freedom without moral responsibility, which is anarchy. By contrast, theism provides for freedom with moral responsibility. George Washington asked the following in his farewell address to the American people in 1796:

> Where is the security for property, for reputation, for life if the sense of religious obligation deserts the oaths which are the instruments of investigation in court of justice?[17]

Where, indeed? We used to place one hand on the Bible, raising the other one, saying, "I swear to tell the truth, the whole truth, and nothing but the truth." Today there is no Bible; we simply raise one hand. We have lost our biblical foundation.

Man is, however, still responsible to obey God's higher law. Anytime the law of the state violates the moral law or an explicit command of God, then, in the words of Peter, "We must obey God rather than men!" (Acts 5:29).

Economics

Concerning economics, are free markets really necessary to apply God's moral law and express God's kingdom in this world? Are they merely one way of doing things, perhaps merely a counterpoint to the Marxist explanation of reality? Free markets acknowledge that wealth's origin comes from mind and morality. It is not something we haul up from the ground. Therefore, free markets protect people, made in the image of God, from the depredations of mercantilists, monopolists, and Marxists. Private property allows man to control the products of his own creative labor. If man is not free, he cannot create.

I am in no way advocating a secular consumerism. With freedom comes responsibility. John Wesley* summed it up beautifully:

> Work as hard as you can, save as much as you can, and give as much as you can.

Besides the responsibility to do one's best and provide for one's own is the command to provide for one's neighbor. Giving is a moral imperative. Free individuals and a competitive market are balanced by our responsibility to the community. We are to love our neighbors as ourselves. "It is more blessed to give than to receive" (Acts 20:35) is not merely a nice saying; it is a fundamental principle of life. In contrast to the failed tenets of Marxism, we are to give willingly, cheerfully, and voluntarily.

Separating economics from its moral foundations leads on the one hand to the kind of hedonistic consumerism we see in the West, with avarice and corruption running rampant. The amoral economic system found in communism, for its part, is no better. Man's creativity is destroyed, making him a cog in the state's machinery of production.

Politics

In the political realm, as Martin Luther King said, "Let freedom reign!" Because man is a sinner to the core of his being, power must not be concentrated too densely, or else tyranny will follow. Lord Acton's famous dictum applies here: "Power tends to corrupt and absolute power corrupts absolutely." Man must be protected from himself.

In America this is done by separating the executive, legislative, and judicial branches of government in a system of checks and balances. While this approach is not mandated in the Bible, it has proven to be a remarkably effective and durable form of government nonetheless. The Swiss take it one step further: They place the separate branches of government in different cities to make it harder for the politicians to collude.

Political freedom, it must be reiterated, is the freedom to do right. It is never a license to do wrong. We live in a moral universe. This allows us to live together.

The law is not a punishment or an oppressive burden imposed upon the people. On the contrary, it was the precious gift of Jehovah by which Israel might exist in justice. The Law of Jehovah was the means for living with one's self and living with one's neighbors; it was the means for regaining order in the soul and in the community.[18]

Study Questions

What is the difference between the classic and modern concepts of "morals"?

Why is it important to mark this distinction?

What is the nature of morals?

What was the impact of the Ten Commandments upon the animistic world?

Why were the Ten Commandments important for the development process?

What is natural law?

Identify several examples of natural law in the culture where you live and work.

How can you encourage and reinforce these?

How can these be used as a bridge to introduce people to God's written Law?

What were some of the consequences of man's sin?

Identify four or five ways you see sin creating poverty in your community:

1.

2

3.

4.

5.

In your own words, why is moral development an integral part of the development process?

How can you begin to use moral development to fight poverty? Be specific.

Moral laws create a foundation for building civil societies in three critical areas: justice, economics, and politics. Pick one area. Devise a lesson plan or teaching tool that would help begin engaging leaders in a discussion of how this can be used to build their community.

What questions or challenges do you have in response to the ideas presented in this chapter?

His Kingdom

In the beginning God created the heavens and the earth.
God saw all that he had made, and it was very good.

Genesis 1:1, 31a

Creation left to itself is incomplete, and humans are called to be co-creators with God, bringing forth the potentialities the creator has hidden. Creation is full of secrets waiting to be discovered, riddles which human intelligence is expected to unlock. The world did not spring from the hand of God as wealthy as humans might make it.

Michael Novak
The Spirit of Democratic Capitalism

CHAPTER SEVEN

Creation's Open System
Expanding the Boundaries

BENGALIS SOMETIMES TELL this unflattering story about their Indian Hindu neighbors:

> One day a genie appeared to a farmer in India. The being told the man he would grant him one wish— anything he desired. Overjoyed, the man began to think of great wealth. Then the genie told him, "There is only one condition: Whatever you receive will be given doubly to your neighbor." Suddenly subdued, the farmer asked the spirit to let him think about it overnight, to which the genie agreed. The next day, the genie returned. The farmer told him, "I have decided on my wish. Put out my right eye."[1]

This parable illustrates the worldview of most people who do not hold to biblical theism. In a closed system, for one person to gain, another must lose. Trust and love of neighbor are absent. Not only is this the prevailing approach in animism, it is also true of secularism. But "nature," because it is the product of a Person instead of impersonal forces, is an *open system*. Creation can be stewarded; in fact, it was designed for this purpose. *Everyone* can gain. Development is thus more about discovering and exploring God's world than merely trying to help people survive. It is about creating new resources, not redistributing scarce ones.

Secularists, and those influenced by their teaching, have a hard time with this. They are locked into a worldview that takes as an article of faith the idea that "spaceship earth" is headed for a crash. Like all pessimists, the ecological glass for them is always half empty. They believe we live in a closed system. Their brothers in the mindset of poverty, the animists, do not believe in natural laws, which cuts at the knees any kind of scientific progress. Those who look at the world as God's creation, however, have a radically different outlook. They see a world of potentialities limited only by their own creativity and moral stewardship.

> Countless parts of God's creation lay fallow for millennia until human intelligence saw value in them. Many of the things we today describe as resources were not known to be resources a hundred years ago. Many of those which may come to be of value still lie fallow today.[2]

The Real World: Three Views

Each of these stories—secularism, animism, and biblical theism—sees man and "nature" in radically different ways. They are opposed to one another and cannot all be right. Using the chart in Figure 7.2, we see these differences clearly.

Secularism's "god" is man, since he is at the top of the evolutionary food chain. This approach, as might be expected, is thoroughly anthropocentric. At least from his own perspective, man is seen as the center of the universe. The universe exists for him. But man's swagger is tempered by the belief that reality is impersonal and purely physical, that matter is all that matters.

"Nature" is seen as a closed system. The choice of terms for the external universe is revealing. We used to call it the creation, implying the existence of the Creator. But

Secularism's view

Figure 7.1

The "Nature" of Nature

	Animism	Theism	Secularism
Ruler	Nature	**GOD**	Man
Perspective	Biocentric	**Theo-centric**	Anthropo-centric
Nature	Capricious (No System)	**Open System (Created)**	Closed System
Man	A Spirit	**A Mind, The Image of God (A Living Soul)**	A Mouth, The Highest Animal
Resources	Limited Good	**Positive Sum**	Zero Sum
Man's Role	Worshipper Victim	**Steward Regent**	Consumer Miner

Figure 7.2

now the politically correct term is *nature*, which refers to what is "natural." Christians use the term without even realizing that they have lost the battle of definition. According to the secularist, nature is all there is (or, as Sagan said, "The Cosmos is all that is, or ever was or ever will be"). What we see is the sum of the chance interaction of the impersonal forces of matter and energy plus time and chance. This system is eternal, without beginning or end. Because there is no Creator, the system is closed, governed solely by the mindless laws of physics and chemistry. We live as cogs in a cosmic machine.

As cogs, we are little more than mouths,* consumers of scarce resources. We're no worse than the "other" animals—but no better, either. Any thought of man being rational or creative is simply a leftover from the theistic worldview. We are reduced to the impersonal— "mankind," or worse, "humankind"— and to mere statistics: Every day 24,000 people die of hunger.[3]

Because secularism has embraced the concept of a closed system, it is a "zero-sum game." One man's gain, by definition, is another's loss. Resources are found in the ground, and matter is all that matters. The word *resources* is almost always preceded by the word *limited*. The concept of earth's "carrying capacity"* is prominent. The "lifeboat" ethic is introduced to children early on. They are told that some people are poor because others are rich. The solution is to redistribute scarce resources to the poor.

Yet secularism has an insoluble contradiction. Despite his professed concern for "limited resources," man, as the miner/consumer, conquers, harvests, and consumes nature. Since he serves no higher authority, man has no moral standard by which to guide his use of resources. Without a moral standard, stewardship quickly lapses into exploitation. Nature is seen only for its short-term economic benefits. Man's goal is to survive in opulence. A 1980s bumper sticker put it: "He who dies with the most toys wins."

Secularism: The Overpopulation "Problem"

How did the West descend from the theistic view to the secular one? The divorce came earlier than you might think. It was not Darwin but Descartes who stood at the divide between these two worldviews. It was René Descartes, the seventeenth-century French philosopher, who turned the world upside down with his famous statement: *Cogito, ergo sum.* "I think, therefore I am."

> How different from the approach of Saint Thomas (Aquinas), for whom it is not *thought which determines existence, but existence,* "esse," *which determines thought!* I think the way I think because I am that which I am— a creature—and because He is who He is, *the absolute uncreated Mystery.*[4]

Truth, therefore, became a matter not of transcendent reality but of something materially present on earth, accessible either through research or through reason. This optimism slowly choked off the need for transcendent reality. Few people during the Enlightenment realized that their optimistic faith in human reason was simply a slick repackaging of the serpent's temptation in the garden.

But three men from post-Enlightenment Europe fleshed out the fearsome implications of a world cut adrift from its Creator. The first to look at a godless world was Nietzsche, whose key idea was "Man is dead." As we saw in Chapter 4, if God is dead, then everything that has its existence in Him is dead as well. This is "all there is." There is no immortality, making our mortal lives pointless, absurd. Death reigns.

MAN
IS
DEAD
—*Nietzsche*

In the midst of this nihilistic milieu, the hero is the individual who rises above the weak, the frail, the hungry, the poor, the feeble-minded through the "will to power." Historian Paul Johnson writes that Nietzsche recognized the "death of God" as a milestone in history.

> But he saw God not as an invention but as a casualty, and his demise as in some important sense an historical event, which would have dramatic consequences. He wrote in 1886: "The greatest event of recent times—that 'God is Dead,' that the belief in the Christian God is no longer tenable—is beginning to cast its first shadows over Europe." Among the advanced races, the decline and ultimately the collapse of the religious impulse would leave a huge vacuum. The history of modern times is in great part the history of how that vacuum has been filled. Nietzsche rightly perceived that the most likely candidate would be the "Will to Power,"….In place of religious belief, there would be secular ideology. Those who had once filled the ranks of totalitarian clergy would become totalitarian politicians. And, above all, the Will to Power would produce a new kind of messiah, uninhibited by any religious sanctions whatever, and with an unappeasable appetite for controlling mankind.[5]

Of course, without the evolutionary theories of Charles Darwin (1809–1882), Nietzsche might never have had occasion to lament the "death of God." Darwin, the British naturalist, paved the way for Nietzsche with his book *The Origin of Species*, which, it is fair to say, turned the world upside down, too. His work provided a naturalistic explanation for the universe that opposed biblical theism. Since,

according to Darwin, life evolved naturally
from lower to higher forms, there was no
longer any need to believe in a Creator.

SURVIVAL OF THE FITTEST

—*Darwin*

Darwin's theory can be summed up with
the phrase "survival of the fittest." Like
Nietzsche, Darwin enthroned man at the center of the universe, the most complex and
therefore highest product of the evolutionary
processes of random selection and mutation. *Homo sapiens*, the fittest of
all the animals, therefore can use his raw power to conquer not only
nature but also the weaker and more infirm members of his own species.
It is not hard to see where Nietzsche came up with his idea of the totalitarian "superman." Darwin's theory, in the hands of his secular followers, quickly became an ideology, blindly accepted by Western society as
an unquestioned truth by the middle of the twentieth century. This ideology had no room for the sanctity of human life. It spawned eugenics
(the science of human improvement). From there it was a short journey
to genocide—the killing of entire peoples, such as the Jews.

The third member of our trio is Thomas Malthus (1766–1834), an
Anglican priest and deist whose ideas on population and food supplies
have set the terms of the debate for 200 years. Malthus's seminal work
in 1798, *The Principles of Population*, is still highly influential. Ever since,
his followers have been fixated on what they call the "overpopulation
problem," in which population will eventually outstrip food supplies. As
a result of this train of thought, the poor could become disposable;
nature would have its way, as famine would reduce populations to more
manageable levels. Columnist Alexander Cockburn writes:

> In Malthus's era the answer to the problem of the poor
> was definitely given when the British did nothing to
> alleviate the starving to death of about 1 million Irish
> peasants.[6]

THE OVERPOPULATION PROBLEM

—*Malthus*

Neo-Malthusian scientists
have continued to articulate this
position, continually fine-tuning
their pronouncements for
today's issues. In 1968, American
biologist Paul Ehrlich argued in

The Population Bomb that overpopulation directly causes malnutrition and starvation. In 1972, the Club of Rome made an urgent call for zero population growth in *The Limits to Growth*. A report from the Worldwatch Institute stated the following:

> Science and technology can no longer ensure a better future unless population growth slows quickly. Food supply is the most immediate constraint on the Earth's population-carrying capacity.[7]

Thanks to Nietzsche, Darwin, and Malthus, the modern world believes "man is dead," its credo is "survival of the fittest," and it is fixated on an "overpopulation problem" that in the end makes people dispensable. Their basic assumptions, rooted in the Enlightenment, have woven a thick metaphysical fabric that is smothering Western society in, as Pope John Paul II has said, a "culture of death."

One of the key figures in all this was Margaret Sanger,* who started the American Birth Control League, known today as Planned Parenthood. A Malthusian and Darwinist to the core,

> [S]he was thoroughly convinced that "inferior races" were, in fact, "human weeds" and a "menace to civilization"....Her goal was "to create a race of thoroughbreds" by encouraging "more children from the fit, and less from the unfit."[8]

In 1920, Sanger wrote:

> The most merciful thing a large family can do for one of its infant members is to kill it.[9]

The heart of her work, however, is found in her 1922 book *The Pivot of Civilization*. She argued that the crisis civilization faced was not simply one of overpopulation but was one of "indiscriminate breeding,"[10] leading to biological and racial degradation. To Sanger the pivotal issue for civilization is *hunger-sex*, "the opposite poles of a single great life force"; and the pivotal factor, *birth control*.

> Herein lies the imbalance, the great biological menace to the future of civilization. Are we heading to biological

destruction, towards the gradual but certain attacks upon the stocks of intelligence and racial health by the sinister forces of the hordes of irresponsibility and imbecility?[11]

Planned Parenthood has grown from its humble beginning in the 1920s to become one of the West's most powerful advocates of social Darwinism and Malthusian policy. The founding federation in America funds 156 projects in 36 countries. The International Planned Parenthood Federation in London has 134 indigenous family planning associations around the world, many in poor countries.[12] Population control is the means of choice for the eugenics movement. Forced sterilization goes on in India, while China's infamous "one child" policy continues unabated.

Of course, belief in "overpopulation" is more a matter of blind faith than empirical reality. The term itself is a giveaway. It is an assertion without evidence—not a statement of fact. Whether a population is "over" a safe level is a matter of debate. Nicholas Eberstadt, visiting fellow at the Harvard Center for Population and Development Studies, writes:

> The problem is that "overpopulation," a term so familiar and used so frequently as to suggest that it has a fixed and understood meaning, cannot in fact be defined unambiguously. Which is to say, there is no workable demographic definition of the idea of overpopulation.[13]

Animism: Man as Pathogen

Animism, by contrast, puts not man but nature itself on the throne. The universe, which exists for itself, is animated, alive, capricious, divine. It is a manifestation of impersonal spiritual forces, a de-creation, a breaking down of the ultimate reality. Man is merely the sum of his microbiology, which in turn is a tiny fragment of the universe's incomprehensible genetic code. The world is a god to be worshiped, even to the point of human sacrifice. While it is open to the spirits, it is closed to man. Fatalism reigns. "It must be fate." "It's in the stars."

In fact, our modern remakes of animism view man as a cancer, a pathogen, an eco-tumor. Man is seen as a disease destroying the earth.

Peter Berger, director of the Institute for the Study of Economic Culture at Boston University, stated as a critic of neo-animism:

Animism's view

Figure 7.3

> In our essence, we are not individuals. We are small, insignificant parts of the vast, pulsating whole of cosmic life. We become healed as we surrender our delusional individuality to the whole. It is not life that is sacred, but the life process as a whole—Gaia, the living earth, and perhaps the entire physical universe.[14]

Man's purpose, therefore is to free the earth from himself, to cease to exist. In this system, "Mother Nature" is god, but she is a cruel mother, not at all what the modern environmentalists would have you believe. Berger adds:

> Gaia has another face. It has been revealed most fully in India. It is there given the name Kali-Durga, the consort of Shiva, the goddess who both gives and destroys life. She manifests herself naked, four-armed, her mouth gaping to show bloody fangs. In her four hands she holds a noose, a skull-topped staff, a sword, and a severed head. She is dancing on a mountain of corpses. Many people, perhaps even you, think they are not yet ready for this vision. But I assure you it is the future to which she calls us; it is the future we have already embraced.[15]

Like its secular counterpart, the animistic worldview sees resources as limited, but for a different reason. Shortages exist not because there is only so much to be extracted from the ground but because there are no physical laws. Wealth, love, friendship, beauty, and health are in limited supply. They cannot be counted upon in a capricious universe. Who knows what tomorrow will bring? The only way to increase one's supply of "wealth" is to take wealth from someone else. Therefore, many animistic societies discourage people from "getting ahead." But maintaining the status quo robs people of the mental framework they need to create, explore, and discover.

Because nature exists for itself and is higher than man in the cosmic pecking order, nature is to be worshiped and feared. Man is to submit to nature. The goal of the average animist is to survive in poverty in the short run and then be absorbed by nature in the long run.

Theism: The Reality

In contrast to secularism and animism, the story of biblical theism puts God on the throne. Everything exists for His pleasure. Fulfilling God's plan, it is *teleopic*. This God is not only infinite; He's personal, and the universe He created is both material and spiritual. Thus, wealth is found in both spheres. Man uses both mind and body to control and shape matter. Because the cosmos, a manifestation of God's creativity, is also subject to man's creativity, the universe is a marvelously open system. Yet, since it is routinely governed by natural law, we can work in it with the expectation of progress.

NATURE

Theism's view

Figure 7.4

How different from the secular view, which sees the universe as a mechanical system with no intervention from the "outside"—either from God, who is denied, or from man, who is just a cog in the machine. The animist sees the universe as open, true; but it is a wild openness.

By contrast, the biblical system is open to God, angels, and man. God, of course, is no more a part of His creation than is an author a part of a book. God is transcendent, existing in eternity past and in no way dependent on the universe. In fact, it is precisely the opposite. As Colossians says, Jesus Christ upholds all things by His power. God created the universe *ex nihilo*, out of nothing, and continues to sustain it through His omnipotent providence. "He is before all things, and in him all things hold together" (Colossians 1:17).

The Bible, of course, is sprinkled with intriguing narratives indicating that creation is open to the work of angels as well. As the writer to the Hebrews stated so well, "Are not all angels ministering spirits sent to serve those who will inherit salvation?" (Hebrews 1:14).

And the creation is certainly open to human beings. Even though man is "a machine" (being "fearfully and wonderfully made") and "an animal" (a physical being who shares many of the same physical processes with members of the animal kingdom), he is still so much more. As a being created in the image of God, man is able to influence the system, to make a difference. He is even able to influence God, who is both omnipotent and omniscient, in ways we can't even begin to understand. Both Moses and Abraham caused God to change His mind (see Exodus 32:11–14 and Genesis 18:16–33, respectively), at least from our perspective. Jesus' brother wrote, "The prayer of a righteous man is powerful and effective" (James 5:16b).

If man can make a difference in the spiritual realm, is it any surprise that he has an impact in the physical? This is not a new concept. In 1541, Paracelsus wrote:

> God did not create the planets and stars with the intention that they should dominate man, but that they, like other creatures, should obey and serve him.[16]

While creation is dependent upon God, man—as God's steward—has the capacity to unfold God's purpose for it. Think about the Wright brothers, two bicycle mechanics in what was then an "emerging nation." They dreamed of flying and proceeded to build a machine that would allow them to do it. Their invention and its progeny have opened a whole new world for the human family. (See Chapter 11 for a fuller explanation.)

Man, made in the image of God, relates primarily toward God, who is Mind. Mind is the ultimate resource. The ultimate Mind, God, existed before matter was created. The writer of Hebrews explains, "[T]he worlds were prepared by the word of God so that what is seen was not made out of things which are visible" (Hebrews 11:3). Mind created and controls matter. Man has been delegated the ability to act creatively, to originate ideas, and, with his own hands, to bring those ideas into the physical world. Resources are created and discovered. They do not spring from the ground but spring from the mind of man.

Economist Julian Simon put it this way:

> I do not believe that nature is limitlessly bountiful...
> our cornucopia is the human mind and heart, and not
> a Santa Claus natural environment.

> Resources in their raw form are useful and valuable
> only when found, understood, gathered together, and
> harnessed for human needs.[17]

We live, therefore, in a positive-sum universe. Resources are limited only by man's moral imagination, creativity, and stewardship. Theism says that wealth is found primarily in the minds and hearts of people and only secondarily in matter. The problem of poverty can be solved by creating free societies—societies that allow women and men to create new bounty for themselves and their communities.

While some individual resources (such as oil) are limited, others (such as energy from the wind or the sun) are not. Furthermore, in addition to man's natural inclination to discover, he has an economic incentive when a resource becomes scarce to develop alternatives. As examples, wind, solar, and nuclear power are alternatives to fossil fuels, while fiber optics is an alternative to the use of copper cable.

Warren Brookes writes:

> We are learning that all economic activity is…the practice of technology, the use of our unfolding knowledge and intelligence to convert seemingly useless matter into increasingly useful and valuable products, to generate wealth where none existed before. True economics, like true metaphysics, is **antientrophy**,[18*] like constant imposition of the order, utility, and organization on an otherwise chaotic and seemingly depleting material world.
>
> It is this development of the metaphysical or "know-how" component of our wealth, which has both mystified and escaped what I call the "entropicists," those who are constantly citing the Second Law of Thermodynamics as an excuse to impose "limits to growth," and to put dampers on both technology and the growth of wealth itself.
>
> Their premise is a purely engineering and materialistic view of the world which attempts to inventory our physical resources and set a time frame within which we will "run out," using this as a pretext on the one hand for rationing our utilization of these "finite"

resources, and on the other for redistributing them "fairly" around the world. Yet because they take no account of the unlimited metaphysical component of our wealth, these inventories have again and again been completely confounded by actual experience.

Julian Simon's brilliant book, *The Ultimate Resource*, documents with endless statistics the fact that our natural resources are not running out; and indeed, that the history of mankind shows, instead, a constantly expanding resource base. "Because we find new lodes, invent better production methods, and discover new substitutes," Simon writes, "the ultimate constraint upon our capacity to enjoy unlimited raw materials at acceptable prices is *knowledge*...and the source of knowledge is the human mind."

Jesus put it more simply, "It is the spirit that quickenth; the flesh profiteth nothing." This was not merely a religious truth, but a practical statement of an infinite spiritual reality that we are only now beginning to understand, namely that it is in the ideas and concepts of mind that we find real wealth, not in depletable material resources.[19]

While some would quibble with Brookes' application of Jesus' words, between the biblical response to poverty and the secular one "a great chasm has been fixed." Pastor and theologian Dennis Peacocke summarizes the distinction aptly.

The [materialist's] fiction is that there is only a fixed amount of wealth in the world and that therefore one man's gain requires another's loss. The wealthy, therefore, can only become wealthy by exploiting others; the poor become poor by being the exploited *victims*. So the state attempts to restore "justice" by taking from the wealthy and giving to the poor.

The biblical response to poverty...is to call the poor into the Kingdom, disciple them to adopt the mental and moral attitudes of good stewards under God, and train them with the skills to begin to create wealth themselves.[20]

The open system principle establishes limitless opportunities to discover new worlds, expand resources, and create positive-sum societies—where, at least theoretically, everyone has the opportunity to benefit. This story stands in sharp contrast to the closed-system story of the universe, in which man is merely a part of nature and cannot intervene in it.

Wisdom-Based Societies

From time to time the news media carry dire warnings from environmental pessimists such as Paul Ehrlich about the earth's "carrying capacity," about "limits to growth" on "spaceship earth." Though usually well intended, such thinking is simplistic and a one-dimensional way of viewing the world. *Carrying capacity*—used to describe the earth's ability to sustain human life—is a relative term. Just as an ocean has far, far more carrying capacity than does a brook, so the kind of positive-sum societies I am advocating can sustain far more people than the old animistic or secular paradigms. Again, it gets down to the fact that mind controls matter. The following illustration makes the point.

The world can support far fewer people living in hunter-gatherer societies than it can support in a society in which the people are herdsmen and farmers. Similarly, earth's carrying capacity increases as societies become agricultural, then knowledge-based, and, finally (as I am advocating), wisdom-based. Some have estimated that if the world had only hunters and gatherers, it could support only about 250 million

CARRYING CAPACITY

BROOK — *Hunter / Gatherers*

CREEK — *Farming / Herding Societies*

STREAM — *Agricultural Societies*

RIVER — *Industrial Societies*

DELTA — *Knowledge Societies*

AN OCEAN   *Wisdom Societies*

Figure 7.5

people. The estimate for industrial consumer societies is far higher, about 2 billion. The estimates are not all in for today's knowledge-based emerging global economy, but they are going up rapidly.

One thing is for sure: The debate between the pessimists and the optimists shows no signs of ending anytime soon. It is a perennial one. Marx and Weber, Malthus and Adam Smith, and Hal Lindsey (author of *The Late, Great Planet Earth*) and Dutch theologian and statesman Abraham Kuyper (who wrote *The Crown of Christian Heritage*) have all taken one side or the other. Both sides can't be right, however. How do we decide between them? We must examine the facts. Here are a few we don't hear about very often:

1. *Food production vs. population growth.* Confounding the predictions of Malthus and his heirs, food production has outpaced population growth. According to the World Health Organization's *World Health Report 1998 Executive Summary*, "…food supply has more than doubled in the past 40 years, much faster than population growth." Life expectancy has increased in every world region since 1950,[21] and the worldwide child mortality rate has declined from 250 per thousand in 1950 to only 84 in 1998.[22] "The world already produces enough food to feed the people who inhabit it today. And it could produce more."[23]

2. *Hunger-related deaths.* The chart in Figure 7.6 shows this remarkable (and largely unexpected) trend from 1950 to 1992. This is good news! There are fewer people dying from hunger each year! We can be encouraged, but there are still many who need our compassion.

3. *Grain production.* The Food and Agriculture Organization of the United Nations reports that "…over the last 50 years, the increase in global agricultural production has been 1.6 times greater than the total production level obtained in 1950, after 10,000 years of agricultural history.[24] After 50 years of modernization, world agricultural production today is more than sufficient to feed 6 billion human beings adequately. Cereal production alone, at about 2 billion tonnes or 330 kg of grain per caput/year and representing 3,600 calories per caput/day could, to a large extent cover the energy needs of the whole population if it were well distributed."[25]

HUNGER RELATED DEATHS

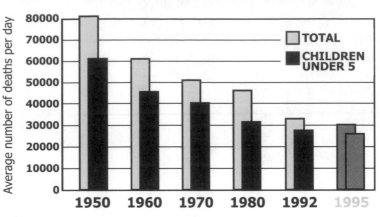

Figure 7.6

The minimum caloric intake per person per day has been set at 2,350, and current worldwide production allows for more than 2,700 calories for every person on earth.[26] People may be dying of hunger today, but it is not due to any lack of food!

4. *Declining food prices.* In spite of the dire warnings of Malthusians that food would become increasingly scarce, food prices have actually fallen over the past 50 years.[27] As any first-year economics student knows, the law of supply and demand dictates that prices fall when there is an abundance of an item and rise when it is scarce.

Knowing all this, Julian Simon made the easiest $1,000 of his life when he decided to put his worldview to the test with a bet against the Malthusian Ehrlich. Simon challenged Ehrlich to choose any five basic metals. The bet was to see whether, between 1980 and 1990, the prices of the metals would rise or fall. If Ehrlich's perspective was right, and we live in a closed system, there would be more people to consume these resources, and the metals would increase in price. If Simon was right and the world was an open system, the prices of the metals would fall. In October 1990, the prices were checked. All five had fallen, and Simon (and the worldview he advocates) was vindicated.[28]

Man's purpose is to glorify God. God's first commission to Adam was to "be fruitful...fill the earth, and subdue it" (Genesis 1:28). Our mandate includes bringing substantial healing to nature, standing

BETTING THE PLANET

For Simon to win, the value of all five wagered metals had to decrease over the ten-year period. That is what happened, and Ehrlich wrote Simon a check for $1000. The wager originally concerned a form of tungsten that is no longer on the market. Both sides agreed to substitute $200 worth of tungsten powder.

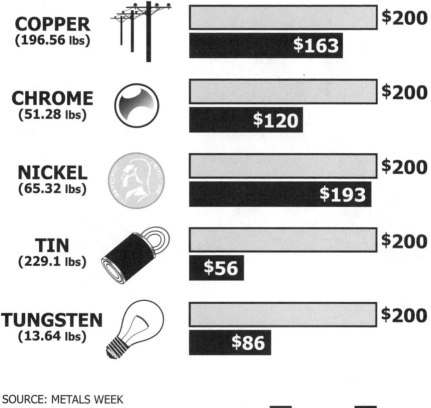

COPPER
(196.56 lbs)
$200
$163

CHROME
(51.28 lbs)
$200
$120

NICKEL
(65.32 lbs)
$200
$193

TIN
(229.1 lbs)
$200
$56

TUNGSTEN
(13.64 lbs)
$200
$86

SOURCE: METALS WEEK
THIS GRAPHIC IS BASED UPON ROSS MacDONALD'S ILLUSTRATION FOR THE DECEMBER 2 1990 ISSUE OF *NEW YORK TIMES MAGAZINE.*

1980 1990

Figure 7.7

against the decay, and causing deserts and gardens alike to bloom. As the apostle Paul wrote to the church in Rome:

> The creation waits in eager expectation for the sons of God to be revealed…the creation itself will be liberated from its bondage to decay and brought into the glorious freedom of the children of God (Romans 8:19–21).

Study Questions

Describe in your own words the three views of nature, man, and the relationship between the two.

Secularism (closed system)

Animism (capricious)

Theism (open system)

Which of these best describes the dominant culture where you live and work?

How would you describe the concept of resources in the culture where you work?

What are the three ideas that have historically shaped the debate over the "population problem"?

According to Margaret Sanger, the founder of Planned Parenthood,
   why is the world "overpopulated"?

How does secularism solve the problem of "overpopulation"?

What is the nature of wealth and resources according to theism?

What is their source?

What is meant by the term *carrying capacity*?

How does one determine the earth's carrying capacity?

What have you learned in this study that has significance for your
   concept of development? or How has your concept of development changed because of this study?

What questions or challenges do you have in response to the ideas presented in this chapter?

CHAPTER EIGHT

Creation's Laws:
Following the Instructions

IN THE THAI COUNTRYSIDE, people often struggle to make a living. Rapid deforestation has slashed the land's productivity. The rainy season seems shorter each year. During the dry season, little grows. A few fruit trees provide welcome shade, but much of the land is arid and harsh.

Songsai and Sii Phot live on a deforested plot in eastern Thailand with their six children. The land, which belongs to Sii's mother, is part of a larger area divided up and given to landless peasants by the government. The family's house is perched on stilts. It has widely spaced wooden slats and a thatched roof.

"The rain comes in through the walls and roof," Sii stated. "It is hard to live here, but we cannot go anywhere else."

The Development Mandate

Cultural relativism poses one of the greatest challenges to human development in our generation. As taught in the "soft sciences" of psychology, sociology, and anthropology, it holds that the values in one culture are no better (or worse) than those in another.[1] But the truth is, all people, groups, and cultures are moving, either from wealth into poverty or vice versa. Our world is constantly changing, and it is our worldview, the story we hold to, that drives most of the change. While secularists and animists would deny the existence of laws that govern this movement, the biblical theist knows that if God exists, His laws, or creation ordinances, have set the parameters for our existence.

The creation narrative in the first chapter of Genesis contains our marching orders. "In the beginning God created the heavens and the earth" (Genesis 1:1)—this affirms God's prior existence and His role as Creator and Developer of the universe. "Now the earth was formless and empty, darkness was over the surface of the deep,..." (Genesis 1:2)—this affirms the incompleteness of the primary creation. Through the next 25 verses, God moves to differentiate and form the raw materials: night and day, land and water, plants and animals, and so on. He does this by *fiat*, or command, showing that intelligence has primacy over matter. Then God forms (see Genesis 1:26–27) the capstone of His creative activity. Finally, God rests (see Genesis 1:31–2:3). Yet creation was unfinished.

> Creation left to itself is incomplete, and humans are called to be co-creators with God, bringing forth the potentialities the Creator has hidden. Creation is full of secrets waiting to be discovered, riddles which human intelligence is expected to unlock. The world did not spring from the hand of God as wealthy as man might make it.[2]

From before the creation of the world, God intended man to participate as co-creator. God gave man, His vice-regent, a creation mandate* for development.

> God blessed them and said to them, "Be fruitful and increase in number; fill the earth and subdue it. Rule over the fish of the sea and the birds of the air and over every living creature that moves on the ground" (Genesis 1:28).

This creation mandate has two aspects: societal (be fruitful and increase in number) and developmental (subdue and rule). Man was never intended to stay in the garden but was to move out to every corner of the earth and extend God's rule and build God's kingdom.

If, as Shakespeare said, "All the world's a stage," then man is a key player on the stage of God's story. He "makes history" with everything he does. He is not simply to survive the vagaries of nature, scrimping and scratching from one meal to the next, as do those poor souls trapped in fatalistic cultures. He is not to simply react to events. He is responsible to be proactive, to have a vision for God's fullness inhabiting the earth. As David so magnificently affirmed:

> When I consider your heavens, the work of your fingers, the moon and the stars, which you have set in place, what is man that you are mindful of him, the son of man that you care for him? You made him a little lower than the heavenly beings and crowned him with glory and honor. You made him ruler over the works of your hands; you put everything under his feet: all flocks and herds, and the beasts of the field, the birds of the air, and the fish of the sea, all that swim the paths of the seas. O LORD, our Lord, how majestic is your name in all the earth! (Psalm 8:3–9).

The prophet Isaiah also implies man's purpose when he says:

> [F]or the earth will be full of the knowledge of the LORD... (Isaiah 11:9).

The earth was delivered to man with "some assembly required." Just as an acorn cannot grow into a mighty oak tree without sun, soil, and time, so the earth required a process of maturation and growth. Creation was to be explored, new worlds were to be discovered, art and music produced, knowledge advanced, people, communities, and cultures built up.

Spreading "the knowledge of the Lord" presupposes and requires purpose, which God has stamped on the very fabric of the universe. According to Nobel laureate Jacques Monod:

> [O]ne of the fundamental characteristics common to all living beings without exception: that of being objects endowed with a purpose or project, which at the same time they exhibit in their performance...we shall call [this] TELEONOMY.[3]

The word *teleonomy* is derived from the Greek word *teleo* (*v.* τελεω), which means "to finish, to bring to an end." Science, as Monod states, implicitly acknowledges a Designer who has imbued the universe with a purpose.

History is moving to fulfill God's purpose. As we have seen, God has revealed Himself and His *telos* (*n.* τελος) to man in four ways. Special revelation reveals God's plan of salvation through the written Word (the Bible) and the living Word (Christ). General revelation reveals God to all humans through their own resemblance to God's image and through creation.

Common grace* is the parallel to general revelation. God's love extends to all people. The created order works the same for all people. As Jesus said of His Father, "He causes his sun to rise on the evil and the good, and sends rain on the righteous and the unrighteous" (Matt. 5:45). All people are created in God's image and thus have the ability to know about their Creator and the laws of creation.

Three primary sets of laws establish the bounds for our lives. Physical or natural laws govern the universe. As man discovers and applies them, he takes dominion over nature. Moral laws reflect the character of God and provide the blueprint for our moral development. Meanwhile, development laws, which I include under the heading of the development ethic, create a cultural framework to guide us in fulfilling the creation mandate to fill and rule the earth. As the image bearer of God, man must discover and apply these laws.

Francis Bacon testified in *The Advancement of Learning* (1605):

> ...Solomon the king, although he excelled in the glory of treasure and magnificent buildings, of shipping and navigation, of service and attendance, of fame and renown, and the like,...maketh no claim to any of these glories, but only to the glory of inquisition of truth; for so he saith expressly, "The glory of God is to conceal a thing, but the glory of the king is to find it out"; as if, according to the innocent play of children, the Divine Majesty took delight to hide his works, to the end to have them found out; and as if kings could not obtain a greater honour than to be God's play-fellows in that game.[4]

These three sets of laws, including the development ethic, are inherent in the created order and are universally applicable. They stand in stark contrast to civil laws, which are instituted by God to set boundaries on civil society. Generally, societies that base their civil law on moral law will prosper; those that don't will wither. Breaking these laws results in natural consequences. Moses wrote:

> See, I set before you today life and prosperity, death and destruction. For I command you today to love the LORD your God, to walk in his ways, and to keep his commands, decrees and laws; then you will live and increase....
> But if your heart turns away and you are not obedient, and if you are drawn away to bow down to other gods and worship them, I declare to you this day that you will certainly be destroyed (Deuteronomy 30:15–18a).

Intended to benefit man, God's laws enable individuals and entire cultures to reach God's purpose for them. Physical laws give structure to nature, while metaphysical laws guide social and human development. The former are descriptive, while the latter are prescriptive. The former work directly in nature and cannot be ignored, even for a second. The latter work indirectly through man and can be set aside, at least for a time. The former tells what is; the latter; what ought to be.

The development ethic is not wishful thinking. Reality affirms it, both historically and practically. Truth is self-authenticating. As Jesus said, "But wisdom is proved right by all her children" (Luke 7:35). Through the principles embedded in the development ethic, people are lifted out of poverty and into prosperity. These principles are universal, fixed, eternal, and absolute—the unity that provides a solid foundation for infinite diversity. They are the form that makes freedom possible, in contrast to the anarchy of freedom without form and the tyranny of form without freedom.

What I call the development ethic is an expansion of Max Weber's Protestant work ethic.[5] Weber noticed the relative prosperity of European Protestant countries and wondered why. He came to believe that their social ethos created a dynamic that lifted them out of poverty. Weber recognized the awesome power of ideas and ideals, vision and values that, when acted upon, transform entire nations. He discerned the interplay of the spiritual with the economic and the political. Creativity and innovation, which come from the mind of man, were seen as the source of bounty.

Distinctions Between Creation's Physical and Metaphysical Laws

Physical Law	Metaphysical Law
Structures The Universe	**Guides Human Development**
Laws of Gravity	The Ten Commandments
Laws of Motion	Christ's New Command
Laws of Physics	The Work Ethic
Laws of Chemistry	Sanctity of Human Life
Direct (in nature)	**Indirect (through man)**
Through Cause-and-Effect Relationships	In Culture and Creation Mandates
	Co-Creators with God
	Tending the Garden
	Naming the Animals
	Creating Beauty (Art)
Can NOT Be Violated	**CAN Be Violated...**
Without Immediate Consequences (e.g., step off a cliff and you will fall)	But Only for a While. The Severity of Consequences Increases Over Time
Mechanically Applied	**Become Manifest**
Consistently Throughout Nature	Through the Exercise of Free Will
Descriptive	**Prescriptive**
How Things **Are**	How Things **Ought To Be**

Figure 8.1

The Reformation swept Europe, leaped the English Channel to Britain, and finally crossed the Atlantic to the United States, carrying a rationale for everyday life that impacted the economic sphere of each of these regions. In the book *The Spirit of Democratic Capitalism*, Novak argues that the Protestant moral philosophy (spirit) and its application to the (democratic) public square and in the marketplace (capitalism) made all the difference between the development of North and South America.

The development ethic is the bridge between the Judeo-Christian worldview and everyday life. It has a dozen moral or philosophical principles in three major groupings: the spiritual, the human, and the creation factors. (These have been the subject and outline of this book. I've been refining my understanding of this concept for over a decade. This information first appeared in print in my article "The development ethic" as part of the book *Christian Relief and Development*. Though it has expanded over the intervening years, it has also become more compellingly clear.)

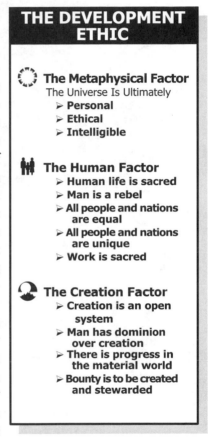

THE DEVELOPMENT ETHIC

The Metaphysical Factor
The Universe Is Ultimately
➤ **Personal**
➤ **Ethical**
➤ **Intelligible**

The Human Factor
➤ **Human life is sacred**
➤ **Man is a rebel**
➤ **All people and nations are equal**
➤ **All people and nations are unique**
➤ **Work is sacred**

The Creation Factor
➤ **Creation is an open system**
➤ **Man has dominion over creation**
➤ **There is progress in the material world**
➤ **Bounty is to be created and stewarded**

Figure 8.2

The spiritual factor deals with what others call "other-worldly" or metaphysical factors. The human factor sets the framework for human existence, for understanding our place in the cosmos. The creation factor sets the parameters of the universe.

These factors are a compass pointing to "true north" in development, toward God's best intentions. They provide the foundation that allows cultures to be built in infinite patterns.

While the development ethic springs forth from the Scriptures and is best articulated by the Judeo-Christian tradition, it is based on transcendent principles manifest around the world. The degree to which

Growing Healthy Cultures

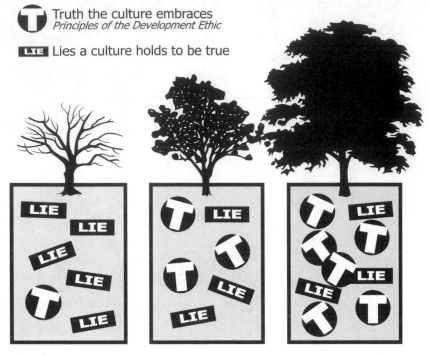

Figure 8.3

this ethic is found in a society, of course, will determine the fertility of the society's soil for development. The more elements of the development ethic that are present in a culture, the more easily that society can progress. The more lies imbedded in a culture, the more hostile its social environment is to development (see Figure 8.3).

But what of those cultures that are developing rapidly without much Judeo-Christian influence, such as several in Asia today? They have elements that are functional equivalents of the biblical ethic. Confucianism, for example, has a work ethic similar to the one articulated by Weber. It works both ways, too. The West's current orientation to the now, with little thought to the future, is a functional equivalent of animist thought.

The development ethic enhances culture by affirming those elements that are life-enhancing and denying those that produce death. It will not—must not—destroy a culture in the name of modernism, development, or change. On the other hand, development is anything but "value neutral." It does not fall in step with the current fad of idolizing culture. The development ethic enables people to become all that God intends, rebuking a culture in some points, affirming it in others.

When it comes to development, the whole is greater than the sum of its parts. The more elements of the ethic a people or society has, the more fertile is the soil for growth in development. Like the strands woven into a piece of cloth, each thread touches the others at different places.

As Christians who care about people who are poor and hungry, our task is to articulate the development ethic and share its values and ideals with our fellow human beings who are trapped in the cycle of poverty. Our task is not to impose a set of values. Articulating this ethic gives the poor an alternative, a way out. Then it's up to them to choose either life or death. Ultimately development is a process of discipling both people and cultures, founded on the creative and redemptive work of God and based on His story.

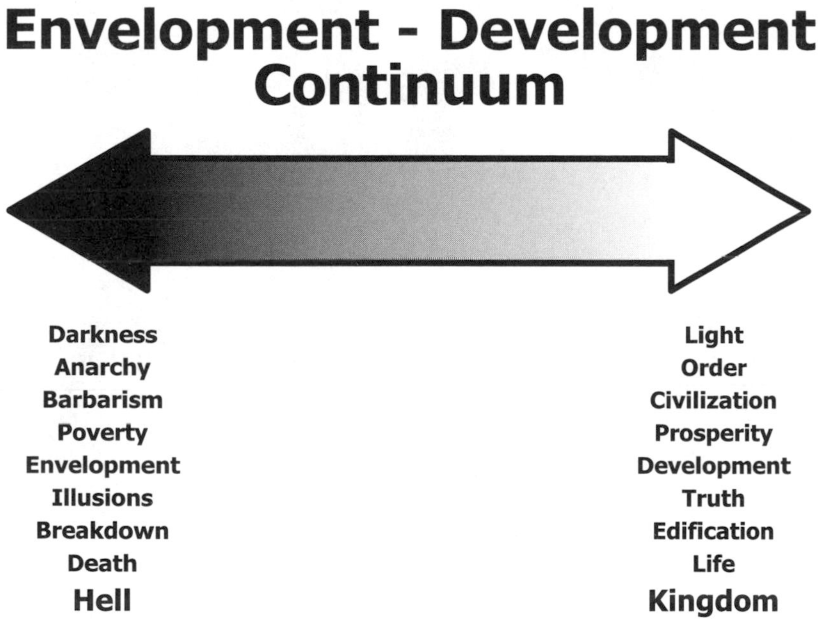

Envelopment - Development Continuum

Darkness	**Light**
Anarchy	**Order**
Barbarism	**Civilization**
Poverty	**Prosperity**
Envelopment	**Development**
Illusions	**Truth**
Breakdown	**Edification**
Death	**Life**
Hell	**Kingdom**

Figure 8.4

Study Questions

What are the two aspects of the creation mandate?

What is the meaning of this phrase: "The earth was delivered to man with some assembly required"?

Describe each of the three primary sets of laws:

Natural laws:

Metaphysical (moral) laws:

The development ethic:

Identify five distinctions between physical laws and metaphysical laws.

Does a person have to be a Christian to appreciate and apply the
   development ethic? Why or why not?

Illustrate at least one way the development ethic is applied and one
   way it is violated in the community where you work.

What questions or challenges do you have in response to the ideas
   presented in this chapter?

His Stewards

So God created man in his own image, in the image of God he created him; male and female he created them. God blessed them and said to them, "Be fruitful and increase in number; fill the earth and subdue it."

Genesis 1:27, 28a

God's purpose as it relates to development find its echoes throughout the Scriptures. The greatest consummation is found suggestively in the book of Revelation, and the first references occur in the opening chapters of Genesis. God said to man, newly created, "Be fruitful and multiply, and fill the earth and subdue it, and have dominion... over every living thing... I have given you every plant for food." This first great commission given to man was a commission to develop. It was world-wide in its scope, but it was to have a direct application to his immediate surroundings. We read that God took the man and put him in the garden of Eden "to till it and to keep it." The suggestion here is that man was to have an active role in development, and that he was to start his work where God had put him. He had a global, but also a local, responsibility. Are we then to imagine that Eden was the location of the first development project? In fact a far greater enterprise preceded it. The whole creation is presented as a work of cosmic development. In the beginning the earth was "without form and void," but with a craftsman's skill God progressively shaped, filled, organized, beautified and peopled it. The framework of the "days" of creation make us think of one who "goes forth to his work and to his labor until the evening." This master craftsman rests, having accomplished his task; like a great artist, he stands back to appreciate his canvas. The writer to the Hebrews adds a final comment: "The builder of all things is God."

In Scripture the Creator is revealed to us as the great Developer, and the development commission is given to man created in his image. It is within man's nature to be creatively engaged in development, because that activity is part of God's nature too. In this respect, as in others, man is called to reflect the divine genius.

Maurice Sinclair
Green Finger of God

· CHAPTER NINE ·

Rebel Servants
The Nature of Man

GENOCIDE! MISSIONARIES DIDN'T THINK SUCH a thing could happen. Roughly the size of Maryland or Israel, Rwanda was the site of the great East African Revival during the 1930s. The vast majority of people living there called themselves Christians. The two main ethnic groups, Hutus and Tutsis (a.k.a. Watutsis), had lived among each other in an unstable peace. Then, starting in April 1994, genocide broke out, as the Hutus systematically slaughtered at least half a million Tutsis. In 1995, long-time missionary to Rwanda Gary Scheer wrote:

> On Sundays in Rwanda, we used to see well-dressed neighbors walking to church on every road. Yet, last year these same neighbors slaughtered each other. I don't assume that all these people walking to church were all walking in the steps of Christ, the Lord. But the committed minority of the church was significant, 5 percent of the population, and the influence of the church was strong in the lives of another 75 percent of the people. Why was there no moderation, no dampening—just hatred and fear, farming tools becoming weapons, neighbors cutting down each other as enemies?[1]

David Rawson, the U.S. ambassador to Rwanda, stated:

> I asked my chauffeur, "Who killed [your] parents and siblings—the army or the militia?" Neither, he said, but rather the people next door who felt authorities had given them the go ahead to kill neighbors and take over their houses and lands. How do you re-knit society where that has happened?[2]

While man is "fearfully and wonderfully made," "a little lower than the angels," he is also in rebellion against God and against God's creation. As the preceding accounts show, a thin "Christian" veneer is no shield against people acting out their basest impulses when presented with the opportunity. Man's entire being has been corrupted; man is prone to evil and is not to be trusted. The development ethic refuses to whitewash man's rebellion, knowing that evil is real, personal, and, since God did not create evil, abnormal. Yet, as we have also seen over and over again, man has dignity because he is created in God's image and is God's steward.

There is a perpetual tension between man's dignity and man's depravity.* Which is true? Both. They must never be separated. Focusing only on man's significance produces tyranny. Forgetting man's dignity leads to a culture of death. Animism denies the sacredness and significance of human life and sees evil as normal. Secularism, on the other hand, while denying the sacredness of life, affirms (without reason) that man is good.

What Is the Nature of Man?

Animism   Theism   Secularism

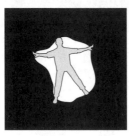  

Figure 9.1

Human Life Is Sacred

Man is a wonder, the crown of God's creation. He is godlike. Man's identity is revealed at the end of Genesis 1 (see Genesis 1:26–28). Man is made in the image and likeness of God and is told to fill the earth and rule over it. There is no comparable story in the sacred literature of any other religion. *Human life is sacred.*

The Attributes of Man

Regarding God's personal attributes—rational, relational, and moral—man differs from God only in the degree to which he possesses them. But man is radically different from the rest of the creation when it comes to these attributes. It is a difference not in degree but in kind. Regarding God's infinite attributes—His omnipotence, omnipresence, and immutability—man is different in kind from God and identical in kind with the rest of creation, because only God possesses them. Figure 9.2 illustrates how Francis Schaeffer described these differences.[3]

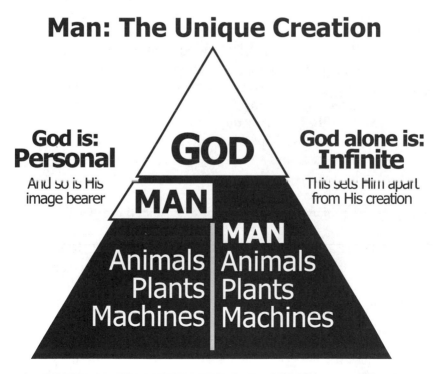

Man: The Unique Creation

God is: Personal
And so is His image bearer

GOD

God alone is: Infinite
This sets Him apart from His creation

MAN

MAN
Animals | Animals
Plants | Plants
Machines | Machines

Figure 9.2

The nature of God's image in man is personal, rational, and moral, as we have seen in previous chapters. Man has been patterned for God's own purpose. Different from the rest of creation, man was made to rule over it as God's vice-regent. As stewards, we are to administer the household, the *oikonomia*, to "fill the earth with the knowledge of the Lord." We exercise dominion over three principal areas: over nature, using technology; over time, as history makers; and over ourselves, as lawmakers. We are to do all this until God's purposes are fulfilled, His *teleos* reached. When we play our part in God's unfolding story as the actors He intended us to be, great and awesome things happen.

Change Agents

William Carey, India's greatest development worker (not to mention its greatest missionary and the "father of modern missions"), wrote:

> As our blessed Lord required us to pray that His Kingdom may come, and His will be done on earth as it is in heaven, it becomes us not only to express our desires of that event by words, but to use every lawful method to spread the knowledge of His name...sin was introduced amongst the children of men by the fall of Adam, and has ever since been spreading...Yet God repeatedly made known His intention to prevail finally over all the power of the Devil, and to destroy all his works, and set up His own kingdom and interest among men, and to extend it as universally as Satan had extended his.[4]

The modern Indian development worker Vishal Mangalwadi comments:

> The tragedy of our times is that while many Christians have confidence in the power of the Lord to return and change the world, many of us do not have confidence in the power of the gospel to transform society now. Carey struggled against specific social evils, just as his friends in England were continuing their struggle against evils. But Carey's confidence was not in his social protest or social action, but in the gospel. This is

the very opposite of those Christians who put their hope for change in their "social action." It is also different from the faith of those who believe that the world can improve only after the Lord Jesus Christ will return. Carey became a reformer because he understood the breadth of the theological concept of "Kingdom of God." He believed that if we disciple nations, we will increasingly see God's will being done here on earth.[5]

By contrast, the mindset of poverty, whether via secularism or animism, denies that progress is possible. Secularism admits that change is possible, but it is limited and impersonal because the universe is a machine. Because there are no moral constraints, nature is for human beings and thus a target for rape. Man dominates nature. Animism, for its part, denies even the possibility of change, seeing life as a series of endless cycles. Man, to the animist, is dominated by nature.

The theistic ethic, unlike secularism or animism, sees man not as a machine or as a drop in the cosmic ocean but as a complex, whole individual. Man has body and soul, heart, mind, will, and strength. Jesus, though He was God, was also man; He shared our humanity in all its complexity. As Luke 2:52 says of Him, "And Jesus increased in wisdom and stature, and in favor with God and man." As the ultimate man, Christ grew in wisdom, in the ability to morally apply truth. He grew physically, spiritually, and socially.

Like Christ, man has a series of relationships with creation. Like the Christian concept of the Trinity, those relationships occur both *within* the person and *without* the person—with God and the rest of creation. Obviously, the analogy is not perfect, but it describes the complexity of man's unity and diversity (which we will examine more closely in the next chapter). This complexity is strikingly different from the mindset of poverty. Secularism sees man as indivisibly physical, while animism sees man as a physical body inhabited by a spirit, with the ultimate goal being union with the spirit.

MAN: *The Image of God*

The fact that man is created in the image of (to use Schaeffer's phrase) "the God who is there" proves that human life is sacred, that every person has dignity: young or old, Jew or Greek, strong or weak, black or white, male or female. All bear the divine imprint. By contrast, secularism's seemingly reasonable "quality of life" standard opens the door to monstrous evil. Once a person is given an intellectual justification that someone else's life is not worth living, the results are nightmarish.

In Nazi Germany, millions of Jewish, Gypsy, enfeebled, and sick people were "weeded out of the gene pool." Before that, the same kind of utilitarian considerations consigned millions to slavery throughout the British Empire and the United States (today in North Africa it still does). The Netherlands has tolerated euthanasia for over two decades, and in November 2000, the lower house of the Dutch parliament approved a bill legalizing it. (At the time of this printing, the upper house is expected to approve the bill soon, making Holland the first nation since Nazi Germany to make it legal for doctors to end their patients' lives.) In October of 1997, Oregon passed the "Death with Dignity Act," making physician-assisted suicide a legal option for terminally ill residents of that state. Female infanticide in China and India, Pol Pot's Cambodia, genocide in Rwanda and Serbia, infanticide, euthanasia, and abortion on demand are other examples of this quite literal culture of death.

Such a worldview can subtly overtake even the well-meaning. A professional colleague told me about a foreign aid worker who watched Rwandan refugee women cutting firewood so they could cook for their hungry children. This "compassion worker" said simply, "There go the trees again."

Sometimes our priorities get completely out of whack. One time, two American relief workers, observing a Cambodian ritual of sucking out the brains of live monkeys, condemned what they saw as the practice's barbarity. But their Cambodian host and translator turned to them and said, "What right do you have to condemn this practice when people in America suck live babies from their mothers' wombs?"

Animism is no better. Many pagan religions, past and present, have sacrificed humans to their gods. (Biblical theism teaches the precise opposite, that God sacrificed Himself for man.) Until William Carey took a stand against Hinduism's practice of *sati*, the immolation of widows on their husbands' funeral pyres went unchallenged.

Our Western concepts of human rights were grounded in the concept of the *imago Dei*, that we are made in God's image and that God (not man) is sovereign. Yet while man is the crown prince of God's creation and of inestimable worth, the Bible and millennia of history teach us that he is a sinner, rotten to the core.

Man Is a Rebel

The story of the fall of mankind is not only valid history but also the best explanation extant of man's depravity. Man was created a free and moral creature, not only morally discerning but also morally good. Man—male and female—was placed in a perfect environment. His freedom was confirmed by a single prohibition.

> Now the LORD God had planted a garden in the east, in Eden; and there he put the man he had formed. And the LORD God made all kinds of trees grow out of the ground—trees that were pleasing to the eye and good for food. In the middle of the garden were the tree of life and the tree of the knowledge of good and evil... (Genesis 2:8–9).
> The LORD God took the man and put him in the Garden of Eden to work it and take care of it. And the LORD God commanded the man, "You are free to eat from any tree in the garden, but you must not eat from the tree of the knowledge of good and evil, for when you eat of it you will surely die" (Genesis 2:15–17).
> "You will not surely die," the serpent said to the woman. "For God knows that when you eat of it your eyes will be opened, and you will be like God, knowing good and evil."
> When the woman saw that the fruit of the tree was good for food and pleasing to the eye, and also desirable for gaining wisdom, she took some and ate it. She also gave some to her husband, who was with her, and he ate it. Then the eyes of both of them were opened, and they realized they were naked; so they sewed fig leaves together and made coverings for themselves (Genesis 3:4–7).

The consequences of this awful choice have reverberated down through history, and their echo continues to be heard as the backdrop to all that our race tries to achieve. At the moment of Adam and Eve's disobedience, their primary relationship was broken, and they died spiritually. All their secondary relationships, as shown by their shame and blame, were fractured as well.

Because their relationship with the Definer of their existence was broken, they no longer knew who they were or what creation was. Metaphysical corruption was added to their moral bankruptcy. At the instigation of Satan, a new explanation of the universe—from an anthropocentric perspective—began. Natural evil was brought into the world (see Genesis 3:16–19), and death reigned, not only spiritually (see Genesis 2:16–17) but also physically (see Genesis 3:22–24). In his fallen state, man quickly learned to love death, as shown by Cain's murder of Abel. So the sorry cycle of death reached full circle: moral evil in man, natural evil in creation, and, finally, cultural death in society.

Man has no one to blame for this but himself. The problem is not in his environment but in himself. As Paul said in Romans 1:21–23, man's thinking has become futile, his heart darkened, and his wisdom exchanged for pure vanity. Worse, man rejects the glory of God in favor of idols.

Because man is significant, his decisions for sin impact the world around him. That which is in his heart eventually manifests itself externally (see Romans 1:24–27), dragging man himself into the depths of sin and depravity. These two words—*sin* and *depravity*—are curiously absent from the modern vocabulary. But evidence of their reality is with us from the dawn of history. Sin means "to miss the mark" of God's holiness and righteousness; depravity indicates man's utter moral corruption. There is enough sin and corruption in the best of us, including Mother Teresa, to kindle the fires of hell.

> The LORD saw how great man's wickedness on the earth had become, and that every inclination of the thoughts of his heart was only evil all the time. The LORD was grieved that he had made man on the earth, and his heart was filled with pain (Genesis 6:5–6).

While man is a sinner, he is of enormous worth. He is a significant sinner, not a zero. We are not helpless victims of uncontrollable forces. Aleksandr Solzhenitsyn aptly noted that the

> line separating good and evil passes not through states nor between classes, nor between private parties either—but right through the human heart.[6]

There is no shortage of people who want to change the world. There are few, however, who recognize that the primary challenge is to change the human heart and mind.

First things must come first, however. The system is broken. Natural evil (death, hunger, drought, suffering, pain in childbirth, weeds in the garden) abounds. In addition, the moral evil of others, and ourselves, wafts across the landscape like mustard gas. These things are natural consequences of the fall. Further, there are natural and inevitable consequences to our moral behavior. The Bible and, indeed, human experience prove that as a general rule blessing comes from obedience to God's law, cursing from disobedience. While it is unquestionably true that sometimes the righteous, like Job, suffer unjustly, and the wicked, as in Psalm 73, seemingly enjoy all life has to offer, these are aberrations. In fact, they are signs of the world's brokenness. God's laws usually lead to bounty. When they are flouted or ignored, they lead to poverty.

A lazy person often ends up impoverished unless someone else cares for him. Believing lies often leads to immoral behavior, such as homosexuality, fornication, or adultery. Engaging in these behaviors can bring horrendous diseases and death. Drunkenness often ruins careers and shatters families. While these consequences shape the daily reality of our existence on this earth, they are not *normal*. Natural evil is an intruder, the result of sin. Sin is to be fought. We are part of a worldwide resistance movement. Medicine stands as a rebel against disease, agriculture against blight, education against ignorance, and law against anarchy.

Ultimately, God stands against the consequences of the fall by providing His plan of redemption from sin and depravity and for the reconciliation of sinners with Himself. To be in conformity with the world is to be in rebellion against God. To be in obedience to God is to be in rebellion against the world. We are all rebels. It's just a question of whom or what we're rebelling against: God or the world. Of course, rebelling against God comes naturally.

So what happened in Rwanda? It is a reflection of man's depravity. Sin touches every part of a person's life, reaching to the very core of his being. Rwanda is a reflection of man's inhumanity to man.

In part, what happened in Rwanda was that the nation was "converted" but not discipled at the profound level of culture. The tribal mindset that sees one tribe as superior to another was not challenged.

The blood of Christ was not applied to the breaking down of the dividing wall of hostility between Hutu and Tutsi (Ephesians 2:14-16). The ancient hostilities of tribalism were not broken by the powerful truth that Tutsis and Hutus are of "one blood," having one set of first parents—Adam and Eve. It was tribalism, this mindset of poverty, that led to the genocide.

The task given to the church in the Great Commission was nothing less than to disciple nations. If the church does not disciple the nation, the nation will disciple the church. Rwanda is an extreme example of this principle.

Systemwide Failure

The problem is systemic. It is not merely a spiritual brokenness, as many pietists would argue. Nor is it merely a structural problem, as many secularists would assert. All of man is affected. All of his relationships are shattered. His primary relationship, with God, is broken. Theology that is biblical tells us how that outward and vertical relationship can be repaired. Then man's four spheres of secondary relationships, all horizontal, also need mending through the other sciences. There is man's relationship with himself, which is studied through psychology; with others, through sociology; with nature, through ecology and economics. Finally, there is man's relationship with the metaphysical world. This involves knowledge, or epistemology; ethology, or ethics; and teleology, or the study of "ends" or purpose. Because man's primary relationship with God has been scrambled, all of these secondary relationships are confused, too.

The consequences of these broken relationships are devastating. Man's vanity creates a world of illusion in his own mind that he projects onto the real world. Thus, man sees what he wants to see (and what Satan desires him to see). Satan, the father of lies, twists truth to build a counterfeit story and blinds the minds of men. This system replaces God in man's mind. With God supplanted as the focus of life, it is no surprise that evil permeates the world system.

The Bible is clear that mankind outside of Christ is spiritually enslaved by the principalities and powers of the kingdom of darkness. Paul wrote:

> For our struggle is not against flesh and blood, but against the rulers, against the authorities, against the

powers of this dark world and against the spiritual forces of evil in the heavenly realm (Ephesians 6:12).

God tells His people about the consequences of obedience (life) and disobedience (death) (see Deuteronomy 30:11–20). Rebelling against God does not lead to a neutral kind of vacuum. It leads to death. "Whoever fails to find me harms himself; all who hate me love death" (Proverbs 8:36).

Herbert Schlossberg describes secular humanism as a "philosophy of death."

> The arguments in favor of abortion, infanticide and euthanasia reveal that the humanitarian ethic wishes to restrict the right to live and expand the right to die— and to kill. Humanism is a philosophy of death. It embraces death, wishes a good death, speaks of the horrible burdens of living for the baby who is less than perfect, for the sick person in pain....The good-death people know nothing of life; have small regard for it, and embrace the enemy as if it were a friend.[7]

Chairman Mao took secularism's culture of death to its logical conclusion by institutionalizing death across China. Millions of peasants, intellectuals, Christians, and entrepreneurs lost their lives to his megalomania. Mao was no aberration. Stalin, Hitler, Lenin, Pol Pot, Idi Amin, and others slaughtered countless people in the name of progress.

Animism, of course, has been killing people for millennia. William Carey fought against not only widow burning, as we have seen, but also the annual festival of *Sagar Puja*. During *Sagar Puja* children were thrown into the Ganges as a sacrifice to the river. There they either drowned or were eaten by crocodiles.

Do societies build their institutions based on the comforting but misguided ideal that man is good? If so, then millions die needlessly when reality fails to match the ideal. Maintaining order in such societies requires a totalitarian state. Or do societies build their institutions based upon the reality of man's sin? Those that do will more likely create institutions that restrain evil, lawlessness, and death. That means there must be some kind of democratic political structures and free-market economics. With all its limitations and warts, the system some call democratic capitalism is significantly better than any other system out there, as the world has come to understand. Why? Because, despite all its abuses and excesses, it is built on the bedrock truth of man's depravity, while its fading rival, socialism, is constructed on a sandy base of nonexistent human goodness.

This is more than ivory tower theory. Francis Schaeffer has said that to understand the differences in history between northern (Protestant) and southern (Catholic) Europe, you need to see the theological roots of Protestantism and Catholicism. Michael Novak had a similar awakening. Novak began his journey as a socialist who was studying to be a Roman Catholic priest. Novak had a heart for the poor, and he couldn't help but notice the divergent paths taken by North and South America. They both had the same number of indigenous peoples and roughly the same number of European settlers. South America had far greater natural resources. Yet North America, which had roots in the Reformation, was far wealthier. In answer to his question why?, Novak wrote his classic volume *The Spirit of Democratic Capitalism*. The difference was not physical, in resources, but spiritual, in ideas and vision. In his essay, Novak wrote:

> There is no use trying to build a republic for saints. There are too few of them, and even the ones there are, are difficult to live with. No, if you wish to build a republic that will last, you must design it for sinners. That is the only "moral majority" there is…a republic of sinners—and, therefore, a republic of checks and balances, as well as other "auxiliary precautions" (to employ the phrase of James Madison, well taught as he was by Christian teachers).
>
> ….No city of man is the City of God. The massive illusion that citizens are inherently and infallibly good, and that government officials may establish happiness on earth, has met reality. Entire realms of social and psychological theory, based upon utopic theories, have failed to account for the ordinary sinfulness of ordinary human beings. Look around you. You see the ruins.[8]

How are these facts, man's significance, and man's depravity, taken into account in the economic and political spheres? Free markets encourage enlightened self-interest—a thoroughly biblical idea (see Romans 12:3; Luke 10:27–28). I am, in a real yet restrained sense, to "love" myself for God's sake. But we are obviously to love others for their sake, too. This is the self-sacrificing love commanded and assumed throughout Scripture (see 1 John 3:11, 16–18; Galatians 5:13–15). Free markets take into account man's sin by "keeping him honest" in an open, competitive system. Yet they are enlightened in that when markets operate as they should, the most people benefit. In economics, you want free markets—not because they are perfect and can magically solve all problems, but because they beat the alternatives (mercantilism, monopolism, and consumerism) hands down.

Likewise, in this imperfect world, you do not want one person to have too much political power. In government, oligarchy and monarchy are the chief dangers. The Founding Fathers of the United States addressed the problem by instituting a system of checks and balances, diffusing power into the executive, legislative, and judicial branches.

During a three-week adult education seminar, I had the pleasure of rooming with a Costa Rican political activist. One night after dinner he told me he was thinking of running for president and asked for the best piece of advice I could give him. "Make sure there are laws to protect the people from you," I said.

"What do you mean?" he retorted, not particularly appreciating my answer.

"Make sure the laws of Costa Rica will protect the citizens of Costa Rica from you and your excesses." I repeated. Now he was stunned!

"Why?" was all he could manage to say.

"Because power corrupts," I said, stealing a page from Lord Acton. "If you don't take into account that you are sinful, the power of the presidency will corrupt you."

I don't know whether he ever took my advice. I hope he did.

Study Questions

In your own words, summarize the two main aspects of human nature.

Human Life Is Sacred:

All Men Are Sinners:

What implications do they have for our work among the poor?

How is man like God?

How is man like the rest of creation?

We have been designed for God's own purpose. What is that purpose?

What does this have to do with development?

What is the importance of being "whole people" for the process of development?

In your own words describe

Moral (personal) evil:

Natural evil:

Give an example of sin and depravity

In your own life:

In your church:

In the community where you work:

Give examples of poverty in the community where you work that are a *direct* result of **moral evil.**

Because **natural evil** is not *normal,* we are to fight against it. Identify examples from the community where you work of

> Fatalism in the face of natural evil (e.g., not building a dam to prevent annual floods):

> People combatting natural evil:

What impact did the Protestant understanding of man have on

> The church?

> The economic systems Protestants favored?

> The political systems Protestants established?

What questions or challenges do you have in response to the ideas presented in this chapter?

· CHAPTER TEN ·

One, Yet Many
The Nature of Community

IN RUSSIA, DESPITE A LOT OF RECENT TALK about individual rights and democratic capitalism, communism has shaped more than just political views over the past 70 years. These days, to keep their friends happy, students in Russian secondary schools routinely cheat for one another. One student informed author Eleanor Randolph (*Waking the Tempests*, 1996), "If someone asked you to help and you said, 'No, I abide by the law,' you would be an outcast." Sixty-five-year-old retiree Klara Gladkova told Randolph, "Before Gorbachev, it was a good life. Under Brezhnev, it was better."[1]

Throughout history, societies have struggled to organize themselves around the individual or the community, the one or the many. Soviet communism, the vestiges of which remain in Russia and the former Eastern Bloc nations, is one example that came down on the side of the community—at the expense of the individual. The current "anything goes" climate of the U.S. exemplifies the other extreme, radical individualism.* Unfortunately, most societies have fallen to the extremes: individualism or communalism,* tribalism or egalitarianism.*

Balance is hard to find; extremes, easy to slip into. Which story a culture chooses to live out is ultimately a religious question. What I call the radical middle has a metaphysical starting point: the Trinity.

Societies that find this balance value both freedom (which emphasizes the individual) and justice (which emphasizes the community).

The Roots of "The One" and "The Many"

Societies that start with "the one" usually come from three basic religious perspectives. (1) *Monism* holds that the only reality is spiritual and that "all is one." Hinduism and Buddhism are prime examples of this Eastern vision of unity. (2) *Pantheism* holds that the only reality is natural or physical (matter and energy). Reality is the sum of the forces and laws of the universe. Folk animism, Greek and Roman mythology, Baal worship in the ancient Holy Land, even Mormonism, are examples. Naturalism, secularism, and materialism are variants. (3) *Unitarianism,** a form of monotheism, holds to belief in one infinite God (with which Christians would heartily agree), but who exists as only one "person." Examples include Islam, Unitarianism, modern Judaism, and cults such as the Jehovah's Witnesses.

Those societies that start with "the many" have their roots in polytheism, the belief in a plurality of personal gods and impersonal forces or spirits. At their most basic levels, societies that start with "the many" have deep similarities that far outweigh their surface dissimilarities.

Those that start with both views, "the one" and "the many," are few and far between. These few are founded upon belief in the Trinity. Does it really make a difference whether a culture is founded on the tenets of this difficult-to-grasp theological doctrine? As I have said, ideas have consequences. Everything a people does, the way it lives, is ultimately based on metaphysical assumptions. For example, the current deemphasis on "facts" in many school subjects goes back to an unspoken belief in relativism, which in turn is rooted in a rejection of biblical absolutes. So why can't Johnny add? Perhaps because his Western culture has drifted from God.

This God is unabashedly the "three-in-one" presented in the Scriptures—the "One and Many" God—Father, Son, and Holy Spirit. This God, "in whom we live and move and have our being" (Acts 17:28), exemplifies both unity and diversity, since He is simultaneously one God and three Persons. Others have plumbed the theological depths of this bottomless mystery far better than I ever could.[2] But a key point to remember for our purposes is that this one God is a community of Persons.

Implications of the Trinity

British economist Brian Griffiths discusses the radical implications of this awesome God for our social, political, and economic lives. Concerning the nature of God, Griffiths notes:

> It affirms that before time there was plurality of persons in the Godhead. God was not alone. He was not some solitary figure, unable to communicate, for whom love was a meaningless idea. The Trinity was a community, a fellowship. The persons of the Trinity related to each other and always have done.[3]

Concerning the significance of the Trinity for human society, Griffiths states:

> This has two important implications. It suggests that the idea of community is crucial to the life of society. Any view of society which analyses behaviour as if the individual were some form of automaton is deficient because it fails to capture the importance of relationships. We were not created to live as Crusoe-like figures. As well as this, there is also the relationship which the Trinity expresses between the one and the many, unity and diversity. In the Trinity the one God does not take precedence over the many persons, neither do the many have priority over the One.[4]

The practical implications for political and economic life, Griffiths avers, are profound.

> When in religion the One is given preference, as in Islam, the consequence has been a form of totalitarian state which attempts to discern the will of Allah. When the many are given priority the result is anarchy. But the tension is one which extends to economic philosophy. Fascism and Marxism are both an attempt to emphasise the one to the exclusion of the many and to find salvation in economic terms through the state.

Animism

Conformity

Figure 10.1

Theism

Community

Figure 10.2

Secularism

Individualism

Figure 10.3

Libertarianism is an attempt to emphasise the many at the expense of the One and is a prescription not just for laissez faire but also for anarchy. The relevance of the Trinity is to emphasise both the individual and the state, as well as a large variety of mediating institutions which form the basis of a pluralist society. As far as economic life is concerned these include corporations, partnerships, trade unions, professional associations, committees concerned with setting standards, and so on.[5]

Thus, "the one" focuses on the unity of the community. Instead of diversity, there is uniformity as the state reigns supreme over the individual. Anyone who has visited the drab gray apartment blocks of Moscow or Warsaw can see the results of this depressing uniformity. "The many," for its part, elevates diversity and individualism, the logical conclusion of which is the dissolution of the state. In his 1992 book *The Disuniting of America*, historian Arthur Schlesinger argues that the current fixation with multiculturalism* is eroding the foundational values of the United States.[6]

The way out, therefore, is through what I call the radical middle, where both the one and the many are properly balanced. To borrow a phrase from Robertson McQuilkin, chancellor of Columbia International University, we must live "in the center of biblical tension." In this case, the rights of the community and the individual must be held in tension if we are to have a state that is both free and just.

FOUNDATIONS FOR COMMUNITIES

	MANY	ONE-MANY	ONE
THE VALUES	Outward to Others	**From Self to Others**	Inward on Self
	We	**Thou (I+We)**	I
	Communalism	**Community**	Individualism
	Other-centered	**God-centered**	Self-centered
	Self-depreciation and Degradation	**Sanctified self-interest**	Selfish
	Dependent	**Interdependent**	Independent
	Paternalism	**Insufficiency**	Egoism
	Group Rights	**Personal Responsibility**	Individual's Rights
	Boran Tribe	**The Church**	Marlboro Man
THE RESULTS	Tyranny	**Liberty & Freedom**	Anarchy
	Injustice	**Justice**	Chaos

Figure 10.4

Arthur Koestler coined a word in English to express a combined one: *holon*. It is derived from *holos* (whole) and the suffix "on" (from proton or neutron, meaning "part").[7] While this word has not exactly captured the imagination of the public, it captures perfectly the meaning of the one and the many together.

Please note, in the pages that follow, a distinction between the Brian Griffiths quotes, which set up this chapter, and my use of the terms "One" and "Many." The point we are making is similar, but the way we are using the terms is different. Griffiths uses the term the ONE to refer to the imbalance of totalitarianism or UNIFORMITY, while I use the ONE to refer to the imbalance of INDIVIDUALISM, focusing on the individual at the expense of the community. Griffiths uses the term the MANY to refer to the anarchy of LIBERTARIANISM, while I use the MANY to refer to the imbalance of COMMUNALISM, focusing on the group at the expense of the individual.

The chart in Figure 10.4 portrays the three basic foundations for establishing a community. While "the one" focuses inwardly on self and "the many" focuses outwardly on others, "the one and the many" focuses both outwardly and inwardly. Outwardly, the focus is upward to God, downward to creation, and sideways to man. Inwardly, the focus on the self is preserved, but it does not predominate.

The well-known psychological/sociological concepts of the I, the We, and the Thou will help clarify. The I focuses on the individual. This is well illustrated by the Marlboro Man, the personification of the rugged individualist. Under this system, the We disappears and the Thou, by definition, does not exist. The We, by contrast, emphasizes communalism. With a focus only on others, the I disappears and the Thou, if it exists, has no diversity. The group is worshiped. For example, the Boran tribe of northern Kenya and southern Ethiopia has no first-person singular possessive pronoun such as "my." A Boran person cannot say "my child," "my house," or "my goat." He or she can only say "our child," "our house," or "our goat."

Only when we include the Thou as God and worship Him do the I and the We find their proper places. From this perspective we get community, which is based on respect for God's authority, the self, and others. The basic currency of community is relationship. Relationships are found on various levels: in the family; in the extended family; in the neighborhood; in the various cultural, civic, and religious groups (the so-called mediating institutions); in the nation; and in the world community.

The proper relationship between the I and We can be maintained only if we are properly related to the Thou, who is God. As the great theologian Charles Hodge said, the glory of God must be the "governing motive" of our actions.

> The sun is the center of the system. Men of the world have themselves for the end of their actions. Philosophers tell us to make the good of others the end; and thus destroy the sentiment of religion, by merging it into philanthropy or benevolence. The Bible tells us to make the glory of God the end. This secures the other ends by

making them subordinate, while at the same time it exalts the soul by placing before it an infinite personal object. There is all the difference between making the glory of God (the personal Jehovah) the end of our actions, and the good of the universe, or of being in general, than there is between the love of Christ and the love of an abstract idea. The one is religion, the other is morality.[8]

The Individual and the Community

As I mentioned before, sanctified self-interest is biblical. This involves having, first of all, an objective view of oneself or, as Paul put it, having "sound judgment" (Romans 12:3). Christ's command to love one's neighbor as oneself (see Matthew 19:19) implies, at a minimum, a healthy self-regard.

We are to be, as far as possible, independent as individuals yet dependent in our social responsibilities and interactions. We *need* each other in community. Yet, above all, we are to be *theo*dependent, acknowledging God's sovereign rule over our lives and His creation. We are insufficient in ourselves. The Church, the body of Christ, ceases to function without its head, who is Christ.

What things does the human family share that provide the foundation for unity? Because we have all been created in the image of God, we are equals in value and dignity. With Adam and Eve as our parents, we are members of the same family (see Genesis 3:20), made by the same Lord, capable of moral choice, and thus morally accountable. Likewise, we are all sinners by nature, living in a fallen world replete with trials, affliction, and suffering. We are all dependent on God for life, meaning, significance, and salvation. Moreover, we have all been given the development mandate to rule over creation (see Genesis 1:28), and we all participate in significant ways to the unfolding of God's story, using the varying gifts that God has provided.

Yet we are all unique. No two people are exactly alike. Beyond the sexual differences mandated at creation (see Genesis 1:27), we have all been equipped with different gifts physically, emotionally, intellectually, and temperamentally. Our talents, abilities, interests, and (for the Christian) spiritual gifts are as diverse as our individual genetic codes. Widening the differences, people are born into different cultures, histories, and economic conditions. People of similar circumstances receive radically different callings, all have divergent roles, motives, and outcomes. Variety is certainly a part of God's plan for us. As C.S. Lewis said:

> I cannot conceive how one would get through the bore-
> dom of a world in which you never met anyone more
> clever, or more beautiful, or stronger than yourself.[9]

Let's look a bit more closely at some of the similarities and differences that are part and parcel of our existence. The most basic is on the
level of male and female. Some will say that equality between the sexes
is an absolute equality, that male and female are the same, with only
surface differences. Such people reject gender distinctions. Radical
feminists take this approach. Others will emphasize the differences
between male and female—usually to the detriment of women. In this
approach, *machismo* rules, and women are treated as beasts of burden,
with wives the property of their husbands.

But the biblical approach embraces both the equality of men and
women and their differences. The creation of man and woman in the
image of God is our guide (see Genesis 1:26–27). Both male and female
are shown to be equal before each other and the law. Neither male nor
female is to dominate the other. But since they were made male and
female, they are different, a difference we are to appreciate, even celebrate. Just as God is both "one and many," so human beings must be in
community, with unity and diversity. If someone had rewritten
Genesis 1:26 so it read, "Let *me* make man in *my* image, in *my* likeness,
and let *him* rule…," we would have something closer to Islam (one person, one God), not Christianity (three Persons, one God). The image
of God would be unitary, not community.

But God said, "It is not good for the man to be alone. I will make
a helper suitable for him" (Genesis 2:18). Far from being alone, the
man already had a perfect relationship with the personal God of the
universe. But the man was "alone" in kind; there were no other people.
So God made a helper suitable, that is, equal but different, someone to
complement the man.

Men and women are equal but are given different roles.

> Submit to one another out of reverence for Christ. Wives,
> submit to your husbands as to the Lord. For the husband
> is the head of the wife as Christ is the head of the church,
> his body, of which he is the Savior. Now as the church
> submits to Christ, so also wives should submit to their
> husbands in everything. Husbands, love your wives, just
> as Christ loved the church and gave himself up for her to

make her holy, washing her by the washing with water through the word, and to present her to himself as a radiant church, without stain or wrinkle or any other blemish, but holy and blameless (Ephesians 5:21–27).

This is mutual submission, reflective of equal stature. But the roles are distinct. The wife is to submit to the husband as to the Lord, while the husband is to love his wife as Christ loves the Church. Yet distinct roles do not imply different statures. Paul wrote "the head of every man is Christ, and the head of the woman is man, and the head of Christ is God" (1 Corinthians 11:3). Headship does not imply superiority. Note that the head of Christ is God, but no Christian would argue that the Father is better than the Son. The man is not better than the woman, but he does have a different responsibility.

Societies that emphasize one extreme either will tend to emphasize a dominant sex (*machismo*) or will destroy sex distinctions (radical feminism). But beginning in the radical middle allows for both legal equality and the honest celebration of sexual diversity.

Ethnicity and Culture

Another arena for the interplay of equality and diversity is on the level of ethnicity and culture. Nationalism* emphasizes unity at the expense of diversity. In such situations, individuals and minorities can be dominated and their human rights taken away. Examples of nationalism, including tribalism (its micro form), are legion in the twentieth century. Nazi Germany (Aryans vs. lesser races), Mao's China (peasants vs. intelligentsia), Bosnia (Muslims vs. Croats), Central Africa (Hutus vs. Tutsis), and the Caucasus (Turks vs. Armenians) all illustrate extreme nationalism.

Multiculturalism, as we have seen, emphasizes diversity at the expense of community, with individual rights seen as paramount. Examples of this approach include India, Pakistan, Bangladesh, the republics of the former Soviet Union, Canada and Quebec, and the U.S. at the end of the twentieth century. Even with an emphasis on diversity, feelings of hostility between groups often break out. India and Pakistan regularly experience communal violence, while group preferences sometimes stir latent racism in America.

The balance between nationalism and multiculturalism is found in what I call moral nationalism. In it, unity and diversity are both valued in the community. Unity is structured around a vision or set of ideas (freedom, democracy, law). Mutual respect and cooperation are the rule. A minority may be assimilated into the society; it is never annihilated in a moral system. Minorities are protected by the rule of law and participate in the nation, but they do not come to dominate it.

Nations figure prominently in God's economy, from Genesis to Revelation. God told Abram (later Abraham) that he and his seed (the nation of Israel) are blessed to be a channel of blessing to other nations* (*ethnos*) (see Genesis 12:1–3). God intends to bless all nations, to have them become all He designed them to be. Part of the Great Commission is to "make disciples of all nations" (*ethnos*) (see Matthew 28:18–20). In his vision John saw kings bringing the splendor of the nations into the City of God (see Revelation 21:22–26). The glory and honor of the nations *will* be brought before the King of the universe. All the precious things of an *ethnos* will be saved, the dross destroyed. Christ's stated task for the Church is to disciple every *ethnos*—all the nations.

Community

	Egalitarianism THE MANY	Community THE ONE AND MANY	Individualism THE ONE
Synonyms	Communalism	**Fellowship**	Libertarianism
Root	Envy	**Contentment**	Greed
Focus	Status	**Responsibility**	Rights
Time Frame	Past	**Future**	Present
Concept of Equality	Numerical	**Equitable**	To the Conqueror the Spoils
Examples	USA Welfare Socialism	**The Body of Christ**	Western Consumerism
Fruit	Enslavement to Envy	**Service to God and man**	Enslavement to Self
Values	Equality	**Justice**	Privilege

Figure 10.5

Finding a Balance

The chart in Figure 10.5 shows the differences between the extremes of the radicalism of "the one" (individualism) and "the many" (egalitarianism), as well as the values of community. Community by definition implies a balance between unity and diversity. Community is destroyed when either extreme is pursued.

Individualism, despite its laudatory press today, is nothing more than the endless search for personal fulfillment, where gratification of "me" or "my class" is the first principle of life. Irving Kristol writes, "[A]s the history of twentieth-century modernism...demonstrates, the pursuit of self suffers the same fate as the pursuit of happiness: he who is merely self-seeking shall find nothing but infinite emptiness."[10]

Egalitarianism, meanwhile, focuses on equal outcomes or equal distribution of resources. While some may think this approach was buried under the rubble of communism in many parts of the world, unfortunately this is not the case. Even in America, "the land of the free," the politics of resentment and victimization are alive and well. While the individualist emphasizes the basic inequalities of people, the egalitarian rejects all social and economic rankings, since all are presumed "equal." The egalitarian, therefore, puts great stock in numerical outcomes and quotas. He or she is perfectly comfortable with the redistribution of wealth—unless, of course, it is his or her own!

Once again, the biblical theist tries to occupy that sliver of real estate known as the radical middle. This middle ground allows for community, which is a group of individuals living in *unity* under *common* laws. The root of *community* is neither the greed of individualism nor the envy of egalitarianism, but is contentment, which comes as we relate properly to God.

> ...give me neither poverty nor riches, but give me only my daily bread. Otherwise I may have too much and disown you and say, "Who is the LORD?" Or I may become poor and steal, and so dishonor the name of my God (Proverbs 30:8b–9).

The apostle Paul said, "I have learned the secret of being content in any and every situation, whether well fed or hungry, whether living in plenty or in want" (Philippians 4:12b). The focus in a community is not **rights**—either for individuals or for groups—but **responsibilities**.

We are primarily responsible to God, and this filters down to all our relationships—to self, family, and neighbor. Our primary values are to be not "freedom" (personal privilege) *or* "justice" (absolute equality regardless of merit), but both freedom *and* justice. "The one" celebrates freedom; "the many" demands justice.

Paul Johnson writes concerning the Judeo-Christian tradition:

> [T]he outstanding moral merit is to invest the individual with a conscience and bid him follow it. This particular form of liberation is what St. Paul meant by the freedom men find in Christ. And, of course, it is the father of all other freedoms. For conscience is the enemy of tyranny and the compulsory society... The notions of political and economic freedom both spring from the Christian conscience as a historic force...[11]

Liberty

Egalitarianism THE MANY	Community THE ONE AND MANY	Individualism THE ONE
Totalitarianism	**Liberty**	Anarchy
Compulsion	**Freedom within limits**	Unrestrained Freedom
No Freedom	**Freedom based on the rule of Law**	No Law
Serfdom	**Moral Freedom**	Natural Freedom
Fascism (right) Marxism (left)	**Democracy Free Markets**	Anarchists Libertarians

Figure 10.6

Figure 10.7

Form and Freedom

Let's explore the nature of freedom a bit more deeply. Each of the three metaphysical stories defines liberty differently. Thus, it's no surprise that they end up with vastly different results.

"The one" mindset focuses on the absolute freedom of the individual (freedom without form), and it leads to anarchy. Freedom is the goal and can be the freedom to do wrong: "Everyone does what is right in his own eyes" (Judges 21:25), convincing evidence that a society has forgotten God.

For its part, the perspective of "the many" leads to totalistarianism (form without freedom).

By contrast, emphasis on "the one and the many" leads to true liberty (form *and* freedom), as illustrated in Figure 10.7. Liberty under law is freedom based on morality and responsibility: the freedom to do good. As Micah 6:8 says so powerfully:

> He has showed you, O man, what is good. And what does the LORD require of you? To act justly and to love mercy and to walk humbly with your God.

As Paul admonished the Galatians, who were tempted to abuse the very freedom Christ had given them:

> You, my brothers were called to be free. But do not use your freedom to indulge the sinful nature; rather, serve one another in love (Galatians 5:13).

The Nature of Justice

As with liberty, so with justice: Each paradigm defines justice differently.

Justice

Egalitarianism THE MANY	Community THE ONE AND MANY	Individualism THE ONE
Injustice	**Justice**	Chaos
Class	**Individuals in Community**	Individual
Economic Equality (numerical)	**Equality before God and the Law**	Maximum Personal Freedom
Group Advancement	**Responsibility**	My Individual Rights
No personal responsibility. Victimization (Class responsibility)	**Personal responsibilities to myself and my community**	Limited personal and NO social responsibility
"Liberal"	**"Progressive"**	"Conservative"
Internationalist Welfarist	**Incarnationalist**	Nationalist Isolationist

Figure 10.8

Because "the one" (individualism) idolizes the individual, justice is morphed into a rationale to maximize personal freedom. Justice for the individualist is an environment free of restrictions. Personal responsibility is a dominant theme; social responsibility is, at best, an afterthought. Conservatives are often caricatured as hard-headed and cold-hearted isolationists who say, "I'll let you alone if you let me alone."

On the other hand, the egalitarian (the many) focus on the injustice of life on a class or group of people. Individual rights are secondary.

The egalitarian looks to government to enforce "justice" through quotas, preferences, and the redistribution of wealth. Personal responsibility is eclipsed by a victim mentality. Liberals are often portrayed as warm-hearted, soft-headed dupes who believe all solutions rest with the government.

A consistent biblical theist surpasses the best that both the egalitarian and the individualist have to offer. He or she cares about the individual and the community as a whole. The theist recognizes what the others see only in part, that people are equal before God and before the law. Thus, the theist is free (theoretically, at least) of prejudice, racism, and classism. Regarding the law, he or she is truly "colorblind," judging people by the content of their character, not the color of their skin. The theist supports justice by protecting all human life, liberty, and property. To do this, individual moral discipline and the civil government of the community work hand in hand. Neither can work alone. As John Adams said about the nascent political experiment that was America:

> Our Constitution was made only for a moral and religious people. It is wholly inadequate to the government of any other.[12]

In such a system, our focus shifts from rights to responsibilities. People have a *personal* responsibility not only for self and the family but also for their larger community. And through our responsibilities as citizens we are to enact laws that protect the weakest and most vulnerable among us. The unborn, children, minorities, our families—all should be protected through civil rights laws, child labor protections, and so on. The theist resists any pigeonholing; he or she is both liberal and conservative, as commonly defined; personally responsible and socially engaged. "I am my brother's keeper" might be the theist's creed.

Hospitals, hospices, schools, senior homes, job training for the able-bodied poor, churches, school boards, political parties are all examples of ways we care for our communities as individuals. Edmund Burke called these kinds of private voluntary associations "little platoons." Tocqueville,* after a tour through the United States in the 1830s, observed:

Americans of all ages, all stations of life, and all types of disposition are forever forming associations. There are... a thousand different types—religious, moral, serious, futile, very general and very limited, immensely large and very minute... Thus the most democratic country in the world now is that in which men have in our time carried the objects of common desires... Nothing, in my view, deserves more attention than the intellectual and moral associations in America.[13]

Little Pushes

The United States is commonly called a capitalist society. By this the country's vast economic capital is usually meant. But there are other kinds of capital: intellectual, moral, and social among them. Robert Putman described social capital as a "social organization such as networks, norms, and social trust that facilitate coordination and cooperation for mutual benefit."[14] Together, social capital contributes to the health of the individual, a society's economic growth, and a strong and functioning representative government.

Thus, worldview is critical far beyond the spiritual realm. Its influence is felt in the most mundane events of daily existence. Augustine knew well the power of worldview, of story.

According to Augustine, culture is not a reflection of a people's race, ethnicity, folklore, language, or heritage. Rather, it is an outworking of a people's creed. In other words, culture is the temporal manifestation of a people's faith. If a culture begins to change, it is not because of fads, fashions, or the passing of time; it is because of a shift in worldview—it is because of a change of faith. Thus, race, ethnicity, folklore, politics, language, [and] heritage are simply expressions of a deeper paradigm rooted in the covenantal and spiritual matrix of a community's church and the integrity of its witnesses.

The reason he spent so much of his life and ministry critiquing the pagan philosophies of the world and exposing the aberrant theologies of the church was that Augustine understood only too well that those

things matter not only in the realm of eternity determining the spiritual destiny of masses of humanity, but
in the realm of the here and now determining the temporal destiny of whole civilizations.[15]

Yes, man is the history maker. Each of us has more influence than
we think, and it all starts in our minds. Again Grant notes:

> The extraordinary was achieved by the ordinary. That
> is actually the great lesson of all history. It has always
> been ordinary people who ultimately were the ones to
> shape the outcome of great human events—not kings
> and princes, not masters and tyrants. It has always
> been laborers and workmen, cousins and acquain-
> tances who have upended the expectations of the bril-
> liant and the glamorous, the expert and the
> meticulous. It has been plain folks, simple people, who
> have changed the course of history—because they are
> the stuff of which history is made.[16]

No matter who we are, we can have an impact. Helen Keller said it this
way:

> I long to accomplish a great and noble task, but it is my
> chief duty to accomplish humble tasks as though they
> were great and noble. The world is moved along not
> only by the mighty shoves of its heroes, but by the
> aggregate of the tiny pushes of each honest worker.[17]

Two Ethics

Societies tend to form around one of two ethics: "the one" or "the
many." Either way, they tend to live out a mindset of poverty. What I
call the development ethic begins with a recognition of the Trinity, the
embodiment of "the one and the many." The culture of development
demands that people take individual responsibility for their lives and
be actively engaged and personally responsible for their communities
and civic life. People must value both freedom and justice before they
can create free and just societies. Only then can they begin to fulfill
their role in God's story as stewards in His house.

Study Questions

Describe in your own words the three models of community

The One:

The Many:

The One-Many:

Which of these models is most like the communities where you live
and work?

How are they similar?

List four ways that people are

Created equal:

Created unique:

How has God created you unique?

One of Satan's greatest lies is this: Men are better than women. How could men show more honor to women, acknowledging their equality while also recognizing their unique role?

What three things could you do to encourage more honor for women?

How does tribalism manifest itself in your country?

Describe in your own words what God intends for all the nations.

In what ways are development workers disciplers of nations (or nation builders)?

Which forces of individualism or egalitarianism are the greatest ene-mies to community in your country?

What is one activity in your community that could promote

Liberty?

Justice?

What are "private voluntary associations"?

Give examples from your society of these "little platoons."

How can they be encouraged to form and grow?

What questions or challenges do you have in response to the ideas presented in this chapter?

The Task

O LORD, our Lord, how majestic is your name in all the earth! You have set your glory above the heavens.... what is man that you are mindful of him, the son of man that you care for him? You made him a little lower than the heavenly beings and crowned him with glory and honor. You made him ruler over the works of your hands; you put everything under his feet: all flocks and herds, and the beasts of the field, the birds of the air, and the fish of the sea, all that swim the paths of the seas.
O LORD, our Lord, how majestic is your name in all the earth!

Psalm 8:1, 4–9

Wherever man may stand, whatever he may do, to whatever he may apply his hand, in agriculture, in commerce, and in industry, or his mind, in the world of art, and science, he is, in whatsoever it may be, constantly standing before the face of his God, he is employed in the service of his God, he has strictly to obey his God, and above all, he has to aim at the glory of his God.

Abraham Kuyper
An Adequate Philosophy of Religion

CHAPTER ELEVEN

Stewardship
Creating and Managing Bounty

IT BEGAN AS PART OF A MOUNTAIN in Italy. Then one day a workman came along and began chiseling out a block of marble. Using his discerning eye and powerful hands and arms, he worked for weeks. When the block was finally hewn from the mountain, another man, with a horse-drawn wagon, hauled it to Florence. A third fellow bought the stone and had it put on a pedestal in his studio. That man was Michelangelo. As he went about his other work, the artist would often pause to gaze at the immense, flawed block. Perhaps months later, Michelangelo saw what lay hidden in the stone. Finally, he picked up his hammer and chisel and began to reveal it. Today we call what was once a buried chunk of marble a priceless masterpiece—*The David*.

Bounty, or abundance, is not primarily found in natural resources. It comes from the cornucopia of personal creativity. Man, the "secondary creator," can use his rational mind and intuition to create wealth, art, scholarship, and poetry.

Stewardship is a major theme of the Bible. I would estimate that 100 percent of Christ's teachings deals with stewardship of life, while just 20 percent focuses specifically on money and material possessions. Stewardship in the physical realm, which is what we will focus on here, involves progressing in God's story toward the City of God—tending His creation so that it becomes increasingly fruitful.

Animism

Worshiper

Figure 11.1

Theism

Steward

Figure 11.2

Secularism

Consumer

Figure 11.3

What does God have to say about economics? Plenty! Remember the choice that God has given us? Obedience brings blessing, while disobedience brings cursing. Biblical theism, rightly applied, leads to bounty. Animism, as we see only too well around the world, produces material poverty. (I know of not a single animist society where the great masses of people are wealthy.) Secularism, while it can lead to physical opulence, produces a metaphysical vacuum, a profound spiritual poverty. The true goal of man, of course, is to worship and serve God. Bounty is the happy byproduct of this joyful task, not its goal.

God and Economics

Those of us from the West—even in today's post-Christian climate—take for granted the idea that "In the beginning, God…." Even most secularists among us are familiar with the creation account in Genesis. We believe that the universe was created, or at least that it began in a "big bang." Not all cosmologies, however, begin with a Creator. Those that don't, deprive people of the ability to understand creativity and man's awesome potential. You don't have to read Carl Sagan to find this "Godless" approach.

Daniel Boorstin writes:

> For the Hindu the creation was not a bringing into being of the wonder of the world. Rather it was a dismemberment, a disintegration of the original Oneness. For him the creation seemed not the expression of a rational, benevolent Maker in

wondrous new forms but a fragmenting of the unity of
nature into countless limited forms. The Hindu saw
the creation of our world as "the self-limitation of the
transcendent."... [T]he aim of the Hindu was to be
uncreated.[1]

The heart of Buddhism, which has its roots deeply lodged in
Hinduism, is suffering and death. The goal of the Buddhist is not to
combat them but to escape from them and the world. Again, Boorstin
shows the way:

> Is it any wonder that the Buddha dismissed those who
> asked when and how the world was created?.... What
> soul en route to Buddhahood would waste energy on
> the mystery of creation? The Buddha aimed at Un-
> Creation....If there was a Creator, it was he who had
> created the need for the extinction of the self, the need
> to escape rebirth, the need to struggle toward Nirvana.
> The Lord of the Buddhists was the Master of Extinc-
> tion. And no model for man the creator.[2]

The theistic cosmology begins not just with a creator but with *the*
Creator. Yet He is not some weak figment of a deist's mind; the Creator
remains actively involved in all He has made. Not only did He design
and make the house, but He owns it and continues constructing it.
David paints a picture of a King who is not so much Artist (although
He is that and so much more) as He is Contractor and Builder:

> He wraps himself in light as with a garment; he
> stretches out the heavens like a tent and lays the beams
> of his upper chambers on their waters. He makes the
> clouds his chariot and rides on the wings of the wind.
> He makes winds his messengers, flames of fire his ser-
> vants. He set the earth on its foundations; it can never
> be moved (Psalm 104:2–5).

Representatives of the King

This same King has constructed us not to be beautiful sculptures
set on our own pedestals but to be His representatives on this earth.

Paul said "we are God's workmanship, created in Christ Jesus to do good works, which God prepared in advance for us to do" (Ephesians 2:10). We are "built on the foundation of the apostles and prophets, with Christ Jesus Himself as the chief cornerstone. In him the whole building is joined together and rises to become a holy temple in the Lord" (Ephesians 2:20–21). We are both God's workmanship and God's workers as God quarries living stones from every tribe and nation. What a marvelous narrative we have been privileged to join!

God began history by planting a garden (see Genesis 2:8) and will end it by building a city. Another way to view this process is that God is the Architect and we are his coworkers, building toward His ends, using His blueprints. God told man to "work" the garden and "take care of it" (Genesis 2:15). We are to make the earth—God's kingdom—more productive by working it. We are to conserve it by taking care of it.

Jesus' stewardship parables made the unmistakable point that the Master owns everything and that we are accountable for what we do with His capital. Luke records one of Jesus' parables in which the Master gives 10 of His servants 10 minas apiece and tells them to put it to work until He returned. God entrusts His ownership of earth to man to do His will there as it is done in heaven. And man will be held accountable for his stewardship (see Luke 19:12–15). One of the criteria by which man will be judged is whether he conserves the earth. Those who destroy the earth will be destroyed (see Revelation 11:18b).

Let's examine the creation mandate for development:

> Then God said, "Let us make man in our image, in our likeness, and let them rule over the fish of the sea and the birds of the air, over the livestock, over all the earth, and over all the creatures that move along the ground." So God created man in his own image, in the image of God he created him; male and female he created them. God blessed them and said to them, "Be fruitful and increase in number; fill the earth and subdue it. Rule over the fish of the sea and the birds of the air and over every living creature that moves on the ground" (Genesis 1:26–28).

The passage makes clear that God creates man like Himself so that man may rule in His place. After creating man, God blessed him for the purpose of developing the earth. Man was to be a channel of God's blessing. Note the close parallel between God's covenant with Abram to be a blessing to all the nations (see Genesis 12:1–3) and the Great Commission of the Church by Christ to make disciples of all the nations (see Matthew 28:18–20).

Man is given the societal mandate to inhabit the earth: "Be fruitful and multiply and fill the earth (see Genesis 1:28b). The earth is to be filled not with consumers or mouths to be fed but with co-creators—those with intellect and passion—scientists, artists, farmers, and educators. We are also given the developmental mandate to "subdue and rule over" the earth. The Hebrew word for "rule," *radah*, means "to have dominion (or authority)." Starting out by tending the garden and naming the animals, we are to build "the City of God."

As we have seen in previous chapters, we are not to be God's mindless lackeys, although that in itself is more than we deserve. No, God has given us the unfathomable privilege of being *co-creators* with Him. Man, made in God's image, is given the awesome task of bringing forth all the potential of creation. Man is the source of earth's bounty as well as its poverty. As the sovereign God's vice-regents, we are stewards for His household, coworkers in His kingdom, caretakers of His garden, builders of His city, and actors in His story. In some ways, like our Master, we transcend nature. Of course, He is completely above the natural order, while we live in it and in some sense are bound by the universe's physical processes. Yet the minds God has given us allow us to move ahead, to leap over barriers, to devise new ways, to solve problems. As Novak has said, "Creation is full of secrets waiting to be discovered, riddles which human intelligence is expected by the creator to unlock.[3] Created "a little lower than the angels," we have a task to perform, a purpose to fulfill.

While our creatureliness binds us to nature, God's image stamped on us allows us to move beyond the physical reality we see daily. We can dream of a better world and then begin to make it happen. Where there is darkness we can create a lightbulb, where there is desert drill a well, where mountains are barren plant a forest, where people are forgotten and ignored set them free through the power of the gospel, where people are ignorant build them schools and libraries, where the land is wasted plant a garden, where people are sick develop a cure, where there is silence hear the music and play it. Man is the discoverer, explorer, innovator, initiator, creator, and composer.

As the Mind, So the World

The earth will be filled with what is in our hearts and minds. If our minds are empty, our world will be barren. If our hearts are hard, our world will lack compassion. As Solomon said, "As a man thinks in his heart, so is he"—and so is his world! Kuyper stated:

> We with our own human nature are placed in nature around us, not to leave that nature as it is but with an urge and calling within us to work on nature through human art, to enable and perfect it…Human art acts on every area of nature, not to destroy the life of nature, much less to juxtapose another structure, but rather to unlock the power which lies concealed in nature; or again to regulate the will power that springs from it.[4]

Just as God conceived of the universe and then "worked" to create it, so man is to transform the world through his work. Man—not nature—is the source of wealth. The more man applies God's laws and uses the gifts God has given him, the more bounty is produced. But the opposite is also true: The more he follows counterfeit laws and principles and fails to use his heart and mind, the greater the destruction of life and creation. It is disobedience, not a growing population, that produces poverty. E. Calvin Beisner notes:

> [O]n the average people produce considerably more than they consume in their lifetimes. That is why growing human populations, far from threatening to create poverty and to exhaust natural resources, promise instead to create wealth and to multiply resources. Remember this: on the average, every mouth born into this world is attached to two hands—and, more important, to a *mind* made in the image of God to be creative and productive. That is why wealth is increasing.[5]

Human creativity is the source of wealth. More and more thinkers are recognizing what George Gilder has called the "overthrow of matter." I'd take it further. As we recognize the primacy of the human mind, we overthrow the primacy of matter along with the superstitions of secularism and the superstitions of animism. The Mangalwadis remind us:

> Being made in the image of God means that even as physical beings, we can transcend some of the physical limitations of nature and alter physical reality. For example, in a dark room animals have to resign themselves to darkness, but we don't have to. Similarly, in a desert we can bring water. We are not completely limited by the external reality. God has made us creative. We are free to imagine a different and better physical, social, and political world. Where there is oppression, we can dream freedom and dignity for the smallest individual.[6]

Before the end of the Cold War, on May 31, 1988, Ronald Reagan gave the students of Moscow University a preview of what was to come. The U.S. president challenged them to replace the tired ideology of materialism with the idea of freedom.

> Like a chrysalis, we're emerging from the economy of the industrial revolution—an economy confined to and limited by the earth's physical resources—into the economy of mind, an era in which there are no bounds on human imagination and the freedom to create is the most precious natural resource.[7]

Creativity within a moral framework creates an endless wealth of ideas, and thus bounty in the material world.

The Secondary Creator

Man uses his creativity to create whole new worlds through art, music, poetry, fantasy, and science fiction. The wealth he creates is found not in the ink or the paper but in the ideas. Though Beethoven was deaf, he "heard" great symphonies in his head. Mozart said he was not so much working at composing as he was writing down the melodies that he heard. J.R.R. Tolkien, author of the beloved world of Middle Earth in *The Hobbit* and *The Lord of the Rings*, pointed out that man, the secondary creator, must mimic God, the primary Creator, for his own work to ring true. The artist creates vivid new worlds when they mimic the primary reality.

> Probably every writer making a secondary world, a fantasy, every sub-creator, wishes in some measure to be a real maker, or hopes that he is drawing on reality: hopes that the peculiar quality of this secondary world (if not all the details) are derived from Reality, or are flowing into it. If he indeed achieves a quality that can fairly be described by the dictionary definition: "inner consistency of reality," it is difficult to conceive how this can be, if the work does not in some way partake of reality. The peculiar quality of the "joy" in successful Fantasy can thus be explained as a sudden glimpse of the underlying reality or truth. It is not only a "consolation" for the sorrow of this world, but a satisfaction, and an answer to that question, "Is it true?" The answer to this question that I gave at first was (quite rightly): "If you have built your little world well, yes: it is true in that world." That is enough for the artist.[8]

We transform the world not only through our hearts, of course, but also through our minds. Mathematics and its systematic, predictable order has been called the language of creation. God has given man the ability to discover the design behind nature (science) and to apply those laws (technology) to attack the ravages of natural evil, the "thorns and thistles."

> The creation waits in eager expectation for the sons of God to be revealed. For the creation was subjected to frustration, not by its own choice, but by the will of the one who subjected it, in hope that the creation itself will be liberated from its bondage to decay and brought into the glorious freedom of the children of God. We know that the whole creation has been groaning as in the pains of childbirth right up to the present time (Romans 8:19–22).

Here we learn several critical facts: (1) creation's fate and ours are inextricably bound together; (2) God's work of restoring all things to Himself is a process, a story, that will one day be consummated; (3) man has been commissioned to be a part of that process; and, by extension, (4) science and technology are tools in this process.

If mathematics and the other scientific disciplines are languages of God, then science is the thinking of God's thoughts after Him. We use our God-given reason and analytical ability to penetrate creation's secrets. Technology is the moral application of science to benefit mankind and creation to the glory of God. Of course, the stories of abusive science are far too common. Hitler's doctors performing cruel experiments on Jews, the Tuskegee experiments on poor black men in the U.S., and the current push for "harvesting" the organs of aborted fetuses are just three examples of science gone awry. The problem with science today is that it has been divorced from the pursuit of Truth. The problem with technology is that it has been separated from morals. Cut from their transcendent moorings, we are set adrift in a "brave new world," full of pollution, dehumanization, and death. Man loses his place in the universe and becomes a slave to technology.

Technology applied to moral ends, however, benefits mankind in many ways. First, it improves the quality of life. Medicine, energy sources, agricultural advances (ensuring a food supply that can feed a world population at least four times larger than today's), and the incredible information explosion have all improved not just the quality of life but also its quantity.

Another thing technology does is generate bounty and new resources. Think about oil for a minute. For thousands of years, oil was a nuisance—an insoluble mess to be scrubbed from your feet if you were unlucky enough to step in it. Then one day someone had the bright idea of burning it to provide energy. Suddenly oil was a resource, not a nuisance. Soon dark streets could be lit, homes heated, cars driven. The oil hadn't changed. But man's ingenuity had made this formerly worthless substance into something we call "black gold." Can you imagine the world without it?

Now let's examine sand. Sand is so common in our world that the Bible has a saying about it: "as numerous as the sand on the seashore." Sand is everywhere. Like oil, sometimes it's hard to get rid of! A grain of sand by itself has no value. But a man can take that grain and transform it into a silicon chip, and suddenly it has value. Another man can then take that chip and impregnate it with data, making it worth even more. And when someone else connects that chip to a computer, it is worth quite a lot. Multibillion-dollar companies like Intel have been built on grains of sand. The sand, of course, remains basically worthless. It must wait for man to give it its value.

Technology also provides benefits that are not so immediately tangible, although they are just as real nonetheless. One of the key benefits, of course, is how it provides a framework for equity and community. Technology allows people and societies the opportunity to leapfrog over centuries of deprivation overnight. Technology, when shared, is a great equalizer. John Empuili is a member of the nomadic Masai tribe. He did not enter school until he was 15, yet through hard work, talent, and the vistas opened to him through modern education and technology, he earned a doctorate. For decades now he has served his people as an educator, pastor, and development consultant.

Technology provides a way for people to share in a larger community. The electronic media allow billions to share in the World Cup, the Olympics, a moon landing, or a sermon by Billy Graham. Information is theoretically available not just to the elites but also to the masses. Technology creates its own momentum and builds on itself. One discovery leads to another. People hear about it and want it. Witness the sudden clamor for satellite dishes in places like China and Iran, where the state attempts to control what people see and how people think.

Man creates bounty not just with his heart and mind but also with his hands. Our bodies produce the labor that manifests our dreams and discoveries into the physical world. Of course, we are not confined to our own "tools": eyes, ears, hands, legs. We can create tools to do so much more than what we could do alone. For eyes, a microscope or telescope; for ears, a microphone; for hands, tweezers or robots; for legs, a car to carry us across a continent.

Another key tool man has to transform the world is the word. In the Bible, words are used to establish dominion, both by God (see Genesis 1:3; Psalm 33:6, 9; and John 1:1–3) and by man (see Genesis 2:19–20a). God speaks to create and sustain the universe. Man speaks to create and shape culture. God's Word informs man about what is (see Genesis 1:1) and what ought to be (see Proverbs 6:20–23), to teach us that "man does not live on bread alone but on every word that comes from the mouth of the LORD" (Deuteronomy 8:3). Reflecting on Deuteronomy 8, author, lawyer, and educator Udo Middlemann stated:

> We do not take our cue from what is, but from what ought to be. We live by every word that proceeds from the mouth of God and not just by natural conditions or statistical averages....God's word does not only address our spirituality, it also informs us of how to make a living in a world that does not tolerate human existence but punishes us with the consequence of our earlier transgression. It is out of that mindset that we give a different shape to the flow of rivers, that we put limits on the life of bacteria....It is out of that mindset that we move mountains and rocks in order to give a place for human existence, when nature sheds no tears, when starvation ruins human existence.[9]

As an actor in God's story, man uses his own word to establish dominion, to create culture, even to assign human identity. Adam named his wife Eve, which means "life-giver," "because she would become the mother of all the living." Parents name their children today. The name a parent gives a child is the name that the God of the universe will call that child for all eternity. By his words, man brings civilization to society through law, progress to the world through language and science, and beauty to the world through literature and music.

Stewardship: A Metaphor for Development

Despite all this rich evidence for a biblical understanding of development, I must admit that the word *development* appears nowhere in Scripture. According to the Oxford English Dictionary, it actually comes from the French *developer*, which means to unfold or disclose; the growth and unfolding of what is in the germ. (The antonym, *enveloper*,* means to enfold, enclose, cover, or wrap.)

Since the word is not strictly biblical, for years I have wondered: Do Christians who work in the development field look at "development" the same way their secular counterparts do? Is their approach to development also rooted in the secularism of the French Enlightenment? Do they tend to "Christianize" their work only by saying that they are motivated by Christ? Or does their work flow from a comprehensively biblical worldview?

Since the definition of "development" has been established by a largely secular industry, what should Christians do? We obviously cannot just go along, since so many things—good and bad—flow from our choice of words. Do we then coin a new word and hope we can convince people to understand and adopt it, or can we find a functional equivalent for development already in Scripture? I have opted for the latter course, since both testaments speak of the concept of stewardship, which is a rich metaphor for development.

Rooted in the Bible are two images that picture God's activity: planting a garden (see Genesis 2:8) and building a city (see Revelation 21). Man began his journey in a garden and will end it in a city. The New Testament employs the concept several ways. First, people are seen as slaves of the Master's house, responsible to administer the entire estate. This concept was broadened to include the apostolic office. The apostle was to faithfully pass on the Good News of salvation in Christ. Second, the concept in the New Testament referred to God's unfolding plan of redemption. Third, stewardship implied the accountability of the stewards. God's stewards have been given a limited period of time to accomplish the task—God's *telos*. Besides this, we are to preserve what is valuable from injury or loss (see Matthew 28:19–20).[10] We are not only to win souls but also to grow in every area of life: morally, physically, intellectually, socially, and spiritually. Thus, the history between Genesis 2 and Revelation 21 is the story of *oikodome*, the story of development.

Development, understood as stewardship, maintains a dynamic tension between conserving and progressing. The biblical development worker, then, is best described as a progressive conservative (or a conservative progressive). What a contrast with secularism, which progresses without conserving, or animism, which conserves without progressing.

The Role of Faith

"Without faith, it is impossible to please God" (Hebrews 11:6). It is also impossible to have a biblically informed stewardship without faith. Man gives substance to the things he knows to be the truth by his words and deeds. Faith sees spiritually what is not yet present physically, understanding that the visible comes from the invisible (see Hebrews 11:3). With Abraham as his model of encouragement, the man of faith is willing to risk all, even life itself, for the kingdom of God.

> By faith Abraham, when called to go to a place he would
> later receive as his inheritance, obeyed and went, even

though he did not know where he was going. By faith he made his home in the promised land like a stranger in a foreign country; he lived in tents, as did Isaac and Jacob, who were heirs with him of the same promise. For he was looking forward to the city with foundations, whose architect and builder is God…All these people were still living by faith when they died. They did not receive the things promised; they only saw them and welcomed them from a distance (Hebrews 11:8–10, 13).

Faith sees God's good intentions for men and women, families, communities, nations, and the world. Where the land is barren it sees a garden. Where there is filth it recognizes the dignity of man in God's image and builds latrines. Where there are bare walls it sees beauty and paints a picture. When it dreams of distant lands it builds a ship and sails there.

In contrast, people in poverty are dominated by fear. They have a gut-level understanding of Jesus' words of warning that "to him who does not have, even what he has will be taken away." Unfortunately, this is how most people throughout history have lived. Peter Berger says this form of existence

was characterized by very high rates of infant mortality, low life expectancy, (both at birth, where of course it was determined by the infant mortality rates, and at later points in the individual life cycle), inadequate nutrition and frequent starvation, very high vulnerability to diseases and pain, very high vulnerability to the ravages of nature, with all this sustained by a simple and relatively unchanging (more precisely, very slow-changing) technology and by a zero-growth subsistence economy. In this form of existence both the life of individuals and of societies were determined to a large degree by the pressures of the physical environment and of the sheer demographic facts upon the feeble structures of human technology and economic arrangements. Fernand Braudel has coined the apt phrase "the biological ancien regime" to denote this millennia-old shape of human existence. It forms the stable underside of all the glittering events that are conventionally evoked by the word "history." Most of it is a reality of pain beyond the experience of virtually all people, even the poorest, in an advanced industrial society.[11]

Zero-growth, zero-risk societies are still with us, unfortunately. They are found anywhere from our inner-city slums to our well-manicured upper-middle-class suburbs among those who are afraid of appropriate risk taking. The comparative language table in Figure 11.4 focuses on the different mindsets of fatalism and faith.

Mindset

FATALISM	FAITH
Fear of failure	Courage to risk
I can't do it	All things are possible
I am a victim	I'm a responsible person
Resign myself to my fate	Rebel against the world
Life happens to me	Life is what I make it
Man is like a pebble in a still pond; *he does not move the water, the water moves him*	Man is like a pebble thrown into a still pond; *his impact creates ripples that go on forever*
Dependent / Responder	Interdependent / Initiator
Tradition / Unchanging	Progress / Innovative
Bureaucratic	Entrepreneurial
"We" Centered	"They" Centered
Luck (Fail)	**Hard Work** (Achieve)

Figure 11.4

Barriers to Risk

There are, of course, several barriers to risk. The first is simply the lack of a compelling vision. If you don't see anything worthy of your life and health, why should you risk them? One of the characteristics of our modern age is the perpetual quest for success with security, personal affluence without conflict. We live in a truly *bourgeois* society, composed of people with small ambitions but huge appetites: for health, for entertainment, for a big house, for a second (or third) car, for "stuff." There remain but a few who want to do something significant with their lives.

A second barrier to risk is a mentality that deifies the past. This is an overly conservative stance in which the past is held sacred. Whole societies are held in thrall to the "tradition of the elders," to fear of the wrath of the ancestors. A third barrier is fatalism, which takes many guises. In animism, the fates are held to be omnipotent. In Islam, the Muslim is to submit to the omnipotence and inscrutable will of Allah. In Japan, the response to an event like an earthquake can be the saying, *shogonai*, which means "this is the way it is," "(I) cannot help it."

Other hurdles to risk taking include a fear of failure, a fear of losing face, a fear of the unknown, a fear of the future, and simple selfishness. Jesus strongly condemned those who refused to be faithful in taking risks for the kingdom (see Luke 19:11–27).

Repentance: Transformation of the Mind

The attitudes of fear and faith reveal the state of the heart. To move from fear to faith requires a change of mind. It requires repentance. Four things underpin true repentance: (1) an acknowledgment of sin in the society or individual; (2) a recognition that fundamental change is possible; (3) an ability to envision a different future; and (4) a willingness to risk the future—commonly referred to as faith.

The barriers to risk must be removed. We must replace the fear of failure with a healthy freedom to fail. We need to balance the traditions and richness of the past with a spirit of adventure and discovery. As William Carey said, "Expect great things; attempt great things!" Balance, of course, is critical to healthy individuals and societies. A risk is no more than an invitation to suicide if it is not carefully weighed first. We need to properly balance risk with insurance, competition with cooperation, individuality with community, and investing with giving.

Professor David G. McClelland of Harvard explored "The Achievement Motive in Economic Growth." McClelland was interested in why some countries grew rapidly and others did not. He focused not on external factors, such as trade and resources, but on internal ones— "in the values and motives men have that lead them to exploit opportunities, to take advantage of favorable trade conditions; in short, to shape their own destiny."[12] McClelland called this attitude "the need for achievement."

Three words, all beginning with the letter g, will help us get a better handle on the internal motivation for development: (1) *gumption*, which is an English word meaning initiative, resourcefulness, stamina, and courage; (2) *ganas*, which is Spanish for desire, will, longing to, and hunger for; and (3) *gambare*, a Japanese word meaning "try harder, never give up."

For the Christian, of course, there is a "fourth *g*"—God. Jesus repeatedly encouraged His followers to take risks for the kingdom, since they had the ultimate insurance policy: God Himself. Here are a few slightly paraphrased examples: "With God anything is possible!" (Matthew 19:26). "If you have the faith of a mustard seed you can move mountains!" (Matthew 17:20). "Look, I am with you always" (Matthew 28:20). "Nothing shall be impossible for you" (Matthew 17:20).

The life of Mother Teresa of Calcutta, described by Robert Fulghum as "a little old lady in sari and sandals," has given us a model of someone who is not very powerful but who is willing to give all she has in the service of God. At a conference of quantum physicists and religious mystics in Bombay, Mother Teresa once said, "We can do no great things; only small things with great love."[13]

Are we ready to risk all for Christ and His kingdom? Are we prepared to try, win or lose? Hear the bracing words of Teddy Roosevelt:

> Far better it is to dare mighty things, to win glorious triumphs, even though checkered by failure, than to take rank with those poor spirits who neither enjoy much nor suffer much because they live in the gray twilight that knows neither victory nor defeat.[14]
> It is not the critic that counts; not the man who points out how the strong man stumbles, or where the doer of deeds could have done them better. The credit belongs to the man who is actually in the arena, whose face is

marred by dust and sweat and blood; who strives valiantly, who errs, and comes short again and again, because there is no effort without error and shortcoming; but who does actually strive to do the deeds.[15]

Of course, no bounty can be created without sweat—usually a lot of it. Genius, it is often said, is 1 percent inspiration and 99 percent perspiration. In Chapter 12 we'll look at how work fits into the biblical story.

Study Questions

What are some of your culture's commonly held beliefs about how creation occurred?

As you reflect on your life, what ways can you see that God, the Master Builder, has sculpted you as a living stone?

Give examples from your culture of ways that the stewardship mandate (Genesis 2:15) is being disobeyed by failing to

Develop creation (work it):

Conserve creation (care for it):

How can man transform the world through

His imaginative heart (the arts)?

His analytical mind (science and technology)?

Consider the culture where you are working. Where is it filled with beauty, discovery, and advancement? Give examples of strengths and weaknesses for each of these areas.

	Strengths	Weaknesses
Art		
Science & Technology		
Work *Labor and manifested dreams*		

How can you encourage the areas of strength and challenge the areas of weakness?

How do words establish dominion?

Give examples of cultural words that encourage development and those that encourage poverty.

Summarize your understanding of these terms:

oikos (οικος):

oikodome (οικοδομη):

oikonomia (οικονομια):

Review the mindset comparative language chart (Figure 11.4). Circle the words that best describe the people you work with.

If there is a pattern, what is it?

What does this tell you?

Identify a person or a group of people in your community who have what David McClelland calls an "achievement motive."

Identify a specific way you can encourage them.

How might you disciple them so that they can motivate and teach others?

GOD IS building His kingdom. How will His kingdom expand in the communities where you live and work? What would you like to do in the next six months as a worker for **Jehovah & Sons Building Company?**

What questions or challenges do you have in response to the ideas presented in this chapter?

· CHAPTER TWELVE ·

Lifework
Reconnecting Vocation
to the Transforming Story

DESPITE SOME SETBACKS, Thailand has developed rapidly in the economic realm. When compared with the development of Western nations, this phenomenon, true across much of Asia, has occurred relatively recently. Why did it take Thailand so long?

Let's look at some of Thailand's stumbling blocks. Three cultural values hindered and impeded Thai people, keeping them from exercising their God-given ability to improve their lives. These three "S's" are *sanuk*, *saduak*, and *sabai*.

The first S, *sanuk*, means "to have fun." The Thais love to have fun. Of course, the work necessary for development is not always fun; sometimes, in fact, it requires sacrifice and deferred gratification. Thus, *sanuk* is a real barrier. The two other S's—*saduak*, "convenience," and *sabai*, "comfortable"—present similar problems. The "three S's" traditionally have had a higher place in Thai society than have hard work and discipline. Once a Thai says, "*Mai sanuk*" (it is not fun), "*Mai saduak*" (it is not convenient), or "*Mai sabai*" (it is not comfortable), any effort to move forward is futile.

The Protestant Work Ethic Revisited

Man, standing as God's steward over creation, was designed to be a worker. Our life work is a calling that affirms our dignity and glorifies the Divine Worker. As the apostle Paul stated:

> So whether you eat or drink or whatever you do, do it all for the glory of God (1 Corinthians 10:31).

The great Reformed theologian, educator, and diplomat Abraham Kuyper put it this way:

> Wherever man may stand, whatever he may do, to wherever he may apply his hand, in agriculture, in commerce, and in industry, or his mind, in the world of art, and science, he is in whatsoever it may be, constantly standing before the face of God, he is employed in the service of God, he has strictly to obey his God and above all, he has to aim at the glory of his God.[1]

As we saw in Chapter 1, Max Weber articulated the Protestant work ethic. Weber grasped that ideas have consequences. He knew that matter is far from all that matters and that the worldview undergirding the Protestant ethic made all the difference.

Figure 12.1

While Weber is an icon in the pantheon of the social sciences even today, it was left to John Wesley (1703–1791), the English revivalist and social reformer, to distill the essence of the as yet undiscovered work ethic into an easy-to-grasp rallying cry. Wesley urged the Christians of his day:

> Work as hard as you can; save as much as you can; give as much as you can![2]

Wesley's three commands referred to three basic principles of biblical economics[3]—diligence (capital formation), thrift (capital savings), and charity (capital sharing). He was clearly working in a larger context than the leaders of today's consumer society. That context was the Judeo-Christian worldview.

Biblical economics reflects a number of critical assertions including freedom (free markets), private property, personal and communal responsibility, stewardship of creation, and justice under the law. It was not just about hard work. Saving, for instance, shows confidence that there will be a future, that history is going somewhere, and it eschews immediate gratification. Giving, meanwhile, reflects man's God-ordained responsibility to help first the family of God and the family of man, and then to steward creation.

This is a triadic model of working, saving, and giving. It provides synergy, as each component feeds off the others. Unlike so much of what passes for capitalism in our day, the Protestant ethic is other-centered in its conception and function. It serves not primarily the self but God, others, and the future. It lays a solid foundation for business and economic enterprise. While it appreciates physical wealth, it is not mainly about money. The fact that so much of modern culture is money-mad shows how far we have strayed from this ethic.

As we saw earlier, the word *economics* comes from the Greek word *oikonomia* (οικονομια), which means "stewardship of the house." The word reflects a moral philosophy, even if it has been largely forgotten today. God cares about all spheres of life, including the economic one. In contrast to today's trend toward compartmentalizing every area of life into discrete and unrelated units, we need to remember that the principles that enliven the economic sphere are the same ones that work in the spiritual and moral spheres.

Westerners are not the only people with access to these principles. A similar ethic is found in Confucian cultures. Two aspects of this alternative "work ethic" are found in the East: hard work and *jen*, which is benevolence or enlightened self-interest. *Jen* is illustrated by the Confucian functional equivalent to Jesus' words in the Golden Rule: "Do unto others what you wish to do unto yourself." The Confucian ethic, based on some of the same principles as its Protestant counterpart, is one major reason for the economic boom sweeping much of Asia.

Economic Premises

	Animism	Theism	Secularism
Economic System	Barter	Capitalism	Consumerism
Ultimate Reality	Spiritual	Personal	Physical
Man	Ghost	Mind	Mouth
Nature	Limited Good	Positive Sum	Zero Sum
Time Frame	Past	Future	Present
History	Life is on a wheel	History is going somewhere	Time is running out
Work	To survive	To glorify God	To consume
Ethics	Amoral	Moral absolutes	Immoral
Knowledge	Ignorance is a virtue	Truth is absolute	Relativism

Figure 12.2

Obviously, the differences in the economic aspects of theism, secularism, and animism are vast. Figure 12.2 encapsulates the key premises of each. These differences have been discussed extensively in this book. Our modern world is replete with cultures that show how secularism inevitably leads to selfish consumerism,[4] and animism consistently produces abject poverty. Behind the amazing prosperity that accompanies biblical economics we will always find principles that flow from a theistic worldview. It will be helpful to examine each component of Wesley's three-part command to better grasp why Kuyper and Weber were right—and why the secularists and animists are so wrong.

Diligence—"Work as Hard as You Can"

Work, including labor, is sacred. Why? God is a worker. Genesis 1:1 reminds us that "in the beginning God created the heavens and the earth." God worked, then He rested from His creative labor on the seventh day (see Genesis 2:2–3). While the Bible does not depict the omnipotent Creator as tired from His work, it does describe what He did (and does) as *work*. The writer of Hebrews describes God as the Architect and Builder of the heavenly Jerusalem (see Hebrews 11:10). The Greek word rendered "architect" is *technites* (τεχνιτης), from which we get the words *technique* and *technology*. The Greek word for builder, *demiourgos*, comes from *demos* (δεμος), "the people," and *ergon* (εργον), "to work or toil." God is a worker for the people and a master technician. When He chose to come in the flesh in Christ, He came as a blue-collar carpenter. Unlike most kings and statesmen, God is not afraid to roll up His sleeves.

It comes as no surprise that human beings, made in God's image, are also called to work (see Genesis 2:15). Giving our work even more dignity, we are called to be coworkers with the Lord of the universe (see Genesis 1:26, 28). Man is to have dominion over God's creation as His vice-regent. As incredible as it sounds, God works through man to achieve many of His divine purposes. God created a bountiful universe; man is to increase that bounty through his own productive labor.

Thus, *no work is menial when done for God*. Our lives, as I have said, are to be lived *coram Deo*, "before the face of God." Even the injustice and oppression of slavery can be redeemed for God's glory.

> Slaves, obey your earthly masters in everything; and do it, not only when their eye is on you to win their favor, but with sincerity of heart, as working for the Lord, not for men, since you know that you will receive an inheritance from the Lord as a reward. It is the Lord Christ you are serving (Colossians 3:22–24).

Work is a calling if we are listening. The story is told of three men working on the construction of a building. A reporter asked each of them, "What are you doing?" The first answered with a note of irritation and sarcasm, "Can't you see that I am carrying these blocks?" The second answered, with a note of pride, "Why, I am building this magnificent structure, which will be a tribute to my craftsmanship and to my generation." The third, however, said with a tinge of awe in his voice, "Why, I am serving the Master Architect. I am helping to build the kingdom of God."

WORK

Theism's view

Figure 12.3

WORK

Secularism's view

Figure 12.4

WORK

Animism's view

Figure 12.5

We live and work in a larger context, what I like to call the divine economy. Man's work receives its significance as he fulfills God's calling and does God's work. Man is to work not primarily for himself but for the glory of God. Man has been given, along with the foundational principles of the development ethic to get the job done, the charge to develop and care for the earth. Christians have been given the additional tasks of reconciling the lost creation to its Maker and destroying the works of the Enemy. We are God's soldiers claiming territory for our King. We are His heralds announcing that His kingdom is at hand. Thus, work is not simply something that we must do. History is going somewhere, and we get to take it by the hand and lead it to God's consummation, the New Jerusalem.

Secular societies have strayed far from this ideal. People made in the image of God, with eternity in their hearts, have been reduced to consumers and producers of the products of industrial and post-industrial society. Work is no longer a sacred task. We no longer follow our vocations;* now we merely "have jobs." Work is a means to an end. As the pop song says, "Everybody's working for the weekend." The idea of one's calling has been silently replaced with the anemic concept of career. What was God-focused has become self-focused.

While secularism exalts the individual, animism seeks to dissolve him. Work is a necessary evil—part of the suffering we must endure in this life. Vishal Mangalwadi says:

[T]he idea of individual destiny is alien to Hindu culture which emphasizes the dissolution of one's individuality, not its fulfillment. In fact, most people who speak Hindi, my mother tongue, would not even know that a Hindi equivalent for the word "destiny" exists in dictionaries.... The word commonly used, and the idea that dominates Hindi literature is "fate"—the exact opposite of what the Christian concept of destiny means.[5]

In the divine economy, there is no dichotomy between sacred and secular, for we all serve *coram Deo*. I like the wall plaque adorning some kitchens that reads, "Worship services held here three times a day!" The issue is not sacred versus secular; it is consecrated versus unconsecrated. A person, even a pastor or missionary, may be doing "spiritual" work without being sanctified. Meanwhile, a homemaker may prepare meals for her family as a true act of devotion to God. A farmer can milk his cows as an act of worship. The place of work is a place for worship.

The development ethic further requires the generation of abundance, or more than what is needed for just today. We are to work not merely for our immediate needs but for future ones as well. The goal moves well beyond survival to encompass helping the needy in our communities, saving and investing for the future, and planning for both drought and rain. The whole concept of the Sabbath rest implies that we must have more than what we need each day in order to enjoy a day of rest.

In the kingdom economy, diligence, or industry, is a virtue. This stands in contrast to the sloth, laziness, and idleness of some cultures. The work-rest cycle that we find in the First Worker (Genesis 2:2-3) contrasts with the addiction to work found in many materialistic societies.

The surest route to abundance is to encourage creativity and give people the fruit of their labor. Property rights are not a modern invention. Private property and personal freedom and responsibility go together. The command in the Decalogue against stealing (Exodus 20:15—"You shall not steal.") assumes that people are entitled to own property and keep what they produce.

Beyond abundance, hard work brings glory to the Master Worker in whose name it is done, fulfilling His purposes and advancing His kingdom. Wealth is not to be spent on mere personal pleasures. The real bounty is internal, in knowing God. The external sign of this internal abundance is a simple lifestyle, which flows from contentment. The wealth emanating from a life that is both frugal and faithful to one's calling results in savings. Savings generate capital for investment in new enterprises and for giving to the "widow indeed" (I Timothy 5:3,16).

Thrift—"Save as Much as You Can"

Working hard at one's calling may produce bounty. However, this bounty is not a reflection of man's merit, but of God's *grace*. While many people in today's society—even Christians—justify their extravagant lifestyles with the statement, "I've earned it," the person who is working primarily for God's glory will not work to consume. He will work to save. He knows the true nature of enduring wealth, which has to do with relationships, with God's kingdom, with righteousness. The rewards of work are moral and spiritual. Enduring wealth is only tangentially related to physical wealth, which too often becomes a trap to pull us from God. But the wise person keeps physical wealth—and poverty—within the context of enduring, eternal wealth. As Job said:

> Naked I came from my mother's womb, and naked I will depart. The LORD gave and the LORD has taken away; may the name of the LORD be praised (Job 1:21a).

Yet because he knows history is going somewhere, the wise person saves. The biblical worldview informs him that there will be a tomorrow, and it will be different from today. Time is not circular, an endless cycle of the four seasons. History is being made, and man is making it. There is past, present, and future, and man appreciates all three. Because he can see beyond past and present, he can truly plan. As Solomon observed:

> In the house of the wise are stores of choice food and oil, but a foolish man devours all he has (Proverbs 21:20).

The future demands delayed gratification, sacrifice, and self-denial. Those who live only for today may well be poor tomorrow. The hedonist's motto is "Eat, drink, and be merry, for tomorrow we die." Perhaps it should be "Eat, drink, and be merry, and tomorrow we will be poor." Excessive spending today is often a predictor of future poverty. A wealthy country such as Saudi Arabia could well become poor if it does not wisely invest its oil wealth. In fact, we can expect this.

In addition to having a keen sense of chronological time, the biblically minded saver grasps something of eschatological time. History is moving to fulfill God's good purpose, and man is to be a part of it. The bounty produced by hard work is to be invested in the coming kingdom through enterprise and ministry. The multiplication and investment of wealth for the coming kingdom is a barometer of a life committed to God's *telos* (τελος).

Another reason we save is because there is a curse upon the earth. There will be days of drought and days of harvest. As Joseph did in Egypt (see Genesis 41), we must save during days of plenty so that we will survive during days of want.

As savers, we have multiple responsibilities. Man is to provide for his own needs (see 2 Thessalonians 3:10b) and those of his family (see 1 Timothy 5:7–8). Man also has a responsibility to his fellow man in his community, his church, and the mediating institutions (see Galatians 6:9–10). I *am* my brother's keeper. I *am* to love my neighbor as myself. I *am* significant—and responsible. With the compassion that springs from the heart of God, I am to extend myself for others.

A final word about frugality. Unlike consumeristic secularism, theism places moral constraints on the gain and use of wealth. Weber knew that the Protestant work ethic held man accountable as a steward.

> Man is only a trustee of the goods which have come to him through God's grace.... He must...give an account of every penny entrusted to him, and it is at least as hazardous to spend any of it for a purpose which does not serve the glory of God but only one's own enjoyment.[6]

External asceticism and hard work are the heart of the Protestant ethic. It was this frugality, this ideal of "neither poverty nor riches" (see Proverbs 30:7–9)[7] that "set the clean and solid comfort of the middle-class home as an ideal." "Neither poverty nor riches" means sufficiency—in contrast to destitution on the one hand, and opulence on the other.

Thrift sets limits to one's personal consumption of material wealth, but not to the creation and giving of wealth. The creation and giving of wealth are virtues; excessive personal consumption is a vice. The focus of biblical economics is not on self, but on God in worship, others in service, and creation in stewardship. As economist and former Dutch parliamentarian Dr. Bob Goudzwaard challenged, we need "to build an economy of care, an economy of *enough*."[8]

In this system, wealth is a consequence of hard work and frugality, which are valued because of a belief in God. Today, however, it is increasingly wealth that is the value. Wealth has become secularized, an end in itself. Wesley, who did so much to encourage personal development, saw it coming.

> I fear that wherever riches have increased, the essence of religion has decreased in the same proportion. Therefore, I do not see how it is possible, in the nature of things, for any revival of true religion to continue long. For religion must of necessity produce industry and frugality, and these cannot but produce riches. But as riches increase, so will pride, anger, and love of the world in all its branches.[9]

As Christians, our goal should not be for material excess, but rather for adequacy (neither wealth nor poverty). God blesses many people with abundance, but this abundance is not for personal consumption. It is to be shared generously with our neighbors and the larger community.

Charity—"Give as Much as You Can"

The bounty that has been produced through work and saving is to be invested in enterprise and gifts for charity (see Acts 20:34–35). C.S. Lewis wrote:

> Charity—giving to the poor—is an essential part of Christian morality…I do not believe one can settle how much we ought to give. I am afraid the only safe rule is to give more than we can spare…If our charities do not at all pinch or hamper us, I should say they are too small. There ought to be things we should like to do and cannot because our charitable expenditure excludes them.[10]

There are two primary biblical motives for our giving. The first is
God's love. We are to give because God first gave to us (see 1 John
4:10–11). Like God, we are to give freely, sacrificially, and abundantly.
As Paul said about Christ:

> [T]hough he was rich, yet for your sakes he became poor,
> so that you through his poverty might become rich (2
> Corinthians 8:9).

God's concern for the poor is to be manifest in our own lives. We are
to practice the same kind of self-emptying love for others. The book of
Proverbs is replete with encouragements to generosity as well as warnings about stinginess (see Proverbs 11:24–28; 14:31; 19:17; and 28:7).

A second biblical motive for generous giving is self-interest. At
first, this seems a paradox. How, after all, can we benefit ourselves by
giving our resources to others? An even more fundamental question: Is
it really biblical to act in one's self-interest? Isn't the term just a
euphemism for selfishness?

The fact is, we cannot be more spiritual than the Bible. Quoting the
Old Testament, Jesus said to "love your neighbor as yourself" (Mark
12:31). This assumes a certain amount of self-interest, an existing and
healthy self-love. This is not wrong, because we are made in the image
of God. Our lives have significance. God established our worth beyond
all doubt by sending His Son to die for us. English banker Brian
Griffiths says self-interest is evidence that we are created

> [in the image of God], possessed of a will and a mind,
> able to make decisions and accountable for them.

On the other hand, Griffiths says:

> Selfishness is the consequence of the fall and it is the
> distortion of self-interest when the chief end of our
> lives is not the service of God but the fulfillment of our
> own ego.[11]

Self-interest is set in the context of community. We are not isolated
individuals fixated on fulfilling our every whim and appetite. We live
among others and must consider their needs as well. Giving is actually

in our self-interest. We are living *coram Deo,* and we will answer for every act of greed. God designed us to give and so contribute to the larger community. Jesus Himself articulated this fundamental principle when he said:

It is more blessed to give than to receive (Acts 20:35).

A human being who does not give is not godlike, because God is the ultimate Giver. Yet we are not to give indiscriminately. Generosity is not enough; we need discernment. When a killer tornado hit the town of Jarrell, Texas, in the spring of 1997, actor Paul Newman trucked in more than 23,000 heads of lettuce and 1,800 bottles of his salad dressing. His response, though generous, swamped town officials, who had not asked for this particular form of bounty. One official worried about creating "a disaster within a disaster."[12]

In recent years, language has devolved. Helping "the poor" is still fashionable, as shown by all the benefits for farmers, refugees, and inner-city residents. However, the word *poor* has come to represent a class of people lacking in physical resources. It says nothing about *how* they got that way. But we have to find that out if we are to help them. The apostle Paul certainly made distinctions (see 1 Timothy 5:3–6), and so should we.

Relational Giving

Personal	☑ **Personal Responsibility** ☑ **Immediate Family** ☑ **Extended Family**	**MORE PERSONAL**
Communal	☑ **Mediating Structures** (churches, civic clubs, etc.) ☑ **Private Charitable Organizations** ☑ **Local Governments** (municipal, county)	⬆
Governmental	☑ **Regional Governments** (state, province) ☑ **National Governments** (USAID, Socialist Welfare, etc.) ☑ **International Agencies** (United Nations, IMF, etc.)	⬇ **LESS PERSONAL**

Figure 12.6

For our purposes, the poor can be divided into three broad classes. The deserving poor—widows, orphans, the disabled, and others—are those who would work if they could. These deserve our giving, which in this instance is properly called charity.

A second group is the working poor. These people, not surprisingly, are able and willing to work, but they still need our help, which in their case means investing in their enterprise or sharing our expertise with them. Many microenterprise loan programs fall into this category. In a well-managed program, the investor is repaid or the money is rolled back into a revolving loan program to provide opportunities for others.

A third group—the undeserving poor—consists of people who are able but unwilling to work. They deserve not our gifts but our loving confrontation. As Marvin Olasky has said, we need to have "hard heads" and "warm hearts" with such people and challenge them on a personal level.[13] To give indiscriminately to the undeserving poor is to increase their poverty. To fail to challenge them is to condemn them in their poverty. We must do all we can to restore and maintain the dignity of the poor, regardless of which class they fall into. The more personal and relational we can be in our giving, the better. This is not always possible, but it is usually the most effective way to do our giving. The chart in Figure 12.6 describes three levels, extending from more personal to less personal.

On one level, the most personal one, we are to give to our immediate and extended family. Paul said that the person who fails to provide for his own family is "worse than an unbeliever" (1 Timothy 5:8). On the second, communal, level, we provide private charity through any number of mediating institutions: churches, synagogues, civic organizations, and so on. Like personal charity, this is private, freely given, and with personal accountability.

On the third level, that of government, we come to the least personal (and least effective) form of giving. Rather than being private and voluntary, giving is public and compulsory, financed by taxation. There is much less accountability for results, which is evident when you see how thoroughly the well-intended welfare state has failed in America. As the size of government increases—ranging in scope from local to state, national, and international—personal involvement disappears like the Cheshire cat, while bureaucratic "solutions" appear and proliferate. Charity is deformed into welfare, the responsibility of individuals to the entitlement of classes, and voluntary association into coercion. In this case, "giving" does very little to help the poor.

To help the poor, whoever they may be, we must remind them, and ourselves, that even though it's not always fun, convenient, or pleasurable, work is sacred. That is the part of the story we cannot forget if we are to see peoples and communities develop.

Study Questions

What barriers to development (like the Thai concepts of *sanuk, sad-uak,* and *sabai*) exist in the community where you work?

In your own words, define "Protestant work ethic."

Review Figure 12.2 and mark each premise that is prominent in the community where you work. What conclusions do you draw from your observations?

Read endnote #3 for this chapter (p. 305). What term would you use to describe the economic mentality of theism? Why?

Work is a calling. How is your life contributing to the building of God's kingdom?

What areas of your life are denying or tearing down God's kingdom?

The motto "Save as much as you can!" was not just for the rich.
In fact, when it was taught in churches and Sunday schools,
it was the motto of the common people. At the time of the
Reformation, all the nations of Europe were poor and undevel-
oped. The thrift of the people made northern Europe's development possible. How can you encourage the teaching of thrift and
the establishment of savings programs for the people in the community where you work?

What is the distinction between *selfishness* and *self-interest*? Is there
an inherent contradiction between self-interest and generosity?

Review Figure 12.6. In your community, to whom do the people look
for help?

Which kinds of programs are you working to create in your ministry?

If you've been looking increasingly to governments, what con-
crete steps can you take to encourage or reinforce personal
and communal responsibilities for charity?

John Wesley articulated the Protestant work ethic this way, "Work as much as you can, give as much as you can, save as much as you can." Write a motto that captures the work ethic of the culture where you are currently working.

What questions, challenges, or further examples do you have in response to the ideas presented in this chapter?

CHAPTER THIRTEEN

History Makers
Obeying All He Has Commanded

THE LINEAR CONCEPT OF TIME in Western thought, with an indefinite past, present, and future, is practically foreign to African thinking.

> Actual time therefore is what is present and what is past. It moves "backward" rather than "forward," and people set their minds not on future things, but chiefly on what has taken place.
>
> This time orientation, governed as it is by the two main dimensions of the present and the past, dominates African understanding of the individual, the community and the universe...[1]

In this book we have examined man's awesome privilege and responsibility: serving as God's vice-regent on the earth, sharing a gospel that includes but goes beyond evangelism and discipleship into nation building. Only biblical theism's story provides a firm foundation for this kind of life. Like shifting sand, neither secularism nor animism can support a just, responsible, healthy society. Man's calling is to fulfill God's *telos,*[2] His ultimate plan. Only people with a biblical understanding of time are equipped to meet that high calling. This final chapter will show why.

Where Is History Going?

Every man must face the question, "Why am I here?" Every generation must address the question, "What is our place in history?" While these may be universal questions, they have generated a multitude of contrasting answers. Worldview makes all the difference.

Built upon Judeo-Christian theism, the development ethic introduces a radical concept of time—that it is linear, with a past, present, and future. Time has a beginning that will extend forever into the future (at least until time is swallowed by eternity, and the mortal puts on the immortal). History is open, also; God, angels, and men can intervene to change its course. It's no wonder, then, that cultures rooted in this ethic expect that life can get better, that progress is possible in the material world. These societies have hope for the future, a sense of optimism, a sense of ambition, action, and discovery. *History is going somewhere.*

In fact, progress is inherent in God's design. God intends for man to "develop" the earth. There is a purpose for creation (*ontology*) and an end for creation (*teleology*). We can see this from the very beginning:

> Then God blessed them, and God said to them, "Be fruitful and multiply; fill the earth and subdue it; have dominion…" (Genesis 1:28 NKJV).

MAN'S PURPOSE
Fulfilling our "Telos"

In The Beginning…

… On That Day…

The Course of History

Ontology*
Creation
Primal Time
Ultimate Design

▶ **DEVELOPMENT** ▶

Teleology*
Consummation
Final Time
Ultimate Purpose

***ontology:** the study of origins.
"Where did everything come from?"
"Why are things the way they are?"
"Who designed everything?"

***teleology:** the study of ends.
"Where is everything going?"
"What is the goal of the story?"
"What is this designed for?"

Figure 13.1

God blessed man to be His steward over creation—to develop the earth. The blessing was repeated to Abraham so that he might be a blessing to all nations (see Genesis 12:1–3). It continues in the Great Commission where Christ has blessed His disciples with eternal life, the presence of the Holy Spirit, and freedom from the fear of death so that they might disciple nations. And why is the blessing to be extended to all nations? Why are we to disciple nations? So that when the King returns, the glory of the nations will be brought by the kings of the nations into the City of God.

> The city does not need the sun or the moon to shine on it, for the glory of God gives it light, and the Lamb is its lamp. The nations will walk by its light, and the kings of the earth will bring their splendor into it. On no day will its gates ever be shut, for there will be no night there. The glory and honor of the nations will be brought into it (Revelation 21:23–26).

History—with a beginning, a middle, and an end—provides a sure pathway for development. Two metaphysical questions, like hedges, guard either side of that path. The first is ontological: "Where have we come from?" The second is teleological: "Where are we going?" Only theism provides the fullest answers, allowing man to stay on the path of development.

Animism, as we have seen, answers both questions with a resounding, "No-where!" To the animist, life is like a wheel—not a wheel that moves us forward into the future but one that turns in place, endlessly. History is tribal or provincial, with little sense of the outside world. Life is a series of endless cycles: birth, marriage, death; spring, summer, fall, winter. The human soul, the individual, transmigrates from one life to another. Prince Siddhartha, the founder of Buddhism, said of man's dilemma:

HISTORY

Animism's view

Figure 13.2

> Surely this world is unprotected and helpless, and like a wheel it turns round and round.[3]

African Concepts of Time

Analysis of African concept of time, as illustrated by a consideration of verb tenses among the Akamba and Gikuyu of Kenya

	Tense	Kikamba	Gikuyu	English	Approximate Time
Sasa	1. Far or Remote Future	**Ningauka**	**Ningoka**	**I will come**	About two to six months from now
	2. Immediate or Near Future	**Ninguka**	**Ninguka**	**I will come**	Within the next short while
	3. Indefinite Future or Indefinite Near Future	**Ngooka** ngauka	**Ningoka**	**I will come**	Within a foreseeable while, after such and such event
	4. Present or Present Progressive	**Ninukite**	**Nindiroka**	**I am coming**	In the process of action now
	5. Immediate Past or Immediate Perfect	**Ninauka** ninooka	**Nindoka**	**I came** I have just come	In the last hour or so
	6. Today's Past	**Ninukie**	**Ninjukire**	**I came**	From the time of rising up until about two hours ago
Zamani	7. Recent Past or Yesterday's Past	**Nininaukie** nininookie	**Nindirokire**	**I came**	Yesterday
	8. Far Past or Remote Past	**Ninookie** ninaukie	**Nindokire**	**I came**	Any day before yesterday
	9. Unspecified Tene (Zamani)	**Tene ninookie** Nookie tene	**Nindokire tene**	**I came**	No specific time in the "past"

Figure 13.3

SOURCE: **John S. Mbiti**, *African Religions & Philosophy* (Heinemann, Oxford, 1969), p.18.

This is why G.K. Chesterton noted:

> [I]t is fitting that the Buddha be pictured with closed eyes; there is nothing important to see.[4]

African animistic culture, for its part, sees history as moving backward from the present to the past. There is no messianic hope, no concept of progress, no place for development (see Figure 13.3). The golden age, called *Zamani*, is always in the past, never in the future. Mbiti writes:

> Man looks back from whence he came, and man is certain that nothing will bring this world to a conclusion....According to this interpretation of African view of history, there are innumerable myths about Zamani, but no myths about any end of the world, since time has no end.[5]

Secularism answers the question about where we are going with an emphatic, "To the grave!" Its symbol is the hourglass. Time and resources are running out. And while the secularist can indeed see time passing in a way the animist cannot, he has no transcendent historical perspective. As John W. Montgomery has written:

Secularism's view

Figure 13.4

> The basic problem thus becomes clear: Since no historian or philosopher—or anyone else for that matter—sits "in a house by the side of the road" and watches all of history pass by, no one, from a secular, humanistic viewpoint, can answer the question, "Where is history going?"[6]

Secularism has no answers to life's ontological and theological questions. Nihilism, Nietzsche's term for the absurdity of life, reigns in Western secular society. We have exchanged a culture of life for a culture of death. The evidence is all around us, and it grows more insistent by the day: fascination with suicide, abortion, infanticide,

HISTORY

Theism's view

Figure 13.5

euthanasia, genocide, hedonism. First considered evil, then normal, these things are now considered morally good.

Animism sees time as a wheel. Secularism sees time slipping away like grains of sand in an hourglass. Only biblical theism reveals that time is optimistically linear. We are on a journey. History is going somewhere. We have examined the beginning of history, along with God's creation mandate for development (see Genesis 1:26–27). We have seen also that history has an end, with God reconciling the world to Himself through Christ (Colossians 1:20). But what about the "middle" of history, where we live our daily lives? What practical effect does this knowledge of ontology and eschatology have? Theologian Wim Rietkerk writes:

> God created the world, began history, and saw that it went wrong. But he did not stop. Rather, he was faithful to his creation, faithful to mankind, and gave history the full opportunity to develop.
> ....The result was a flow of human history in which God's creation could develop in spite of sin....[God] gave people and nations the freedom to live and to act responsibly towards nature. This biblical teaching gives tremendous emphasis to the validity and importance of culture.[7]

History, then, is objective. It is outside of man and can be studied and understood. Man is a player, not scenery, on the world stage. He is to be neither passive nor reactive but active. Life is to be lived. Time, pictured as an arrow, is God's gift to man. Man is thus a creator of history, not its slave.

Concepts of Time

Time is so much a part of our lives that we seldom stop to think about it. We assume that everyone "sees" time the same way. Not so. Each of the three basic worldviews defines time differently.

Animist societies are based on what is called *event time*, which is defined by natural phenomena, the cycles and rhythms of the seasons. Years have little meaning in such cultures. Western reporters were sometimes surprised that old Rwandan refugees in Zaire could not tell them their ages. Such people rarely count days. Instead, they count catastrophes such as earthquakes, floods, and illnesses. While a person used to watching the clock might rise every morning at 6:00, people living in event time would likely be more flexible and arise with the sun, whether it be 5:15 or 7:00. The event—sunrise—would be more important than the clock. Such thinking does not function well in modern industrial society, however!

Three Concepts of Time

	Animism	**Theism**	**Secularism**
View of History	The Circle of Life	**History is going somewhere**	"One damn thing after another."
Symbol	Wheel	**Course**	Hourglass
Concept of Time	Events Seasons Cycles	**Chronos Eschatos Kairos**	Hours Minutes Seconds
Time Focus	Past	**Past Present Future**	Present
Values	Status Quo	**Progress**	Change
Nature	"Open"	**Open**	Closed
Goal	Harmony with nature Power over others	**"Fill the earth with the knowledge of the Lord**	Survival of the fittest Pleasure
Result	Envelopment	**Development**	Envelopment

Figure 13.6

TIME

Animism's view

Figure 13.7

Mbiti points out that the Ankore people of Uganda define their lives by their cattle. Each day is bounded by events related to the cattle's existence. In many African cultures, the calendar is lunar rather than numerical. The years are endless, changeless agricultural cycles punctuated by major events. In such societies, people savor the moment. They see time as abundant because the cycles never end. Relationships, not tasks, dominate life. By Western standards, time is wasted; but animists think time is without limit, and therefore it has no value, so it cannot be wasted. While much in African culture is to be admired (particularly the honor and value placed on relationships), such an outlook can have profoundly negative consequences on the economic aspects of life.

This view is not confined to Africa. On one occasion, a Western agriculturist was talking to a farmer in Colombia. The Westerner wanted to know why the farmer had not gotten his crops planted during that year's planting season. "Don't worry," the farmer responded. "It will come around again!"

In modern secular society, on the other hand, the clock—or the appointment book—rules. There is no transcendent or moral context for time. It is simply ticking down mechanically to the ultimate heat death of the universe. Precision is critical. Secularists stay up late

TIME

Secularism's view

Figure 13.8

thinking of ways to measure millennia, centuries, decades, years, months, weeks, days, hours, seconds, even nanoseconds. We are always glancing at our wrists, always watching the clock, always jotting down our appointments. We wish there were 25 hours in every day. Time is running out. There is not enough of it. And the secular goal is not quality relationships but material affluence. I remember the advertising slogan that put it, "You only go around once, so grab for all the gusto you can."

The West has not always looked at time as the enemy. The evidence is found in our art and architecture. Art historian Erwin Panofsky shows how our forebears depicted time with

> symbols of fleeting speed and precarious balance, or by symbols of universal power and infinite fertility, but not symbols of decay and destruction.[8]

The symbol of death was the Roman agriculture god Saturn (Greek, *Cronos*). Montgomery writes,

> Panofsky shows that the humanistic Renaissance was responsible for fusing a personification of dynamic classical time with the frightening figure of Saturn— thus creating the image of Time the Destroyer. And today? Today the drawings of Father Time retain visually none of the visual force of their ancient counterparts; for us, time is seen as a debilitating agent—a symbol of the decay to which all life is subject.[9]

This shift in worldviews from Judeo-Christian to secular has taken us from a comprehensive view of time to today's materialistic orientation of the consumer. T.S. Eliot once remarked:

> [W]e have been condemning the rising generation to a new form of provincialism: to the provinciality of time, which imprisons men and women in their own little present moment.[10]

Theism helps us see so much more. Like modern physics, which sees light as both wave and particle, theism sees time from different angles. These viewpoints are not mutually exclusive but rather work together to give us a complete perspective.

The Bible's View of Time

To the Greeks, the simplest aspect of time was *chronos* (χρονος), chronological time, the natural pattern we observe from the rotations of the sun, moon, and stars. Day follows day, month follows month, year follows year. This is time as a measurable quantity. When Jesus

TIME

Theism's view

Figure 13.9

said, "I am with you for only a short time" (John 7:33), He was using this word. It is used throughout the New Testament letters. For example:

> We were in slavery under the basic principles of the world, but when **the time** (χρονος) had fully come, God sent his Son…to redeem… (Galatians 4:3–5).

Kairos (καιρος) is similar to the animist's understanding of event time, but it is much, much more. *Kairos* refers to the fullness of time, the perfect time for an event to occur. *Kairos* looks past the *quantity* of time to its *quality*. The distinction is difficult for many Westerners to grasp. Kirk summarized it well:

> [M]odern men generally think of what we call "time" much as the Greeks thought of time: that is, time seems "linear," extending in a kind of line from some point in remote antiquity to the present. But the Hebrews thought of time as "psychic"—that is, related to the soul, to spiritual experience. For God, all things are eternally present: God is not bound by human conventions of "time." What occurred to Moses and the prophets was a breakthrough in time, so to speak: for certain moments, or rather in certain abrupt experiences, time and the timeless coincided, and the Hebrews were given a glimpse of God's eternity.
> For the Hebrew… to survive physically as an individual is not the aim of existence. The Hebrew's "time" is not merely the days and nights of individual life, but rather the existence of a people under God.[11]

The "*kairos* moments" in the Bible include: Creation; God's blessing upon Adam and Eve; the fall of humanity; the giving of the Abrahamic covenant; the giving of the Mosaic covenant; the birth of the Christ, His passionate life, atoning death, and victorious resurrection; the giving of the Great Commission; and Christ's ascension to the right hand of His Father. The long-awaited consummation of history, when Christ returns, death is destroyed, and all things are completely restored, will be another "*kairos* moment."

> And he made known to us the mystery of his will according to his good pleasure, which he purposed in Christ, to be **put into effect** (οικονομια) when **the times** (καιρος) will have reached their fulfillment—to bring all things in heaven and on earth together under one head, even Christ (Ephesians 1:9–10).

Our individual lives as believers also have an element of *kairos* about them. God told Jeremiah that He would forgive Jerusalem if the prophet could find just one honest truth seeker (see Jeremiah 5:1). One life can transform the world if that life is yielded to the Creator of the universe. If we accept the fullness of God's blessing and keep the fullness of His commands, we become the "great men" of our generation. This is living *coram Deo*, as our lives become marked by *kairos*. Linking time and eternity, *kairos* is where we worship Almighty God and serve our fellow man.

> [God's] intent was that **now** (νυν: *noon*), through the church, the manifold wisdom of God should be made known to the rulers and authorities in the heavenly realms... (Ephesians 3:10).

Our lives have more potential impact—for good or ill—than we will ever know, this side of eternity.

The third Greek time perspective we find is *eschatos* (εσχατος)—transcendent time. It is time that is both before the beginning and after the end. While it recognizes a past orientation, the dynamic of *eschatos* points to the future. We get the word *eschatology*, or study of the end, from *eschatos*. Christ's conquest of death and enthronement as Lord of creation occurred in chronological time, but they were anchored in eschatological time. The author of Hebrews wrote,

> In the past God spoke to our forefathers through the prophets at many times and in various ways, but in these **last** (εσχατος) days he has spoken to us by his Son, whom he appointed heir of all things, and through whom he made the universe (Hebrews 1:1–2).

This view of time can be achieved only from outside the time-line—so we are dependent on revelation. God Himself must reveal His *eschatos* to us. We are tied to our place in chronological history, but He is not. God stands outside of time.

> With the Lord a **day** (ημερα: *haymerah*) is like a thousand **years** (ετη: *etay*), and a thousand **years** (ετη) are like a **day** (ημερα). The Lord is not slow in keeping his promise, as some understand slowness. He is patient with you, not wanting anyone to perish, but everyone to come to repentance (2 Peter 3:8–9).

From His unique perspective, God can reveal to us His ultimate purposes—including the end of time. Of course, God need not tell us everything. As the apostle Paul said:

> **Now** (αρτι: *arti*) we see but a poor reflection as in a mirror; **then** (τοτε: *totay*) we shall see face to face. **Now** (αρτι) I know in part; **then** (τοτε) I shall know fully, even as I am fully known (1 Corinthians 13:12).

Such confidence, trusting God despite our incomplete understanding, is the benefit of this biblical concept of time. Even Jesus admitted His ignorance of the Father's *eschatos*. But He was still confident in those things that the Father *had* revealed to Him. And what he received, He passed on to His disciples (see John 17:8) with the command to be alert and watchful.

> No one knows about that day or hour, not even the angels in heaven, nor the Son, but only the Father. Be on guard! Be alert! You do not know when that time (καιρος) will come (Mark 12:32–33. See also Matthew 24:1–51 and Luke 21:5–36).

Values

Only theism, therefore, has a solid grasp of time—past, present, and future. The secularist is enslaved to the clock, fearing his personal extinction with every tick of the second hand. He has little concern for the past, to his own harm. Richard Weaver said it well:

> Those who have no concern for their ancestors will, by simple application of the same rule, have none for their descendants.[12]

The animist, however, is enslaved to the past, unable to see his present opportunities or to plan for the future. In contrast, the theist's broad time focus encompasses past, present, and future. The theist can celebrate all of life. Each time period is unique and valuable in God's story.

We appreciate the past and learn from it. We enjoy our traditions, culture, and sense of rootedness. We enjoy the present, since this is the time in which we live and act, experiencing all life has to offer. We anticipate the future: building for it, fulfilling God's good purposes along the way, manifesting the kingdom, and hastening Christ's return. Balancing all three time frames creates freedom. Focusing on just one enslaves us.

The animistic mindset focuses on the past. It is profoundly conservative; progress is unheard of. Those with this kind of attitude say things like, "Our fathers did it like this," or "That's the way we've always done it." To the animistic thinker, change is sacrilegious. Fatalism rules in sayings such as, "Que sera, sera," "It is written," or "Allah wills."

The Pakkred Children's Home in Thailand is filled with youngsters with physical and mental handicaps. Most are there not because their families cannot take care of them but because they refuse to. You see, Buddhism's concepts of reincarnation and karma teach that people are born with disabilities for sins committed in their previous lives. If they are ever to escape this world of suffering, they must work off their bad karma. From a family's perspective, the most compassionate thing it can do, therefore, is abandon its children with handicaps.

The secular approach focuses on the present. It is radically liberal: Secularists are constantly looking for change for change's sake. Marketing professionals know that one of the best ways to sell a product in today's consumeristic society is to slap the word *new* on the package, whether or not it has actually been improved. Change is merely a hollow substitute for progress. If one defines it as progress, it is a progress devoid of moral purpose or direction. C.S. Lewis noted:

> Mere change is not growth. Growth is the synthesis of change and continuity, and where there is no continuity, there is no growth.[13]

Time is meaningless to the secularist, good only to be "killed" through insatiable appetites for sex, drugs, work, or any other distraction. That's a big reason why we have so many alcoholics, workaholics, sexaholics, and all the other "aholics." Russell Kirk observed:

> [T]he unhistorical or anti-historic attitude is peculiar to our era. It parallels the widespread seeming indifference to the reality of the soul and the prospect of the life everlasting. Quite conceivably men and women uninterested in the soul may forfeit their own souls, and a people uninterested in their history may cease to have a history or to remain a people.[14]

The theist, however, enjoys both progress and tradition. He is neither a radical liberal nor a hidebound conservative but someone characterized by progressive-conservatism. In theism, history is going somewhere. The theist knows that as a person, he will be "perfect and complete," physically, intellectually, morally, and socially. Eschatologically, all his hopes will be fulfilled as the kingdom is built. Life will not be merely different in the future but will better. The theist, unlike the secularist, has cause for hope. As Lewis noted:

> If things can improve, this means that there must be some absolute standard of good above and outside the cosmic process to which that process can approximate. There is no sense in talking of "becoming better" if better means simply "what we are becoming"—it is like congratulating yourself on reaching your destination and defining that destination as "the place you have reached."[15]

Living in the Arena

Time is the arena of human activity. In time we either unfold and reveal God's kingdom or do Satan's heartless bidding. Each person has been granted a limited amount of time to invest in God's story. Therefore, we are to redeem the time using the multitude of Christian virtues. Prudence means we wisely order our time. Discipline means we fight procrastination, the "thief of time." Perseverance means we "keep on keeping on," even in the hard times. Stewardship compels us to obey the Lord's command to "occupy until I return!"

Man is the history maker. Secularists can only react, and animists are relegated to inactivity, but the theist is active. Our choices are significant, each day. Schaeffer said that we create ripples that go on forever. To follow Christ is to consciously accept this awesome responsibility. Russell Kirk said:

> To embrace Christian teaching wholeheartedly meant that the person reborn in Christ must make moral choices every day of his life. No moral choice could be revoked: for good or ill, it would endure forever.[16]

History is not already written. Yes, we know how it will all turn out, but we do not know what our own roles in the cosmic drama will be. Only God knows, and He isn't sharing that information! (see Deuteronomy 29:29a). We are free to act. Not only that, we are responsible to do so as God's vice-regents, from the greatest of us to the least. Helen Keller said it so well:

> I long to accomplish a great and noble task, but it is my chief duty to accomplish humble tasks as though they were great and noble. The world is moved along not by the mighty shoves of its heroes, but by the aggregate of the tiny pushes of each honest worker.[17]

In 1989, Kabia de Almonte, a Food for the Hungry promoter in the Dominican Republic, was able to give the world a little nudge—and save the life of a child. During one of her visits to the town of Nizao, Kabia met a woman carrying a child in her arms. The 15-month-old boy, the woman's nephew, was severely malnourished and dehydrated, weighing only 7 pounds. Near death, he could barely open his eyes or move around. The mother, severely mentally disabled, was unable to help. Kabia, a young mother herself, offered to drive the woman and child to the hospital 20 kilometers away using a Food for the Hungry vehicle. But when they arrived, Kabia's hopes for help were dashed. The employees were on strike, so the toddler was only briefly examined before being released. Kabia recalled:

> At that time my infant baby was six months old, and since I was still breastfeeding my own child, I decided to breastfeed this malnourished little boy. Later, I advised this woman to stop breastfeeding her 3-year-old daughter and breastfeed her malnourished nephew instead. At first, she thought it wasn't right to do so. Finally, I ended up convincing her…, for she understood that she would be the one taking care of this dying child.[18]

However, people in the community, and even her own husband, were telling Kabia not to get her hopes up because the child was too far gone and would surely die. Kabia told them that she would prove she could save the boy's life if this was God's will.

It was. The next day the boy opened his eyes and began to move. Each day he got a little better. In only six months, the toddler had completely recovered, even to the point of being of normal weight for his age. All because Kabia de Almonte had provided a series of tiny pushes.

The Goal of Development

Only Judeo-Christian theism can take man off the revolving wheel of animism and the sinking ship of secularism; only Judeo-Christian theism can set man on the path to the City of God, providing bright hope for the future and a new paradigm. Only Judeo-Christian theism brings Good News for today and tomorrow.

The Lord's Prayer gives us the right perspective. When we pray "Thy kingdom come," we acknowledge Christ's coming future kingdom. When we pray "Thy will be done on earth as it is in heaven," we acknowledge our present responsibility to help build His kingdom today. As Jesus said when He inaugurated His earthly ministry:

> The time has come. The kingdom of God is near.
> Repent and believe the Good News (Mark 1:15).

The present aspect of the kingdom places life in a broader context. God is building His kingdom today. I am His coworker and must respond to His calling. There is to be progress in the material world. I am to live *coram Deo* as I contribute to kingdom building, to God's unfolding story. This is the Good News: God, in Christ, reconciling the world to Himself. Anything less is anemic, suppressing the truth, distorting the gospel, stifling the kingdom, disengaging the church, and boring the world.

The goal of human development—our *telos*—is that we become fully human. Man is to assume his rightful role at the pinnacle of the created order to the glory of God. He is to be "perfect and complete," lacking nothing (see James 1:4; Colossians 1:28) mentally, physically, spiritually, or relationally.

> The creation waits in eager expectation for the sons of God to be revealed…in hope that the creation itself will be liberated from its bondage to decay and brought into the glorious freedom of the children of God (Romans 8:19–21).

Man is to participate in and help hasten God's unfolding consummation of history, in which all the Lord's purposes are fulfilled, the transformation completed, and the blessing of the nations fully extended—this is our *telos*. The glory of the nations *will* be revealed, and all man's relationships—with God, himself, and creation—*will* be restored.

When Christ returns, the blessing of Abraham to bless all nations will be completed because God has sworn by an oath. On the day of His return, the earth will be full of the knowledge of the Lord as the waters cover the sea (see Isaiah 11:9). For those of us who work among the poor and hungry, one of the most beautiful passages in Scripture comes from one of Isaiah's prophetic songs.

> *O Lord, you are my God;*
> *I will exalt you and praise your name,*
> *for in perfect faithfulness*
> *you have done marvelous things,*
> *things planned long ago….*
> *You have been a refuge for the poor,*

a refuge for the needy in his distress,
a shelter from the storm
and a shade from the heat....
so the song of the ruthless is stilled.
On this mountain the LORD
Almighty will prepare
a feast of rich food for all peoples,
a banquet of aged wine—
the best of meats and the finest of wines.
On this mountain he will destroy
the shroud that enfolds all peoples,
the sheet that covers all nations;
he will swallow up death forever.
The Sovereign LORD will wipe away the tears
from all faces;
he will remove the disgrace of his
people from all the earth.
The LORD has spoken.
In that day they will say,
"Surely this is our God;
we trusted in him, and he saved us.
This is the LORD, we trusted in him;
let us rejoice and be glad in his
salvation (Excerpts from Isaiah 25).

This beautiful song reminds me of the wedding feast for Christ and His bride.

*Then I saw a new heaven and a new earth… I saw the Holy City, the new Jerusalem, coming down out of heaven from God, prepared **as a bride beautifully dressed for her husband**. And I heard a loud voice from the throne saying,*

*"Now the dwelling of God is with men, and **he will live with them. They will be his people, and God himself will be with them** and be their God. He will wipe every tear from their eyes. There will be no more death or mourning or crying or pain, for the old order of things has passed away."*

He who was seated on the throne said, "I am making everything new!" Then he said, "Write this down, for these words are trustworthy and true" (Revelation 21:1–5).

On that day, with the discipling of the nations complete, the kings of the earth will bring the glory of the nations to the Lamb—our King, Jesus Christ (see Revelation 21:24–26). Until that ultimate day, we all have work to do!

Study Questions

In your cultural setting, among the people with whom you work, where is history going? What is man's ultimate purpose?

In what time context does development occur?

What kinds of barriers to development do you think are formed in animist concepts of history?

Hinduism and Buddhism—life on the wheel: *Samsara*

African/Swahili—history moving backward: *Zamani*

Man is a maker of history. He is to be **proactive**: "Life is something to be lived." Some people are **passive** or fatalistic, letting events unfold: "Life is something that happens." Other people see life in between proactive and passive. They are reactive, responding to events. Describe the people in your community.

How do these attitudes either support development or hinder it?

Describe in your own words each element of the **biblical concept** of time.

Chronos (χρονος)—clock time:

Eschatos (εσχατος)—transcendent time:

Kairos (χαιρος)—the fullness of time:

Each worldview has a different focus of time, and that focus impacts the development process. In what way does each perspective support or hinder the development process?

"Tradition!"—the past

"Eat, drink and be merry, for tomorrow we die!"—the present

"Celebrate life!"—the past, the present, the future

What do people value in the community where you work—the status quo, change, or progress?

How does their perspective impact their development or lack of it?

According to biblical theism, what is the goal of development

For the individual?

For all of human history—*telos*?

Typically, what is the vision for the future for people in your community?

How might you help convey God's vision for the community where you live and work?

What two or three ways might you personally and consciously contribute to nation building—redeeming your culture for the coming King?

What questions or challenges do you have in response to the ideas
   presented in this chapter?

How can you begin to apply the message of this book?

Glossary

activism: Action without reflection.

animism: A set of metaphysical assumptions that see the world as ultimately spiritual, in which the physical world is animated by spirits or gods. In some cases, the physical world may be considered an illusion. Man's highest good and ultimate goal is to return to spiritual oneness while the physical is denigrated. Folk religions, Buddhism, and Hinduism are examples of highly animistic systems, but animistic beliefs can infect any worldview.

antientropic: Serving to prevent, cure, or alleviate the steady degradation and disorganization of a society or system; increasing order; the opposite of entropy's increasing disorder.

axiology: The study of values, ethics, and morals in general and the problem of evil in particular.

biblical theology of vocation: Understanding the place one's work has in God's unfolding kingdom. Can be reached by the conscious process of examining biblical foundations and guiding principles for one's vocational calling. Christ is Lord of every area of life, including work. See *coram Deo*.

bounty: Wealth or prosperity in *all* areas of life: physical, spiritual, social, and intellectual. This ancient idea is closely related to the Hebrew term *shalom*. Bounty is a byproduct of living in accordance with the development ethic.

Buddhism: An offshoot of Hinduism, Buddhism was founded around 525 B.C. To the Buddhist, life is miserable and pointless suffering. The only way to escape one's *karma* and achieve *nirvana* (a state of nothingness) is to cease desiring.

capitalism: Derived from the Latin *caput* (head), an economic system originally based upon the principles found in the development ethic. Man can create "capital" by hard work and thrift and use it to build his nation by generous investment and giving. This historical understanding differs sharply from the modern definition, which is more appropriately labeled "consumerism." The highest form of capital is human creativity.

caput: Latin for "the head," which is the source of wealth.

carrying capacity: Seen as the earth's limited physical ability to sustain a maximum population at a certain quality of life. This phrase always betrays Malthusian assumptions. Malthusians believe the earth is overpopulated or running out of resources.

common grace: God's patient, longsuffering, and generous love—extended to all mankind (see Matthew 5:43–48). There is a biblical distinction between common grace and the grace that saves (see 2 Peter 3:9–15).

communalism: A cultural view that ignores the individual. Each member is to focus only on others. This thinking is closely related to, and sometimes a precursor of, egalitarianism.

compassion workers: Workers who invest their life, time, talent, and treasure to bring the Good News of the kingdom of God to those with apparent physical needs.

coram Deo: A Latin phrase meaning "before the face of God," "under the authority of God," or "to the glory of God." Living each moment "before the face of God" was one of the challenges put forth by the leaders of the Protestant Reformation. *Coram Deo* was one of their rallying cries.

cosmology: The study of the nature of the universe.

creation mandate: God's command to mankind to rule over creation (Genesis 1:26–28) and care for it (Genesis 2:15).

culture: The manifestation of a people's ethos, creed, or sacred belief system. Cultures can change rapidly, slowly, or not at all, depending on the internal dynamics of the culture and shifts in worldview. Ideas spread downward through culture, affecting the way people live and the institutions they build.

Darwin, Charles (1809–1882): British naturalist whose book *The Origin of Species* provided naturalism with an intellectually viable alternative to a Creator: random mutation guided by natural selection—commonly referred to by the amorphous label **evolution.**

depravity: The absolute sinfulness of man. Man is immoral, corrupt, and wicked. Sin touches every area of human life. No one is good by God's standard (see Job 14:1–4; 15:14–16; Psalm 53; Luke 13:1–9; Romans 3:23, 6:23, 7:14–25; and Galatians 6:7–10) . Orthodox Christianity holds this doctrine in tension with the principle of man's significance because he is created in the image of God.

development: From the French *develop*; a self-sustaining process whereby a people, group, or society advances economically, socially, morally, and intellectually; differs from relief in that development is long term while relief is short term.

development ethic: The body of nonphysical laws established by God that, when followed, lead to bounty and prosperity or, when ignored, lead to poverty. The development ethic is an expansion of the Protestant work ethic.

Dewey, John (1859–1952): Humanist founder of modern education who believed that the purpose of education was not to "prepare people for life" but to "prepare them for a job."

ecology: The study of "the house" (the environment), a moral philosophy derived from the Greek words *oikos* (οικος) and *logia* (λογια).

economics: Stewardship of God's "house"; derived from the Greek word *oikonomia* (οικονομια).

egalitarianism: Focus only on the many; numerically equal outcomes, equal distribution of resources.

Enlightenment, the: The Age of Reason. The period following the Middle Ages when intellectuals sought to free man from God's authority and established dogmas and free man for his own autonomy. One manifestation of this shift was the advent of deism, in which God was seen as transcendent but not immanent.

envelopment: The opposite of development; from the nineteenth-century French word *envoloper* (to wrap, cover closely on all sides). It is used to describe the end of the mindset of poverty—death, destruction, and isolation from God.

epistemology: From the Greek *episteme* (επιστεμε: knowledge). The study or theory of the foundations for knowledge and truth, especially referencing its limits and validity. Epistemological questions include *How can we know? What can we know for certain? Is anything always true?*

ethic of poverty: That body of values, exemplified in secularism and animism, that leads to poverty and death.

ethos: A Greek word (εθος) that lived on in Latin and eventually English, though it has recently fallen out of the common vocabulary. *Ethos* means the distinguishing character, sentiment, moral nature, or guiding beliefs of a person or people. It is the root word behind *ethics* and *ethnic*. It is important to note that ethnic groups were originally (by the ancient Greeks) distinguished not by their music, language, skin color, or customs but by their ideas. This connection has currently unexplored ramifications for Christian Mission and our current definition of a people group. If we still used the term *ethos* today, we would have no need of the term *worldview*.

faith: The biblical word *pistis* (πιστις: moral conviction) comes from *pitheo* (πιθεω), which was a legal term meaning "to be convinced by argument" or "to yield to the evidence." This kind of faith will lead one to expose life, property, and reputation to loss or injury. Risk can be accepted because the evidence is compelling. Today the word *faith* is most often used to mean "a position held despite a lack of evidence" or "believing despite opposing evidence." Faith is a precious concept that has seen a perverting deterioration in our language.

general revelation: The message of God revealed in creation and in the conscience of man (Romans 1:19–20).

gnosticism: The Greek dichotomy between the spiritual realm, considered sacred, and the physical realm, considered profane. Gnosticism emphasizes secret knowledge and has ancient and modern variations. In first-century Ephesus, the apostle John fought a heretical gnostic sect led by Cerinthus. Gnostics later produced such works as *The Gospel According to Thomas,* still popular today with groups like the Jesus Seminar. A large portion of the church moved into a form of this heresy around the turn of the century in reaction to the debate with secular science. Christians who view "religious" or "spiritual" activities as superior to "secular" or "worldly" activities are often operating from a gnostic worldview.

Hinduism: An animistic religion that originated on the Indian subcontinent around 1500 B.C., Hinduism holds that the universe is ultimately spiritual. Everything in the physical world is seen as a manifestation of the Divine One; all aspects of reality are manifestations of the One. Hinduism has many forms but is generally polytheistic and holds to a belief in karma and reincarnation—the endless cycle of birth and death.

Hutchins, Robert (1899–1977): University of Chicago president who lost the debate with John Dewey over the purpose of education. Hutchinson advocated the classic liberal position that the purpose of education was "to prepare people for life."

individualism: Focus only on self, personal fulfillment, and gratification.

intellectualism: Study and reflection without action or application (Acts 17:21; James 1:22, 2:14–26).

Islam: Founded in 622 by Muhammad, this monotheistic religion holds that God is wholly Other and unknowable. The role of man is to submit to the revealed will of Allah (in Arabic, in the Qur'an, through the prophet Muhammad). Muslims reject the Christian doctrine of the Trinity, believing that God is absolutely One. Islam, like Catholicism, is often found mixed with local animistic beliefs—the syncretism is known as Folk Islam.

Judeo-Christian theism: The historical worldview of Christendom (the West), theism assumes the existence of a transcendent, infinite-personal God who created the universe both animate and inanimate, spiritual and physical, separate from Himself but not independent of Him. God is both transcendent (outside of His creation) and immanent (present within it). He is everywhere present and involved. The universe is open to God's purpose and intervention. God has revealed Himself through special revelation, first through the written Word, the Bible, and then through the living Word, Jesus Christ. At the same time, man can use his God-given reason to discover truth about God and the universe because God has revealed Himself to all men—general revelation—in creation and in His making man in His image.

Kant, Immanuel (1724–1804): German philosopher who first coined the term *Weltanschauung*, or worldview.

karma: The doctrine in Hinduism and Buddhism that life is an endless cycle of birth and rebirth, that people are reincarnated in higher or lower forms according to what they have done.

Kuyper, Abraham (1837–1920): Dutch theologian and prime minister, he founded the Free University in Amsterdam.

Logos: Refers to the living Word of God, Jesus Christ, the Second Person of the Trinity.

Malthus, Thomas (1766–1834): English political economist and writer who worried about overpopulation and mass starvation because he believed that population will outstrip the food supply.

man's relationships: Primary (outward and vertical), with God (*theology*); and secondary (internal and horizontal), with himself (*psychology*), with others (*sociology*), and with the physical world (*ecology and economics*).

Marx, Karl (1818–1883): German social Darwinist, political economist, and philosopher who laid the theoretical foundation of communism. Marx was a thoroughgoing materialist who believed that "matter is all that matters."

mediating institutions: Private voluntary organizations (churches, synagogues, civic clubs, school boards, and political parties) that mediate between families and the government.

metaphysics: The branch of philosophy concerned with the fundamental nature of reality and being.

mind: A symbol representing biblical theism's view of man. Man, made in the image of God, is rational, moral, spiritual, and creative. Man can intervene in the creation.

monotheism: The belief in one sovereign Creator. Judaism, Islam, and Christianity are examples.

morality: Relating to the practice, manners, or conduct of men as social beings, and with reference to right and wrong, good and evil.

moral nationalism: The positive form of nationalism—when it celebrates a unique culture that is established upon a moral order that values unity and diversity in its populace.

mouth: A symbol representing secularism's view of man. Man is (the highest) of the animals. He is a consumer of limited resources. Man is controlled by nature (genes, instincts, environment).

multiculturalism: Focus on diversity at the expense of unity. Dependent on subjective relativism.

nation: Not merely the modern concept of nation states, but the concept of tribe or ethnic/people group. In the Old Testament *mishpachah* and the New Testament *ethnos*.

nationalism: Focus on unity and conformity at the expense of diversity and dissent.

natural evil: The curse; the condition of toil and strife, hunger, disease, physical death, and natural disasters resulting from man's rebellion against God and His laws.

natural law: God's moral law written into the hearts of men. The understanding of what "ought to be" that comes from observation of the design inherent (teleology) within what is.

New Age: A revival of Eastern and animistic religion masked in Western language. The New Age has been called "Hinduism in a business suit."

Nietzsche, Friedrich (1844–1900): German philosopher and nihilist who foresaw the "death of God" in culture, with the inevitable corollary that if God is dead, then man is dead, also. Nietzsche relied heavily on the now discredited work of Edward B. Taylor, who applied Darwin's theory to the development of religion and culture.

nihilism: A hopeless, angry fatalism that sees life as meaningless. Especially prevalent in the U.S. during the 1960s. Nihilism seeks the negation of everything—knowledge, ethics, beauty, reality (James Sire, *The Universe Next Door*, p. 85).

ontology: From the Greek *ontos* (οντο+λογια). The study of being, existence, and origins. Ontology asks such questions as *"Who am I?" "What is life?" "Where have things come from?" "Why is there something instead of nothing?"*

overpopulation, theory of: First articulated in *The Principle of Overpopulation* (1798) by Thomas Malthus, this evolutionary perspective fears ecological catastrophe because food production is said to increase arithmetically, while population increases geometrically. The theory states that there are not enough resources to provide for everyone. Events of this century have discredited the theory, which still has many prominent proponents.

pauperism: A poverty of mind or mindset of poverty.

physical laws: The laws that God has built into creation to govern nature.

polytheism: Belief in many personal gods (who are ultimately impotent).

presuppositional: The assumption that an idea or thing is true.

progress: The word progress (in contrast to the modern mantra "change") implies moving towards a goal or the fulfillment of God's purpose. If one takes a wrong course, then he is regressing, moving further from the goal. To be progressive, one must repent of the wrong direction and head toward the goal of God's good intentions.

In this way, progress for an individual, community, or nation is to move towards God's purpose. A synonym might be "maturity."

This concept will be developed more fully in Chapter 13.

Protestant Reformation: Era starting in the sixteenth century sparked by Martin Luther and others who reacted against corruption and theological error in the Roman Catholic Church. Guiding principles included the *priesthood of all believers* and *sola Scriptura*, the belief that the Bible alone is God's infallible standard for life. A key Reform belief is that there is no separation between sacred and secular; all of life is to be lived *coram Deo*, before the face of God.

Protestant work ethic: The values—including hard work, saving, and giving—derived from belief in God and a specifically Reformed way of looking at the world. The Protestant work ethic moved northern Europe into prosperity. Max Weber believed that the absence of these values or their functional equivalents caused people to be impoverished.

psychology: The study of man's psyche (soul, spirit, inner self).

reason: Orderliness of mind. A thumbprint of God, revealing His nature in man.

Sanger, Margaret (1883–1966): Founder of the American Birth Control League (now Planned Parenthood) and an advocate of population control, particularly of the poor.

science: The thinking of God's thoughts after Him. A rational evaluation of empirical evidence, combined with a willingness to follow that evidence wherever it leads.

secularism: A system that sees the world as ultimately physical and limited, controlled by the blind operations of impersonal natural laws, time, and chance. Secularism renounces spiritual or transcendent reality. "Man is the result of a purposeless and natural process that did not have him in mind" (*George Gaylord Simpson*). "The human species was not designed, has no purpose, and is the product of mere mechanical mechanisms" (*Douglas Futuyma*). Also known as secular humanism, humanism, or naturalism, this is the increasingly prevalent worldview of the Western world.

sociology: The study of human relationships.

special revelation: The message of God revealed in Scripture and by God's other extraordinary communication with man.

stewardship: To care for and develop God's house for God's glory. Man is God's steward or vice-regent over creation and is responsible to Him.

story: A paradigm or set of assumptions (true or false) by which people view the world. Used as a synonym for worldview.

technology: The moral application of science for the purpose of fighting against natural evil.

teleology: From the Greek word *telos* (τελος). The study of ends and ultimate purposes. Teleology asks such questions as "*Why am I here?*" "*Where is history going?*" "*What is the purpose of my life?*" "*What was [a thing] designed for?*"

theism: The belief or system of belief in one God; sees the universe as ultimately personal.

theology: The study of God.

Tocqueville, Alexis de (1805–1859): French historian who toured the U.S. in the 1830s and called attention to its intellectual and moral associations.

trinitarianism: One God, three Persons of the Deity: Father, Son, and Holy Spirit.

truth: The principle that there is absolute truth that can be known and applied; the moral foundation for freedom, and the assumption behind knowledge. Anything that claims to be true can be subjected to four tests: Is it reasonable? Does it match reality? Does it explain all of life? Is it livable?

unitarianism: One God, one Person of the Deity; examples are Islam and Unity.

vocation: One's calling. Work is a call of God upon an individual's life. It becomes the sphere *through* which, not merely *in* which, a Christian serves Christ and His Kingdom. It is the occupation—the principle business of one's life—through which one occupies territory or a sphere of influence (Luke 19:13) *for* Jesus Christ.

vision of community: People having a growing understanding of God's purpose for their community or nation.

Weber, Max (1864–1920): German sociologist who used the term *worldview* as a tool in his analysis of the relationship between a people's belief system and its economic development. Weber gave us the term *Protestant work ethic.*

Wesley, John (1703–1791): English revivalist and social reformer who coined the dictum "Work as hard as you can; save as much as you can; give as much as you can." The Wesleyan revival transformed every aspect of British culture. It makes an excellent case study for what it means to disciple a nation.

wisdom: The moral application of truth.

wisdom worker: A compassion worker who applies God's truth. The role of the compassion (development) worker is to help people see God and the universe the way He made it by encouraging the thinking of new thoughts: analytical thinking, problem solving, and the envisioning and creating of new worlds.

worldview: A set of assumptions, held consciously or unconsciously, about the basic make-up of the world and how the world works. The word *story* is used throughout this book as a synonym for worldview.

Endnotes

Introduction

1. Bernard T. Adeney, *Strange Virtues: Ethics in a Multicultural World* (Downers Grove, Ill.: InterVarsity Press, 1995), p. 65.

2. Stanley Hauerwas, *Vision and Virtue* (Notre Dame, Ind.: Fides, 1974), p. 3.

3. George Grant, *The Micah Mandate* (Chicago: Crossway Books, 1995), pp. 218–219.

4. Edward Stockwell and Karen Laidlaw, *Third World Development* (Chicago: Nelson Hall, 1981), p. 120.

5. Ronald H. Nash, *Poverty and Wealth* (Westchester, Ill.: Crossway Books, 1986), p. 11.

6. "The Immorality of Our Welfare State," an interview with E. Calvin Beisner, *Christian Perspectives* (Liberty University, Winter 1990), p. 6.

7. Michael Novak, "From the Publisher: The War of Ideas," *Crisis*, March 1989, p. 3.

8. Novak, p. 2.

Chapter 1

1. I first heard this story from Josie in April 1994 at a Youth With A Mission training session in Tyler, Texas.

2. For simplicity I will often use the time-tested nomenclature of "man," "men," or "mankind" when referring to both male and female. Because of current sensitivities over gender, I hasten to affirm that men and women are equal partners in God's kingdom, but with different roles, as the Bible clearly teaches.

3. For the sake of simplicity, we will refer to biblical theism as theism. Of course, I recognize there are other monotheistic models, such as Islam. The evidence, however, convinces me that the views of God as expressed in the Bible are true.

4. This book uses the term *animism* in its widest sense to refer to the philosophies of the East, e.g., Hinduism and Buddhism, as well as the more traditional folk religions around the world.

5. The word *repent* is one of the casualties of our language shift in the West. The Greek verb used in the New Testament is μετανοεω, which literally means "to think differently." It is derived from two Greek words: μετα (meta: change) and νους (nous: intellect). The original idea of repentance was much more than feeling bad about one's sin. It meant changing how one thinks about God, the nature of reality, who man is, God's purpose in history… yielding to God's perspective and changing how we live accordingly.

6. Paul A. Marshall, *Stained Glass: Worldviews and Social Science* (Lanham: Md.: University Press of America, 1989), p. 8.

7. Max Weber, *The Protestant Ethic and the Spirit of Capitalism* (New York: Scribner and Sons, 1958).

8. Quoted by George Grant in *Legacy Communications*, Volume 2, Number 7/8, July/August 1992, p. 2.

9. Thomas Sowell, *A Conflict of Visions* (New York: William Morrow, 1987), pp. 14, 16.

10. Ronald H. Nash, *Worldviews in Conflict* (Grand Rapids, Mich.: Zondervan, 1992), p. 16.

11. Niels Mulder, *Inside Thai Society* (Bangkok: Editions Duang Kamol, 1990), p. xi.

12. This is similar to James W. Sire's definition in *The Universe Next Door* (Downers Grove, Ill.: InterVarsity Press, 1976).

13. Chapter 2 of Phillip Johnson's book *Reason in the Balance* (Downers Grove, Ill.: InterVarsity Press, 1995) is a clearly presented argument for this view.

14. Mel Gabler, National Association of Christian Educators, ©1983.

15. E.F. Schumacher, *Small Is Beautiful* (New York: Harper & Row, 1973), p. 90.

16. Friedrich Nietzsche, *The Madman* (*The Portable Nietzsche*; New York: Viking, 1954), p. 125. For an excellent critic of Nietzsche read Appendix B, Section 1, from Ravi Zacharias' book *Can Man Live Without God* (Dallas: Word Publishing, 1994).

17. The worldview graphics by Tom Steffen were originally inspired by a set of whiteboard illustrations used by R.C. Sproul in his video series *A Blueprint for Thinking: Reforming the Christian Worldview* (Ligonier Ministries, P.O. Box 547500, Orlando, FL 32854).

Chapter 2

1. The actual title of the paper: *An Essay on the Principle of Population as It Affects the Future Improvement of Society*. A copy of the 1798 version can be found edited by Phillip Appleman (New York: W.W. Norton, 1976). Malthus later revised and expanded his theory. Appleman's book also includes the 1803 version titled: *An Essay on the Principle of Population, or a View of Its Past and Present Effects on Human Happiness with an Inquiry into Our Prospects Respecting the Future Removal or Mitigation of the Evils Which It Occasions*. A brief overview of Malthus and his impact is offered by constitutional lawyer John Whitehead in Chapter 10 of his book *The End of Man* (Westchester, Ill.: Crossway Books, 1986).

2. Known as Malthus' Dismal Theorem, the accompanying chart illustrates its essence. The data comes from page 23 of Appleman's collection.

3. Garrett Hardin, from an interview on NBC Nightly News with Tom Brokaw, October 26, 1987.

4. 1994 U.N. Cairo Conference on Population and Development.

5. Of course, Planned Parenthood wouldn't state it so clearly. For an excellent and well-documented history of Margaret Sanger and eugenics in the United States, read George Grant's book *Grand Illusions: The Legacy of Planned Parenthood* (Franklin, Tenn.: Adroit Press, 1992).

6. Sir Francis Galton, *Memories of My Life* (London: Methuen, 1908), p. 323. Galton, Charles Darwin's cousin, created the term *eugenics*. His elitist, evolutionary philosophy helped lay the foundations for Nazi Germany, Mao's Red Army, Pol Pot's Cambodia, the Tuskegee experiments, and our modern white supremacy groups.

7. "All roads lead to the sea." Several Food for the Hungry workers have heard this proverb while serving in Africa. It is used as an excuse for poverty. It refers to the imperial powers that came, built roads, robbed the resources, and took them by ship to the north.

8. For an example of a Christian arguing this closed universe concept of injustice see Ron Sider's book *Rich Christians in an Age of Hunger* (Nashville, Tenn: Word Publishing, 1990) especially Chapter 2—"The Affluent Minority."

   The Big Mac analogy comes from Jeffrey Hollender, *How to Make the World a Better Place* (New York: William Morrow, 1990), p. 124.

9. U.S. Bureau of the Census, International Data Base, 1997.

Chapter 3

1. See Patrick Johnstone, *Operation World*, WEC Publications, 1993.

2. AD2000 and Beyond is a growing network of Christians cooperating in evangelism. Address: 2860 S. Circle Dr., Suite 2112, Colorado Springs, CO. 80906. Phone: (719) 576-2000; Worldwide Web: www.ad2000.org.

3. Dr. Yamamori, the president of Food for the Hungry International, wrote an excellent book explaining the relationship between the poor and the unreached. He also provides practical ways to become one of God's new envoys. Tetsunao Yamamori, *Penetrating Missions' Final Frontier* (Downers Grove, Ill.: InterVarsity Press, 1993).

4. στοιχεια and στοιχειων (*stoicheion*), English doesn't have a single word with the same connotations, but weigh these definitions and you can see where Paul was heading:

   1) any first thing, from which the others belonging to some series or composite whole take their rise; an element, first principle

      a) the spoken sounds of an alphabet, the simplest elements of speech

      b) the elements from which all things have come, the material components of the universe

      c) the elements, rudiments, primary and fundamental principles of any art, science, or discipline (e.g., of mathematics, Euclid's geometry)

   Notice how primary *stoicheion* are. This is Paul's vocabulary for the concept of world-view. This concept directly impacts how we live our lives (at least it was meant to). The word στοιχειων was derived from στοιχεω, which means to "walk orderly."

   1) to proceed in a row as the march of a soldier, go in order; metaphorically, to go on prosperously, to turn out well

   2) to walk, to direct one's life, to live

5. See Gailyn Van Rheenen, *Communicating Christ in Animistic Contexts* (Grand Rapids, Mich.: Baker Book House, 1991), p. 101. For those of us trained to see the world from a Western materialistic perspective, this book is an excellent tool for examining our bias and removing our blinders. I strongly recommend it to anyone living (or planning to live) among animistic people.

6. Joanne Shetler, *And The Word Came With Power* (Portland, Ore,: Multnomah Press, 1992), p. 54.

7. Adapted from the original quote, "… the Kingdom is God's all-out answer to man's total needs," by E. Stanley Jones in *The Unshakable Kingdom and the Unchanging Person* (Nashville, Tenn.: Abingdon Press, 1972), p. 53.

8. Other books to read on this subject include Thomas H. McAlpine, *By Word, Work and Wonder* (MARC Publications, 1995), and Sherwood Lingenfelter's two books: *Agents of Transformation* and *Transforming Culture* (both also printed by MARC Publications, 800 W. Chestnut Ave., Monrovia, CA 91016-3198; call 1-800-777-7752).

Chapter 4

1. Carl Sagan, *Cosmos* (New York: Random House, 1980), p. 4.

2. Daniel Boorstin, *The Creators: A History of Heroes of the Imagination* (New York: Random House, 1992), pp. 45–46.

3. Frank Houghton, "Thou Who Wast Rich Beyond All Splendor" in *Christian Praises* (London: InterVarsity Press, 1973), p. 43.

4. Francis Schaeffer, *The God Who Is There* (London: Hodder and Stoughton, 1968), pp. 94–95.

5. Job is probably the oldest book of the Bible. This is a very ancient text with a very clear opinion on the origin of human life.

6. The most popular may be Stephen Hawkings in books like *A Brief History of Time*. Discerning readers will note that he does not put forth any falsifiable scientific theories but offers metaphysical possibilities that diehard naturalists prefer to accept. Hawkings doesn't even consider the evidence for intelligent design.

7. Now the LORD descended in the cloud and stood with him there, and proclaimed the name of the LORD. And the LORD passed before him and proclaimed, "The LORD, the LORD God, **merciful** and **gracious**, **longsuffering**, and **abounding in goodness** and truth, keeping **mercy** for thousands, **forgiving** iniquity and transgression and sin, **by no means clearing** *the guilty*... (Exodus 34: 5–7, NKJV, emphasis added).

8. ελεωσ (eleos) mercy: kindness or good will towards the miserable and the afflicted, joined with a desire to help them

    a) of men toward men: to exercise the virtue of mercy, show oneself merciful.

    b) of God toward men: in general providence; the mercy and clemency of God in providing and offering to men salvation by Christ.

    c) the mercy of Christ, whereby at his return to judgment he will bless true Christians with eternal life.

9. Stephen Neill, *A History of Christian Missions* (Baltimore, Md.: Penguin Books, 1964), p. 42.

10. C.S. Lewis, *Miracles* (New York: Macmillan, 1947), p. 137.

11. The kinship triangle is borrowed from John Steward's materials. John has worked for World Vision Australia.

12. οικονομια (oikonomia) [management of a household or its affairs, specifically, the management, oversight, administration of others' property; a divine plan, task, work, or responsibility; stewardship]. The word is derived from οικια, ος (oikia, oikios) [house, home, property, family, household, temple, sanctuary, nation, people] and οικεω (oikeo) [live, dwell, live in]. It is easy for us to lose sight of the richness of this concept. Look at these two passages:

    > For he has made known to us in all wisdom and insight the mystery of his will, according to his purpose which he set forth in Christ as a **plan**

(oikonomia) for the fullness of time, to unite all things in him, things in heaven and things on earth.

Ephesians 1:9–10

...stay there in Ephesus so that you may command certain men not to teach false doctrines any longer nor to devote themselves to myths and endless genealogies. These promote controversies rather than God's **work** (oikonomia)— which is by faith.

1 Timothy 1:3–4

When we think of economics as merely "money business" instead of nation building, when we think of ecology as concern for animals and plants (vs. people), we separate things that are really interrelated. We commit a greater sin by separating spiritual from public and financial disciplines. We lose the historical, linguistic, and *very real* mandate of God. He calls us to steward His house: to build, improve, garden, and keep creation— and the priceless agent is man—God's image, bringing glory to our King by keeping house.

Chapter 5

1. Ruth and Vishal Mangalwadi, *William Carey: A Tribute by an Indian Woman* (New Delhi, India: Nivedit Good Books, 1993), p. 15.

2. Quoted by Dr. Vernon Grounds of Denver Theological Seminary in a lecture, Fall 1967.

3. William Wordsworth, *The Prelude*, Book XIV, line 70.

4. Jacques Monod, *Chance and Necessity* (New York: Alfred A. Knopf, 1971), pp. 21–22.

5. Shetler, *And The Word Came With Power*, p. 47.

6. C.S. Lewis, *Mere Christianity*, Book 2, pp. 52–53.

7. George Gilder, *Microcosm* (New York: Simon and Schuster, 1989), p. 382.

8. C.S. Lewis, *Reflections on the Psalms* (New York: Harcourt, Brace & World, 1958), p. 59.

9. Phillip Johnson, *Reason in the Balance* (Downers Grove, Ill.: InterVarsity Press, 1995), p. 108.

10. See *lanthano*, no. 2990, "to lie hid," and *aletheia*, no. 225, in *Strong's Concordance.*

11. George Grant, *The Micah Mandate* (Chicago: Moody Press, 1995), pp. 218–219.

12. Paulo Freire's term is Praxis, *Pedagogy of the Oppressed* (New York: The Seabury Press, 1968), p. 75. I believe the original meaning of the biblical word *wisdom* denotes the same idea, so I've chosen to use it instead.

13. Allan Bloom, *The Closing of the American Mind* (New York: Simon and Schuster, 1987), p. 29.

14. C.S. Lewis, *The Abolition of Man* (New York: Macmillan, 1947), p. 60.

15. John W. Whitehead, *The End of Man* (Westchester, Ill.: Crossway Books, 1986), p. 57.

16. Francis Schaeffer, *The Great Evangelical Disaster* (Westchester, Ill.: Crossway Books, 1984), p. 37.

17. J. Gresham Machen, quoted in J.I. Packer's *Fundamentalism and the Word of God* (Grand Rapids, Mich.: Eerdmans, 1980), pp. 35, 36.

18. Ruth and Vishal Mangalwadi, *William Carey: A Tribute by an Indian Woman* (New Delhi: Nivedit Good Books, 1993), p. 8.

19. Fred Hereen, *Show Me God* (Wheeling, Ill.: Searchlight Publishing, 1995).

20. C. F. Von Weizsacker, *The Relevance of Science* (New York: Harper and Row, 1964), p. 163.

21. Charles B. Thaxton, *The Soul of Science: Christian Faith and Natural Philosophy* (Wheaton, Ill.: Crossway Books, 1994), p. 33.

22. Thaxton, p. 31.

23. Paul Davies, "Physics and the Mind of God: The Templeton Prize Address," May 3, 1995.

24. Daniel J. Boorstin, *The Discoverers* (New York: Vintage Books, 1985), p. xv.

25. Thaxton, p. 30.

26. Thaxton, p. 32.

27. Thaxton, p. 35.

28. Thaxton, p. 35.

29. See *oikonomia,* endnote #12 in previous chapter.

30. George Gilder, *Wealth and Poverty* (New York: Bantam Books, 1981), p. 306.

31. *Newsweek*, "Souls At War" November 20, 1995, p. 59.

32. Warren T. Brookes, "Mind, Not Money, Drives the Economy," *Imprimis*, April 1984.

33. Brookes, p. 3.

34. George Gilder, *Microcosm*, p. 382.

35. George Gilder, *Microcosm*, p. 378.

36. Ruth and Vishal Mangalwadi, p. 68.

37. Quoted in *Table Talk*, a publication of Ligonier Ministries, June 15, p. 31.

38. An Ethiopian businessman said this to me in August 1995 as we sat talking on the flight into his adopted home of Uganda.

39. Edward C. Banfield, *The Moral Basis of a Backward Society* (Chicago: University of Chicago Press and New York: The Free Press, 1967), pp. 7–8.

40. Francis Fukuyama, *Trust: The Social Virtues and the Creation of Prosperity* (New York: The Free Press, 1995).

41. Winston Churchill at the House of Commons, November 11, 1947.

42. Borrowing from Schaeffer again.

Chapter 6

1. Deborah Sontag, "Physicians Say 'Partial Birth' Is Just One Way," *The New York Times*, March 21, 1997.

2. C.S. Lewis, *Mere Christianity* (New York: Macmillan, 1943), p. 21.

3. Katharine Q. Seelye, "House Votes by Large Margin to Ban Late Abortions," *The New York Times*, March 21, 1997.

4. **moral**: *Noah Webster's First Edition of an American Dictionary of the English Language* (San Francisco: Foundation for American Christian Education, 1828).

5. **ethics**: *Noah Webster's First Edition of an American Dictionary of the English Language* (San Francisco: Foundation for American Christian Education, 1828).

Our modern words *ethnic* and *ethics* share the same Greek root *ethos*. Study these three words and you learn that (historically) the important defining differences between peoples were not language, skin color, music, or diet but were their ethos, the way they saw reality, their worldview.

6. Russell Kirk, *The Roots of American Order* (Washington, D.C.: Regnery Gateway, 1991), p. 27.

7. C.S. Lewis, *The Abolition of Man* (New York: Macmillan, 1947), pp. 95–121.

8. C.S. Lewis, *Mere Christianity*, p. 117.

9. David Aikman, "Cambodia: An Experiment in Genocide," *Time*, July 31, 1978, pp. 39–40.

10. David F. Wells, *No Place for Truth* (Grand Rapids, Mich.: Eerdmans, 1993), p. 300.

11. Kirk, *The Roots of American Order*, p. 24.

12. From a museum display in India.

13. Larry Lea, "Garifunas Fret AIDS May Wipe Them Out," *Honduras This Week*, January 6, 1996, p. 1.

14. Maggie Gallagher, *Enemies of Eros* (Chicago: Bonus Books, 1989), p. 16.

15. Bob Moffitt. This quote is from the background paper to "A Narrow View of the Gospel" titled "God's Intentions—Their Irreducible Minimum," p. 3. The article is included in Harvest's *Leadership Development Training Program*, p. 59.

16. Mangalwadi, p. 11.

17. J.D. Richardson, Ed., *Compilation of Messages and Papers of Presidents, Vol. 1* (New York: Bureau of National Literature and Art, 1907), p. 213.

18. Kirk, *The Roots of American Order*, p. 26.

Chapter 7

1. Adapted from W. Merrill Long, "Introducing Social Change Through Community Health," *Evangelical Missions Quarterly*, July 1997, p. 321.

2. Michael Novak, *The Spirit of Democratic Capitalism* (New York: Simon and Schuster, 1982), p. 103.

3. World Health Organization (WHO), 2000.

4. Pope John Paul II, *Crossing the Threshold of Hope* (New York: Alfred A. Knopf, 1994). p. 38.

5. Paul Johnson, *Modern Times: The World from the Twenties to the Eighties* (New York: Harper & Row, 1985), p. 48. For an excellent overview and critique of Nietzsche and other watershed thinkers of modernity, read Ravi Zacharias' book *Can Man Live Without God* or Luis Palau's *God Is Relevant*.

6. Alexander Cockburn, "Malthus and the Modern World," *The Nation*, April 11, 1994, p. 476.

7. Associated Press, "World Population Outstrips Food Production-Savants," *The Philippine Star*, August 14, 1994, p. 1.

8. George Grant, *Grand Illusions: The Legacy of Planned Parenthood* (Brentwood, Tenn.: Wolgemuth and Hyatt, 1988), p. 91.

9. Margaret Sanger, *Woman and the New Race* (New York: Brentano's, 1920), p. 63. Quoted by Francis J. Beckwith, *Politically Correct Death*, p. 174.

10. Margaret Sanger, *The Pivot of Civilization* (Elmsford, N.Y.: Maxwell Reprint Company, 1992, reprinted 1950), p. 136.

11. Sanger, *The Pivot of Civilization*, p. 176.

12. George Grant, *Grand Illusions*, p. 192.

13. Nicholas Eberstadt, "Population Policy: Ideology as Science," *First Things*, January 1994, p. 34.

14. Peter L. Berger, "The Other Face of Gaia," *First Things*, August/September 1994, p. 16.

15. Berger, p. 17.

16. Boorstin, *The Discoverers*, p. 3.

17. Julian L. Simon, *The Ultimate Resource* (Princeton, N.J.: Princeton University Press, 1981), pp. 41 and 346.

18. Antientrophy: increasing order, the opposite of entrophy's increasing disorder.

19. Warren T. Brookes, *Imprimis*, Hillsdale College, April 1984.

20. Dennis Peacocke, "Understanding the Critical Difference Between Justice and Equality." *Crosswinds*, Vol. II, No. 2. Fall/Winter 1994–95, p. 47.

21. United Nations Development Programme, *Human Development Report 2000*, Statistical Annex.

22. United Nations Development Programme, *Human Development Report 2000*, Statistical Annex.

23. Food and Agriculture Organization of the United Nations, *The State of Food Insecurity in the World 1999*, p. 4.

24. Food and Agriculture Organization of the United Nations, *The State of Food and Agrigulture 2000*, PART II: The socio-economic impact of agricultural modernization, INTRODUCTION. Quoted from M. Mazoyer and L. Roudart. 1998. Histoire des agricultures du monde. Paris, Éditions du Seuil.

25. Food and Agriculture Organization of the United Nations, *The State of Food and Agrigulture 2000*, PART II: The socio-economic impact of agricultural modernization, ASSESSMENT AND FUTURE PROSPECTS.

26. Bread for the World, www.bread.org/hungerbasics/international.html, December 2000.

27. Peacocke, *Crosswinds*.

28. John Tierney, "Betting the Planet," *New York Times Magazine*, December 2, 1990, pp. 52–53, 74–81.

Chapter 8

1. For well-documented evidence that proves this assumption wrong, see Robert Edgerton's book *Sick Societies: Challenging the Myth of Primitive Harmony* (New York: The Free Press, 1992). The book also exemplifies just how completely naturalistic assumptions have saturated the field of anthropology.

2. Michael Novak, *The Spirit of Democratic Capitalism* (New York: Simon and Schuster, 1982), p. 39.

3. Jacques Monod, *Chance and Necessity* (New York: Alfred A. Knopf, 1971), p. 9.

4. Daniel J. Boorstin, *The Discoverers* (New York: Vintage Books, 1985), p. ix.

5. Max Weber, *The Protestant Work Ethic and the Spirit of Capitalism* (London: Allen and Unwin, 1904).

Chapter 9

1. Gary Scheer, "Rwanda: Where Was the Church?" *Evangelical Missions Quarterly*, July 1995, p. 324.

2. David Rawson, "Rwanda: Analysis by the U.S. Ambassador," *Evangelical Missions Quarterly*, July 1995, p. 322.

3. Francis Schaeffer, *Escape from Reason* (Downers Grove, Ill.: InterVarsity Press, 1974), p. 26.

4. Ruth and Vishal Mangalwadi, *William Carey: A Tribute by an Indian Woman* (New Delhi: Nivedit Good Books, 1993), p. 73.

5. Mangalwadi, pp. 73–74.

6. Charles Colson, "When History Is Up for Grabs," *The New York Times*, December 28, 1995, p. A17.

7. Herbert Schlossberg, *Idols for Destruction* (Washington, D.C.: Regnery Gateway, 1990), p. 82.

8. Michael Novak, "The Lesson of Lent," *Crisis*, April 1993, p. 7.

Chapter 10

1. Patricia Kranz, "Under Brezhnev, It Was Better," *Business Week*, June 24, 1996, p. 15.

2. See Millard J. Erickson, *Christian Theology* (Grand Rapids, Mich.: Baker Book House, 1985), pp. 321–342; John Piper, *The Pleasures of God* (Portland, Ore.: Fromm International, 1991), pp. 38, 42–44.

3. Brian Griffiths, *The Creation of Wealth* (Downers Grove, Ill: InterVarsity Press, 1984), p. 55.

4. Griffiths, p. 55.

5. Griffiths, p. 55.

6. Arthur Schlesinger, *The Disuniting of America: Reflections on a Multicultural Society* (New York and London: W.W. Norton, 1992).

7. Arthur Koestler, *The Ghost in the Machine* (London: Hutchinson and Company, 1967), p. 48.

8. Charles Hodge, quoted in the June 14, 1996, *Table Talk*, p. 31.

9. C.S. Lewis, "The Grand Miracle" (1945), in *God in the Dock: Essays on Theology and Ethics*, ed. Walter Hooper (Grand Rapids, Mich.: Eerdmans, 1970), p. 85.

10. Irving Kristol, "Of Decadence and Tennis Flannels," *The Wall Street Journal*, September 21, 1976, Section I, p. 24.

11. Paul Johnson, *A History of Christianity* (London: Weidenfield, 1976), p. 516.

12. A. James Reichly, *Religion in American Public Life* (Washington, D.C.: The Brookings Institution, 1985), p. 105.

13. Alexis de Tocqueville, quoted by Robert Putman in "Bowling Alone, Revisited," in *The Responsive Community* (Foundations of Democracy, Spring 1995), p. 18.

14. Robert Putman, p. 20.

15. George Grant, *The Micah Mandate* (Chicago: Moody Press, 1995), pp. 218–219.

16. George Grant, pp. 218–219.

17. Cited by George Grant, p. 220.

Chapter 11

1. Daniel J. Boorstin, *The Creators* (New York: Random House, 1992), p. 18.

2. Boorstin, p. 26.

3. Michael Novak, *The Spirit of Democratic Capitalism* (New York: Simon and Schuster, 1982), p. 39.

4. Abraham Kuyper, *Christianity and the Class Struggle* (Grand Rapids, Mich.: Piet Heirr Publishers, 1950), p. 19.

5. E. Calvin Beisner, "Is There an Invisible Hand to Help the Poor?" *Crosswinds: The Reformation Digest*, Fall/Winter 1994–95, p. 51.

6. Ruth and Vishal Mangalwadi, *William Carey: A Tribute by an Indian Woman* (New Delhi: Nivedit Good Books, 1993), p. 68.

7. Warren T. Brookes, "The Real Wealth of Mankind Is Spiritual," *Conservative Chronicle*, November 29, 1989, p. 10.

8. J.R.R. Tolkien, *Tree and Leaf* (London: Unwin Books, 1964), pp. 70–71.

9. Udo Middlemann, *World Hunger and World Views*, lecture given in June of 1983 at Food for the Hungry's office in Arizona.

10. After Jesus commands his disciples to "μαϑητευω!" (make disciples!: μαϑηευσατε *is the first aorist active imperative plural form of this verb, which means—to make a disciple*), he tells them how to do it: First baptize, second teach them to τηρεω all I have commanded. τηρεω, {tay-reh'-o} means to attend to carefully, take care of, to guard; to observe; to reserve; it is a verb derived from τηρος (a watch, assignment). Τηρεω expresses watchful care and is suggestive of present possession. Like Tolkein's dragon Smaug guarding its gold or a mother watching her children, this is the idea of protecting a precious possession in its entirety. The commands, all of them, are our precious treasure. τηρεω has been translated as keep, reserve, observe, watch, preserve, and hold fast. Just one more example of English translation missing the richness of the original idea.

11. Peter L. Berger, *The Capitalist Revolution—Fifty Propositions About Prosperity, Equality and Liberty* (New York: Basic Books, 1986), p. 35.

12. David C. McClelland, "The Achievement Motive in Economic Growth," in Bert Hoselitz and Wilbert E. Moore, eds., *Industrialization and Society* (Geneva, Switz.: Moutouni UNESCO, 1970), p. 74.

13. Robert Fulghum, *All I Really Need to Know I Learned in Kindergarten* (New York: Ivy Books, 1988), pp. 189–192.

14. Maurice Fulton, ed., *Roosevelt's Writings* (New York: Macmillan, 1922), p. 168.

15. Thomas H. Russell, *Life and Work of Theodore Roosevelt* (New York: L.H. Walter, 1919), p. 257.

Chapter 12

1. Abraham Kuyper, *Lectures on Calvinism* (Grand Rapids, Mich.: Eerdmans, 1983), p. 16.

2. See Wesley's 1872 Sermon 50, The Use of Money.

3. I have used the term biblical economics in lieu of a better label. The Bible reveals principles of economics but does not endorse any one system. Predatory capitalism (consumerism) is a far cry from the fundamentals of biblical economics and capital formation. On the other end of the spectrum, socialism and the defunct communist system do not approach the strengths of biblical economics. Each system applies some biblical principles and is hostile to others. The more biblical principles found in the system, the more honor it brings to God, the more it lifts people out of poverty, and the better care it gives to creation.

4. Brian C. Robertson refers to this idea as "predatory capitalism" in his book *There's No Place Like Work* (Dallas, TX: Spence Publishing Company, 2000), p. 177.

5. Ruth and Vishal Mangalwadi, *William Carey: A Tribute by an Indian Woman* (New Delhi: Nivedit Good Books, 1993), p. 77.

6. Max Weber, *The Protestant Ethic and the Spirit of Capitalism* (New York: Scribner and Sons, 1958), pp. 170–171.

7. *Sayings of Agur Son of Jakeh.*

8. Bob Goudzwaard, *Idols of Our Time* (Sioux Center, IA: Dordt College Press, 1984), p. 107. See also Dr. Bob Moffitt's paper entitled "Jesus and the Concept of Adequacy" available from the Harvest Foundation.

9. Quoted by William J. Danker, *Profit for the Lord* (Grand Rapids, Mich.: Eerdmans, 1971), p. 30.

10. C.S. Lewis, *Mere Christianity* (New York: Macmillan, 1952), p. 73.

11. Brian Griffiths, *The Creation of Wealth* (Downers Grove, Ill.: InterVarsity Press, 1984), p. 69.

12. Associated Press, "*Donated Food Overloading Ruined Town*," June 5, 1997.

13. Marvin Olasky, *The Tragedy of American Compassion* (Wheaton, Ill.: Crossway Books, 1992).

Chapter 13

1. John S. Mbiti, *African Religions and Philosophy* (Garden City, N.Y.: Anchor Books, 1970), pp. 21, 23.

2. The words we've used: *teleo, telos* and *teleios* are all derived from the same root word *tello* (τελλω), to set out for a definite point or goal. The entire family of words has to do with ends, or results. It is important to note that these words have both human and historical aspects. Humanly they refer to our being complete and perfect in Christ—becoming all that God intended for us to be. Historically, they refer to eschatological things—the end of time, the purpose of history. The words you've seen used in this book are

> τελος, ους (a noun; transliterates as TELOS)
> *the end, conclusion, outcome, goal, aim, result*
>
> τελεω (a verb; transliterates as TELEO)
> *finish, complete, end, fulfill, carry out, accomplish, be one's utmost*
>
> τελειοω (a verb; transliterates as TELEIO-O)
> *to make perfect, perfect, to make complete, finish, accomplish, to finish one's work, to reach one's goal, to make mature, to make come true, to make real*

τελειος, α, ον (an adjective; transliterates as TELEIOS)
full-grown, mature, complete, perfect, whole

3. Daniel J. Boorstin, *The Creators* (New York: Random House, 1992), p. 25.

4. Herbert Schlossberg, *Idols for Destruction* (Washington, D.C.: Regnery Gateway, 1990), p. 13.

5. John Mbiti, *African Religions and Philosophy, 2d ed.* (Oxford: Heinemann International, 1989), p. 23.

6. John W. Montgomery, *Where Is History Going?* (Grand Rapids, Mich.: Zondervan, 1969), p. 31.

7. Wim Rietkerk, *The Future Great Planet Earth* (Kromme Nieuwe Gracht: The Netherlands: Nivedit Good Books, 1989), pp. 36–37.

8. Erwin Panofsky, *Studies in Iconology: Humanistic Themes in the Art of the Renaissance* (New York: Harper & Row, 1939, 1962), p. 73.

9. Montgomery, p. 28.

10. Cited by Russell Kirk, *The Roots of American Order* (Washington, D.C.: Regnery Gateway, 1991), p. xviii.

11. Kirk, pp. 41–42.

12. Quoted in George Grant, *The Micah Mandate* (Chicago: Moody Press, 1995), p. 199.

13. C.S. Lewis, *Selected Literary Essays*, "Hamlet: The Prince or the Poem" (Cambridge: Cambridge University Press, 1969), p. 105.

14. Kirk, p. xix.

15. C.S. Lewis, *God in the Dock: Essays on Theology and Ethics*, ed. Walter Hooper (Grand Rapids, Mich.: Eerdmans, 1970), p. 21.

16. Kirk, p. 153.

17. Quoted in George Grant, *The Micah Mandate* (Chicago: Moody Press, 1995), p. 220.

18. Kabia shared her story with me when we were visiting Food for the Hungry projects together in the Dominican Republic.

For Further Reading

Berger, Peter L. *The Capitalist Revolution: Fifty Propositions About Prosperity, Equality, and Liberty.* New York: Basic Books, Inc., 1986.

Bjork, David E. *Unfamiliar paths: the challenge of recognizing the work of Christ in strange clothing : a case study from France.* Pasadena, CA: William Carey Library Publishers, 1997.

Blamires, Harry. *The Christian Mind: How Should a Christian Think?* Ann Arbor, MI: Servant Books, 1978.

de Soto, Hernando. *The Other Path: The Invisible Revolution in the Third World.* New York: Harper & Row, 1989.

Ferrell, John S. *Fruits of Creation.* Shakopee, MN: Macalester Park Publishing Company, 1995.

Grant, George. *The Micah Mandate: Balancing the Christian Life.* Nashville, TN: Cumberland House, 1999.

Harrison, Lawrence E. and Samuel P. Huntington, eds. *Culture Matters: How Values Shape Human Progress.* New York: Basic Books, 2000.

Harrison, Lawrence E. *Underdevelopment is a State of Mind: The Latin American Case.* Lanham, MD: University Press of America, Inc., 1985.

Heslam, Peter S. *Creating a Christian Worldview: Abraham Kuyper's Lectures on Calvinism,* Grand Rapids, MI: Wm. B. Eerdmans Publishing Company, 1998.

Hill, Octavia. *The Befriending Leader: Social Assistance Without Dependency.* Sandpoint, ID: Lytton Publishing Company, 1997.

Mangalwadi, Vishal and Ruth. *The Legacy of William Carey.* Wheaton, IL: Crossway Books, 1999.

Mangalwadi, Vishal. *Truth and Social Reform.* Landour, Musoorie, India: Nivedit Good Books, 1996.

Moffitt, Bob. *BASICS: Wholistic Discipleship for New Believers.* Tempe, AZ: Harvest, 1993.

Moffitt, Bob. *Leadership Development Training Program, levels I and II.* Tempe, AZ: Harvest, 1994.

Noll, Mark A. *The Scandal of the Evangelical Mind.* Grand Rapids, MI: William B. Eerdmans Publishing Company, 1994.

Novak, Michael. *The Spirit of Democratic Capitalism.* New York: Madison Books, 1991.

Olasky, Marvin. *The Tragedy of American Compassion.* Washington, D.C.: Regnery Publishing, Inc., 1992.

Peacocke, Dennis. *Almighty & Sons: Doing Business God's Way.* Santa Rosa, CA: REBUILD, 1995.

Rietkerk, Wim. *The Future Great Planet Earth.* Landour, Musoorie, India: Nivedit Good Books, 1989.

Schaeffer, Francis A. *Pollution and the Death of Man.* Wheaton, IL: Crossway Books, 1992.

Sire, James W. *The Universe Next Door* (Third Edition). Downers Grove, Illinois: InterVarsity Press, 1997.

Van Rheenen, Gailyn. *Communicating Christ in Animistic Contexts.* Grand Rapids, MI: Baker Book House, 1991.

Weaver, Richard M. *Ideas Have Consequences.* Chicago, IL: The University of Chicago Press, 1984.

Wells, David F. *No Place for Truth Or Whatever Happened to Evangelical Theology?* Grand Rapids, MI: William B. Eerdmans Publishing Company, 1993.

Whitehead, John W. *The End of Man.* Westchester, IL: Crossway Books, 1986.

Other Resources

For books contact The MacLaurin Institute, 331 17th Ave. SE, Minneapolis, MN 55414, USA. Phone: 1-(800) 582-8541 or (612) 378-1935
E-mail: maclaurin@maclaurin.org.

For church resources contact The Harvest Foundation, P.O. Box 15577, Scottsdale, AZ 85267. Phone: (480) 968-2600
Email: www.harvestfoundation.org.

The Samaritan Strategy

Transforming Nations One Church at a Time

A partnership between
FOOD FOR THE HUNGRY INTERNATIONAL
and
THE HARVEST FOUNDATION

The Samaritan Strategy is a movement that equips churches around the globe with a biblical worldview and a vision to carry out wholistic ministry in their local communities. The Samaritan Strategy exists to serve the church of Jesus Christ worldwide by assisting her in declaring the Kingdom of God in word and deed. We accomplish this objective by training pastors, missionaries, and church leaders to think and operate with a comprehensive, biblical worldview. We also provide vision, tools, and skills to help individuals and churches bring God's wholistic transformation to their neighbors, churches, communities, and nations.

The Samaritan Strategy began in 1997 as a partnership between Food for the Hungry International and the Harvest Foundation. While its roots are in these two organizations, we continue to develop an expanding network of alliances with individuals, churches and organizations committed to spreading the message of biblical worldview and wholistic church-based ministry.

Jesus' Great Commission to His church was to "make disciples of all nations...teaching them to obey all I have commanded" *(Matthew 28:18-20)*.

The Samaritan Strategy is committed to making disciples of all nations. We believe Jesus Christ raised up His church to *proclaim* the good news of the Kingdom of God and to *demonstrate* the reality of the Kingdom to a lost and broken world.

To learn more about the Samaritan Strategy and how you might get involved, please visit our web site or contact us by email.

> *The Samaritan Strategy is challenging the church to return to a more comprehensive understanding of her calling, and to once again think and operate on the basis of the biblical worldview.*
>
> *The movement inspires the church to proclaim the gospel of the Kingdom of God, explains how to teach the nations to obey all that Christ commanded, and suggests ways to provide practical demonstrations of Christ's love in neighborhoods, communities, and nations.*

Samaritan Strategy
SamStrat@fhi.net
www.fhi.net/samaritan

———— *About the Authors* ————

Darrow L. Miller is the Vice President of the Samaritan Strategy at FHI (Food for the Hungry International), a Christian relief and development organization working to feed both the physical and spiritual hungers of people in more than 25 developing countries on four continents. For nearly 20 years, Darrow has been a popular speaker at conferences and seminars on topics that include the Christian movement worldwide, hunger, servanthood, development and its biblical mandates, volunteerism in missions, Christianity and culture, Christian apologetics, and social issues.

Two memorable experiences significantly shaped Darrow's vocational pursuits. The first occurred during a trip to Mexico at age 19, when he first encountered poverty. The second happened while studying under Francis Schaeffer at L'Abri Fellowship in Switzerland, where he learned that Christianity is objectively true; it is reality, even if no one believes it. The combined effect of these two experiences has motivated Darrow to devote his life to serving the poor and hungry from a thoroughly Christian worldview.

Before joining Food for the Hungry in 1981, Darrow spent three years on staff at L'Abri Fellowship, three years as a student pastor at Northern Arizona University, and two years as pastor of Sherman Street Fellowship Church in urban Denver, Colorado.

In addition to earning his master's degree in higher adult education from Arizona State University, Darrow has pursued graduate studies in philosophy, theology, Christian apologetics, biblical studies, and missions in the United States, Israel, and Switzerland.

Darrow has authored two Bible studies, numerous articles, a chapter entitled "The development ethic: Hope for a Culture of Poverty," which was published in *Christian Relief and Development* (Word Publishing, 1989), and two workshops called "Worldview and Development" and "The Development Ethic."

Darrow and his wife Marilyn reside in Cave Creek, Arizona They have four children and four grandchildren.

Stan Guthrie is associate news editor for *Christianity Today* and author of the book *Missions in the Third Millennium: 21 Key Trends for the 21st Century* (Paternoster, 2000). He has been editor of *World Pulse* and managing editor of *Evangelical Missions Quarterly*. A guest of "The Dick Staub Show" and other radio programs, Guthrie edits *Discernment*, the newsletter of Wheaton College's Center for Applied Christian Ethics. His work has also appeared in *Moody* magazine, *New Man*, *Current Thoughts and Trends*, and other periodicals. Guthrie, his wife Christine, and their children live in Wheaton, Illinois.

FUNDAMentals

Originally designed to help translators convey worldview concepts to large audiences, our goal for the Fundamentals icons is to illustrate *stoicheion*—the basic principles within differing worldviews—so they can be easily identified, compared, and remembered.

Trent Eastman and Darrow Miller deserve credit for the brainstorming session in Korea that launched this project. Additional thanks to R.C. Sproul, whose whiteboard sketches in *A Blueprint for Thinking* provided a springboard for creativity. Highest gratitude to our Creator for gifting and inspiration. He even redeems doodles for the building of His Kingdom.

We continue to welcome recommendations for improving these graphics—especially regarding their use as teaching aids in different cultures. Email your questions and suggestions to Tom Steffen at tom@steffengroup.com. For permission to reproduce these icons or other graphics in this book or for presentation materials, call FHI's Wholistic Ministry Resources Department at (480) 951-5090.